Divine Action, Determinisn and the Laws of Nature

A longstanding question at the intersection of science, philosophy, and theology is how God might act, or not, when governing the universe. Many believe that determinism would prevent God from acting at all, since to do so would require violating the laws of nature. However, when a robust view of these laws is coupled with the kind of determinism now used in dynamics, a new model of divine action emerges.

This book presents a new approach to divine action beyond the current focus on quantum mechanics and esoteric gaps in the causal order. It bases this approach on two general points: First, that there are laws of nature is not merely a metaphor. Second, laws and physical determinism are now understood in mathematically precise ways that have important implications for metaphysics. The explication of these two claims shows not only that nonviolationist divine action is possible but also that there is considerably more freedom available for God to act than that which current models allow.

By bringing a philosophical perspective to an issue often dominated by theologians and scientists, this book redresses an imbalance in the discussion around divine action. It will therefore be of keen interest to scholars of philosophy and religion, the philosophy of science, and theology.

Jeffrey Koperski is Professor of Philosophy at Saginaw Valley State University, USA. He is an editorial board member for *Philosophy Compass* and has published articles in journals such as *Philosophy of Science*, *British Journal for the Philosophy of Science*, and *Zygon*. He is the author of *The Physics of Theism* (2015).

Divine Action, Determinism, and the Laws of Nature

Jeffrey Koperski

Routledge
Taylor & Francis Group
LONDON AND NEW YORK

First published 2020
by Routledge
2 Park Square, Milton Park, Abingdon, Oxon OX14 4RN

and by Routledge
52 Vanderbilt Avenue, New York, NY 10017

Routledge is an imprint of the Taylor & Francis Group, an informa business

First issued in paperback 2021

British Library Cataloguing-in-Publication Data
A catalogue record for this book is available from the British Library

Library of Congress Cataloging-in-Publication Data
A catalog record for this book has been requested

ISBN: 978-0-367-13900-1 (hbk)
ISBN: 978-1-03-208311-7 (pbk)
ISBN: 978-0-429-02911-0 (ebk)

Typeset in Sabon
by Apex CoVantage, LLC

Dictionary of Christianity and Science: The Definitive Reference for the Intersection of Christian Faith and Contemporary Science, edited by Paul Copan et al, 1:186–88. Grand Rapids. Reprinted by permission of Zondervan.

MIX
Paper from
responsible sources
FSC
www.fsc.org
FSC™ C013985

Printed in the United Kingdom
by Henry Ling Limited

To my mother, Karen, whose hopes for my lucrative career in engineering were dashed by philosophy. To my sister, Ruth (a.k.a., Danielle), who started me thinking about such things a few decades ago. And to my brother, Chick, who would have loved this book.

Contents

1 Philosophy and divine action

Deists believe in God but not "organized religion." God created the universe, but that exhausts the deistic job description. Theists – organized or not – believe that God also continuously upholds the universe in existence. Whatever else God might do goes by the name *special divine action*. This might refer in part to miracles, although what a miracle is precisely is a matter of some debate. The term is typically used for God's activity within nature, regardless of whether anyone knows about it.

For the most part, the question of special divine action has been the purview of theologians. There has long been a division between those who believe that God sometimes breaks the laws of nature and those who deny it. Most laypersons and even scholars are initially puzzled by this second camp. "Why can't God break the laws of nature?" As we will see in Chapter 2, some theologians believe that God cannot; others believe that God will not – or at least not often.

Some in this debate not only have backgrounds in theology but were once well-credentialed scientists: John Polkinghorne, Arthur Peacocke, and Robert Russell are prominent among them. I have observed over the years, however, that many of the arguments in the literature are, properly speaking, neither issues in theology nor issues in science; rather, they are matters of philosophy. A few philosophers of religion have made important contributions to the question of divine action, but there is one corner of analytic philosophy that has largely remained silent: the philosophy of science. This book is a step toward breaking this silence, bringing something of an outsider's perspective to the debate. This is sometimes useful. Robert Griffiths was a condensed matter physicist who turned his attention to quantum mechanics only after being asked to teach a course in it. He went on to found one of the standard interpretations of quantum mechanics: the consistent histories approach. Philosopher of science John Earman wrote a short book on David Hume's argument against miracles some years ago, refuting Hume through the rigorous application of Bayesian probability theory (2000). (As one might imagine, Hume scholars were not altogether pleased by this intrusion.) My hope is that bringing philosophy of science to bear on the question of divine action will suggest new ways of approaching the main arguments.[1] At the very least, I intend to present material that one will not generally find outside philosophy of science journals.

Some will not find this perspective helpful. Others will be puzzled by my conclusions, especially those that do not fit well with current trends in theology. Such is the messiness of interdisciplinary work. Among the theologians mentioned in the next two chapters, there is broad agreement on two doctrines: The first is nonviolation: if God acts within nature postcreation, this action ought not violate the laws of nature. The second is determinism: if nature were deterministic, special divine action would entail the breaking of natural laws. Without some sort of openness or plasticity within the natural realm, there is nothing God can do that would not thereby count as a violation. Many believe that the second issue has been resolved by quantum mechanics, which is normally thought to be indeterministic. In other words, nature is not deterministic, and so the second of these two doctrines is no longer a worry.

Philosophers of science reading this literature will have two questions: The first is, what do theologians mean by "laws of nature"? There are a variety of ways in which one might understand natural laws, ranging from those with no metaphysical significance to others that determine every physical event. What, precisely, a "violation of law" amounts to changes depending on which interpretation one holds. This relationship between laws and violations need be made explicit to even know whether there is a problem of divine action to be resolved.

The second question has to do with physical determinism. For most philosophers and theologians, determinism is an obstacle to be overcome. Determinism of this sort, with its roots in the seventeenth-century thought of Spinoza and Leibniz, would preclude moral responsibility. In short, you aren't responsible for your actions if you literally do not have any choice in the matter. This attitude is in contrast with physicists who work hard to *uphold* determinism in the face of *prima facie* violations. They typically take breakdowns in determinism to indicate an error of some kind, with the (possible) exception of quantum mechanics. These differing attitudes between philosophers and theologians on one hand and physicists on the other are due to an important conceptual shift. What "determinism" now means in mathematical physics is only distantly related to its philosophical counterpart.

Sorting this out is important since current models of divine action presuppose indeterminism of some sort. For many of those models, physical determinism in a world of robust laws would prevent special divine action. "Not to worry," we are told, "since quantum mechanics is famously indeterministic." Well, maybe. Deterministic interpretations of quantum mechanics continue to gain adherents, especially Everettian many-worlds. By the end of this century, physicists and philosophers of physics might no longer consider quantum mechanics to be the realm of ontological randomness.

For most science-and-religion scholars working on divine action, the return of deterministic physics would be bad news indeed. Indeterminism opens a range of possibilities that would otherwise have been closed in the deterministic world of classical mechanics (or so it is commonly thought).[2] Consider a parallel argument regarding free will, understood as libertarian freedom.[3] In a deterministic world, there is no free will. One's "choices" are as much the product of the laws of nature as is the trajectory of a tennis ball. Libertarians rejoice, then, that quantum mechanics has refuted physical determinism. Free will is at least possible, although indeterminism alone is not sufficient for freedom. This same indeterminism is likewise thought to allow for avenues of divine action that would be impossible in a Newtonian world. That physics might reembrace determinism is therefore a source of great concern.

For my part, I will argue that this worry is misplaced. Determinism need not be the bugaboo that it is normally portrayed – "bugaboo" being a technical term in philosophy of science. If an older understanding of natural laws is coupled with a physicist's view of determinism, a new approach to divine action emerges whereby God would no longer be constrained to work within the indeterministic gaps of exotic physics. The *neoclassical model* of special divine action is not dependent on any one interpretation of quantum mechanics.[4] But that's getting ahead of ourselves a bit. Let's first consider where things stand today.

1.1 Distinction

There are broadly speaking three approaches to divine action, although the latter two are usually collapsed into one. *Interventionists* believe that God sometimes violates the laws of nature. Many theologians reject this view as naïve, and we will consider some of their arguments in the next chapter. *Noninterventionism* will be restricted here to the view that God created and sustains the universe but does not immediately bring about specific events within nature. Remove the clause about sustaining, and one is left with deism, which few are willing to embrace.[5] Panentheists and others focused on the God–world relationship also fall into this category. What I will call *nonviolationism*, which is usually subsumed under the second group, is a middle position. Like interventionism, it holds that God actively governs creation, causing events that would not likely to have happened otherwise. Like noninterventionism, it holds that God seldom if ever breaks the laws of nature.

Why invent a new category, especially when nonviolationists refer to themselves as noninterventionists? There are two answers. The first is that failing to do so causes confusion. There are important differences between the two approaches to the degree to which God is active in the universe. Second, arguments aimed at one are not always relevant to the other. Consider Alvin Plantinga's work on the question of divine intervention. He begins by showing that, for theologians such as Langdon Gilkey, divine action is limited to God's creating and sustaining the universe. Here Plantinga quotes Gilkey himself:

> Thus contemporary theology does not expect . . . wondrous divine events on the surface of natural and historical life. The causal nexus in space and time which the Enlightenment science and philosophy introduced into the Western mind . . . is also assumed by modern theologians and scholars; since they participate in the modern world of science both intellectually and existentially, they can scarcely do anything else. Now this assumption of a causal order among phenomenal events, and therefore of the authority of the scientific interpretation of observable events, makes a great difference. Suddenly a vast panoply of divine deeds and events recorded in scripture are no longer regarded as having actually happened. . . . Whatever the Hebrews believed, we believe that the biblical people lived in the same causal continuum of space and time in which we live, and so one in which no divine wonders transpired and no divine voices were heard.
>
> (Plantinga 2008, 371)

Gilkey is clearly a noninterventionist. Modern scientific folk cannot rationally believe in miracles or any other sort of divine action after creation itself. This view is further articulated by John Macquarrie:

> The way of understanding miracle that appeals to breaks in the natural order and to supernatural interventions belongs to the mythological outlook. . . . The traditional conception of miracle is irreconcilable with our modern understanding of both science and history. Science proceeds on the assumption that whatever events occur in the world can be accounted for in terms of other events that also belong within the world; and if on some occasions we are unable to give a complete account of some happening . . . the scientific conviction is that further research will bring to light further factors in the situation, but factors that will turn out to be just as immanent and this-worldly as those already known.
>
> (Plantinga 2008, 372)

Plantinga traces this sort of "hands-off theology" back through Rudolf Bultmann. Thomas Tracy (2009, 230) extends it further, starting with deism, through Schleiermacher and the early liberal Protestants, down through Bultmann and Gordon Kaufman. If, as we are told, science has taught us that nature is a closed continuum, theology must give up divine intervention.

One result of such thinking has been the naturalizing of biblical miracles. The feeding of the five thousand (Matthew 14:13–21) might be understood as Jesus prompting his audience to spontaneously share what little food they had with others, thereby feeding everyone. Perhaps the crossing of the Red

Sea in Exodus was made possible by high winds, a tsunami, an earthquake, or some combination, each of which has been proposed as a natural explanation.[6] As William Pollard sums up, "Biblical miracles are, like that in the exodus, the result of an extraordinary and extremely improbable combination of chance and accident. They do not, on close analysis, involve, as is so frequently supposed, a violation of the laws of nature" (1958, 115).

Nonviolationists agree to an extent, consistently arguing against divine intervention. Robert Russell calls his own model of divine action noninterventionist objective divine action (NIODA). One might therefore be forgiven for lumping them in with Bultmann, Gilkey, and Macquarrie.[7] That would be a mistake. As Russell has emphasized, he and other members of the Divine Action Project (DAP) are "hands-on," not "hands-off," in their theology, rejecting deism and typically believing in an active God (private discussion). It isn't special divine action postcreation that worries them or even that God brings about specific events; it is action that requires the violation of the laws of nature. The goal of their program is to find ways in which God could act without such violations. It is unfortunate, then, that this camp self-identifies as noninterventionism. In any case, I believe it would be useful to distinguish the hands-off approach of Leibniz and Bultmann (noninterventionism) from the hands-on view of Russell *et al.* (nonviolationism).

Thoroughgoing noninterventionists do not like this middle position, seeing it as a kind of soft intervention. Even if there are windows through which God can act without breaking natural laws, such approaches have "simply replaced one mode of interference with the world – that in which the laws of nature are set aside – with another, in which those laws are used as tools" (Knight, 2007, 26). Noninterventionists take the other two camps to differ merely by degree of divine manipulation.

Is this fair? To a point, yes. In spirit, nonviolationists agree with interventionists that God takes a more hands-on approach to nature. In practice, however, their models allow for such a limited range of physical effects that they are functionally much closer to hands-off noninterventionists. As I will argue, there is little that God could do by way of the causal pathways proposed by nonviolationists in the divine action literature. For it to survive as a research program requires a reexamination of foundational assumptions about the laws of nature and determinism.

1.2 Overview

Here then is the plan for the rest of the book. Chapter 2 analyzes the current terrain regarding divine action. The first question is, Why not intervention? Theologians point to a variety of issues: conflicts with science, inconsistency on God's part, and the problem of evil prominent among them. These concerns motivate both noninterventionism and nonviolationist models for divine action, several of which will be critiqued. Most of these approaches, I will argue, allow for too little freedom on God's part. In other words, if *that* is the way God interacts with nature, there is not much that God can do.

Chapter 3 is an extended discussion of one nonviolationist model: God working through quantum indeterminism. The central idea behind Russell's NIODA is that God could act through ontologically random quantum events without breaking any laws. The model presupposes that quantum fluctuations are readily amplified into the macroscopic realm. This is not the case. Dynamical systems theory, continuum mechanics, and condensed matter physics show that such fluctuations are prevented from bubbling up within macroscopic systems. While some look to chaos theory to overcome this problem, chaotic systems are not nearly as prevalent as the popular literature indicates. Once all the relevant physics is considered, models of divine action based on quantum randomness and chaos are far more limited than they are generally assumed to be. Unless some sort of new physical mechanism is discovered, the amplification problem cannot be solved.

Having established the need for a new model of divine action, we begin to address some foundational issues in Chapter 4. To this point terms like "violation" and the "laws of nature" have been used as if everyone knew what were meant. Not only is this false, but leaving such concepts at an intuitive level also obscures an important shift in the history of science. The very idea that there *are* laws of nature is a modern innovation. The ancients and medievals did not believe in such laws – a claim that is often met with puzzlement. "Of course they did!" I am told. "Aristotle believed in an orderly world. Ptolemaic astronomy might have been wrong, but it clearly presupposed absolute regularities in nature." Well, yes, all that is true, but it is also beside the point. That nature contains regularities is not a modern discovery. But what is responsible for those regularities? For Plato it was the Forms. For Aristotle, it was essences and natures. While the idea of "natural law" had a long tradition in ethics, at least back to the Stoics, it took Descartes to unambiguously apply the idea to physics. This was no incremental change. If there was ever such a thing as a Kuhnian paradigm shift, this was it. The ramifications for divine freedom, empiricism, and special divine action will be discussed.

Chapter 5 moves into the contemporary philosophical question about the nature of the laws of nature. If intervention entails the breaking of natural law, what precisely is being broken? There are four main approaches in philosophy of science: Humean reductionism, supervenience on causal powers, the structure of possible worlds, and nomological realism. The first denies that laws have any metaphysical significance. They are merely statements that allow us to organize and systematize scientific knowledge. The second takes laws to depend on *dispositions* – a technical term. These are responsible for causal regularities among events in this view, not for the laws themselves. The third agrees that laws are not fundamental; it but grounds them in relations among possible worlds: the ways in which reality could have been different. The fourth take laws themselves to be fundamental: They are metaphysically real and cannot be reduced to any of the other three accounts.

What the problem of divine intervention amounts to is a function of which view one holds. In the end, I argue that early modern natural philosophers largely had it right. Laws are not created entities or powers that act as intermediaries between God and nature; they are best understood as expressions of God's will for nature.

Chapter 6 turns to the question of determinism. While it is a common idea in philosophy, theology, and physics, the disciplines generally do not agree on its meaning. Philosophers and theologians often employ a notion of physical determinism that was introduced in the seventeenth century, pointing to classical mechanics as a paradigm case. Physicists, in contrast, use a mathematical definition based on the underlying differential equations. This latter approach opens new possibilities for divine action. It is not the case that God could only act within a deterministic, classical world by breaking the laws of physics. Nonviolationist divine action would have been possible even under classical mechanics. The search for causal gaps in exotic physics – quantum mechanics, chaos, etc. – was poorly motivated from the start. Moreover, if trends in the philosophy of quantum mechanics hold, the standard interpretation[8] may well be supplanted by the deterministic many-worlds view. A model of divine action is needed that could survive such a shift.

Chapter 7 completes the narrative, showing why all this previous work was required. By this point, we will have considered how the laws of nature were understood at the birth of classical mechanics. For Descartes, Newton, and Boyle, theism was not merely an appendage to an otherwise naturalistic approach but rather an inextricable part of their theorizing. In Chapter 5, we see where their view fits within the current metaphysical landscape regarding laws. Coupling an early modern approach to laws with the mathematical determinism explained in Chapter 6 produces a new view: the neoclassical model of special divine action. It is nonviolationist yet not dependent on any particular interpretation of quantum mechanics. One charge this sort of divine action is liable to is that it violates the conservation of energy. I deny that, but understanding why requires some undoing of the conventional wisdom regarding conservation.

The final chapter will consider a few possible objections. These include whether this model entails a kind of occasionalism whereby God is causally responsible for every physical event. In the history of philosophy, occasionalism is usually considered something to be avoided, yet Robert Larmer (2017) has recently tried to paint me with the occasionalist brush. We will see what options are available.

Philosophers of science are often an intellectually conservative lot by training. Getting the science right is a high priority, but drawing metaphysical lessons is not. If anything, physicists are now far more speculative, positing realms of infinite universes and hidden dimensions. Philosophers of science, in contrast, often disappoint readers for refusing to go out on a metaphysical limb. This, then, is an atypical book. I will venture out on several such limbs in the chapters to come, some thinner than others. And I suspect that few readers will be willing to follow me out onto each one. In any case, a way forward on the question of divine action is presented here that challenges many of the assumptions made today about the laws of nature, determinism, and causal closure. My hope is that most readers will find something helpful along the way.

1.3 Acknowledgments and loose ends

The proposed model of divine action advances a program suggested by C. S. Lewis ([1947] 1978, 57–60) and developed by William Alston (1994, 50), Plantinga (2008; 2011, chap. 4), and Robert Larmer (2008, 149–50; 2014, chap. 5).[9] This is not to say that they would embrace it in every detail. Larmer's own view of the nature of law is at odds with that presented in Chapter 5. And Plantinga accepts the charge of occasionalism that I will attempt to dodge. Such divergences are to be expected given the variety of views possible on the laws of nature. The premise of this book is that my predecessors' ideas can best be advanced when they are more fully integrated with the history and philosophy of physics.

This book develops arguments that I first considered in chapter 4 of *The Physics of Theism* (Koperski, 2015) and draws on material from several previous works: "Divine Action," *Dictionary of Christianity and Science*, Paul Copan, Tremper Longman, Chris Reese, and Mike Strauss, eds. (2017); "Divine Action and the Quantum Amplification Problem," *Theology and Science* 13, no. 4 (2015): 379–94 and "God, Chaos, and the Quantum Dice," *Zygon* 35, no. 3 (2000): 545–559; and chapter 5, "Breaking Laws of Nature," *Philosophia Christi* 19, no. 1 (2017): 83–101.

As for acknowledgements, several people provided valuable feedback on early versions of these ideas, including Jim Bradley, Travis Dumsday, Doug Geivett, Michael Murray, and Robert Russell. Others fielded specific questions along the way: James Hitt, Al Lent, David Nichols, and Peter Rose-Barry. I received especially valuable comments on chapter drafts from Robert Bishop, William Lane Craig, Paul Gould, Rope Kojonen, Ben Nasmith, Brian Pitts, and Del Ratzsch, with extensive feedback from Robert Larmer and Philip West. My thanks also to my editor, Joshua Wells; to an anonymous reviewer for Routledge, who pushed me to consider material that I had not originally intended; to the John Templeton Foundation, which supported this book with a generous grant (ID 61070); and to the Office of Sponsored Programs at Saginaw Valley State University. Finally, my thanks to John Polkinghorne, who first got me interested in the question of science and divine action 20 years ago. Polkinghorne himself believes that physics will in time discover a depth and breadth of openness in nature that chaos and quantum mechanics merely approximate (1996, 36). I believe that Sir John is essentially correct but that the greater openness he predicted has been there all along, waiting to be acknowledged.

Notes

1 Or at least that's what I have talked Joshua Wells, my editor at Routledge, into believing.
2 The conventional wisdom is represented here:

> The far-reaching consequences of this common willingness to accept a "no-inherent-room-for-God" constraint coming from Newtonian physics cannot be overemphasized. Prior to the rise of Newtonian physics, Christian thinkers simply did not perceive the logical difficulty of asserting simultaneously that God acts at specific times and places and that the world retains its own causal efficacy and integrity. However, the supposed compatibility of these two ideas dissolved in the face of Newtonian determinism, which left in its wake human and divine agency as newly felt problems.
>
> (Wegter-McNelly 2008, 162, quoted in Dodds 2016, 159)

> All versions of determinism accept the ontological thesis that the state of the universe up to and including the present time t determines the universe's state in subsequent moments. Obviously, if what happens at time t + 1 is determined by the physical state of the world at t, no place remains for divine action.
>
> (Clayton 2008, 187)

3 Many libertarians hold to the principle of alternative possibilities: Whatever choice one is inclined to make, if that person is free, he or she has the ability to choose otherwise. So while it appears that my pen will remain on my desk for the rest of the afternoon, it is within my power to alter the future ever so slightly by putting the pen in my pocket – a power or capacity that does not depend on circumstances being otherwise. The choice is simply up to me.
4 "Classical" in the sense of classical mechanics.
5 Robert Larmer disputes this characterization of deism, providing textual evidence that even many deists held that God sustains the universe (2018). While Larmer may be correct about this, I will continue to use the more typical view of deism.
6 See (Oord 2015, 136–40) for more examples and discussion. While the Exodus 14 account specifically mentions a "strong east wind," interventionists take the sudden appearance of the wind to be a miracle.
7 I have heard nonviolationists say that Plantinga (2008) wrongly treats them as quasideists. That complaint has some merit, at least *prima facie*. Making a distinction between nonviolationism and noninterventionism should make matters clearer for both advocates and critics.
8 While this is often now called the Copenhagen interpretation, that properly refers to Niels Bohr's approach, which tended toward antirealism about the quantum realm itself. What I am calling the "standard interpretation" is closer to von Neumann's formulation.
9 It would also count as "interventionist determinism" in Leigh Vicens's taxonomy (2012, 328), but she does not recognize nonviolationism as a third possibility.

Works cited

Alston, William P. 1994. "Divine Action: Shadow or Substance?" In *The God Who Acts: Philosophical and Theological Explorations*, edited by Thomas F. Tracy, 41–62. University Park: Pennsylvania State University Press.

Clayton, Philip. 2008. *Adventures in the Spirit: God, World, Divine Action*. Edited by Zachary R. Simpson. Minneapolis: Fortress Press.

Dodds, Michael J. 2016. *Unlocking Divine Action: Contemporary Science and Thomas Aquinas*. Washington, DC: Catholic University of America Press.

Earman, John. 2000. *Hume's Abject Failure: The Argument Against Miracles*. New York: Oxford University Press.

Knight, Christopher C. 2007. *The God of Nature: Incarnation and Contemporary Science*. Theology and the Sciences. Minneapolis: Fortress Press.

Larmer, Robert. 2008. "Miracles, Physicalism, and the Laws of Nature." *Religious Studies* 44 (2): 149–59.

———. 2014. *The Legitimacy of Miracle*. Lanham: Lexington Books.

———. 2017. "Decretalism and the Laws of Nature: A Response to Jeffrey Koperski." *Philosophia Christi* 19 (2): 439–47.

———. 2018. "Theistic Evolution, Intelligent Design, and the Charge of Deism." *Philosophia Christi* 20 (2): 415–28. https://doi.org/10.5840/pc201820242.

Lewis, C. S. (1947) 1978. *Miracles: A Preliminary Study*. Macmillan Paperbacks ed. New York: Macmillan.

Oord, Thomas Jay. 2015. *The Uncontrolling Love of God: An Open and Relational Account of Providence*. Downers Grove: InterVarsity Press.

Plantinga, Alvin. 2008. "What Is 'Intervention'?" *Theology and Science* 6 (4): 369–401. https://doi.org/10.1080/14746700802396106.

———. 2011. *Where the Conflict Really Lies: Science, Religion, and Naturalism*. Oxford: Oxford University Press.

Polkinghorne, John. 1996. *Scientists as Theologians: A Comparison of the Writings of Ian Barbour, Arthur Peacocke and John Polkinghorne*. London: SPCK.

Pollard, William G. 1958. *Chance and Providence: God's Action in a World Governed by Scientific Law*. New York: Charles Scribner's Sons.

Tracy, Thomas F. 2009. "Creation, Providence and Quantum Chance." In *Philosophy, Science and Divine Action*, edited by F. LeRon Shults, Nancey C. Murphy, and Robert J. Russell, 227–61. Philosophical Studies in Science and Religion. Leiden: Brill.

Vicens, Leigh C. 2012. "On the Possibility of Special Divine Action in a Deterministic World." *Religious Studies* 48 (3): 315–36. https://doi.org/10.1017/S0034412511000266.

Wegter-McNelly, Kirk. 2008. "Fundamental Physics and Religion." In *The Oxford Handbook of Religion and Science*, edited by Philip Clayton, 156–71. New York: Oxford University Press.

2 Mapping the terrain

What exactly is the problem with God breaking the laws of nature? If "special divine action" is unfamiliar, there is probably some question about why a theist would be worried about such things. Isn't divine intervention the very thing that distinguishes theism from deism? Isn't intervention in some sense the default position?

The first question is based on a false dichotomy of sorts. There are not only two options: either (i) the disinterested Creator of deism or (ii) the interventionist God who routinely breaks the laws of nature. Most theologians today choose a third option – "none of the above," and this chapter explores the terrain between those two extremes. But in terms of the "default position," I agree that these noninterventionist and nonviolationist alternatives bear the theological burden of proof on this question. Without some argument to the contrary, the biblical God would most naturally be understood as sometimes acting contrary to natural laws.[1] Let's begin then by considering what motivates these alternative views. They are presented here without critique.[2]

2.1 Why not intervention?

The argument that God would not intervene in nature is not new and goes back at least as far as the conflict between Gottfried Leibniz and Isaac Newton.

2.1.1 Leibniz and the divine clockmaker

The many debates between Newton, Leibniz, and their respective camps are well-documented by historians of science (Janiak 2016, sec. 6). Both men appear to have independently discovered calculus at about the same time, which is not as implausible as it might sound. Unlike today, mathematical advances in the seventeenth and eighteenth centuries were largely propelled by the needs of physics. Given that both Newton and Leibniz required new tools to describe the same area of research (mechanics), it is not surprising that they would discover the same underlying mathematics.

On the theological side, Newton's supporters allowed for divine intervention in nature. They believed that such action might be necessary to keep the solar system stable, for example. Leibniz, on the other hand, argued that an omniscient deity would not act that way. The creation of an infinite God would not need maintenance:

> According to [the Newtonian] doctrine, God Almighty wants to wind up his watch from time to time: otherwise it would cease to move. He had not, it seems, sufficient foresight to make it a perpetual motion. Nay, the machine of God's making is so imperfect, according to these gentlemen, that he is obliged to clean it now and then by an extraordinary concourse, and even to mend it, as a clockmaker mends his work.
>
> (Leibniz and Clarke [1717] 1956, 11–12)

In other words, Newton and his follows are positing a lesser god, one that lacked the foresight to make a universe without the need for occasional tinkering. An omniscient, omnipotent deity, Leibniz argues, would have gotten it right in the first place. An infinite clockmaker would make a clock that would keep perfect time forever without winding or adjustments. The same goes for the universe as a whole. A god who needs to intervene in nature would be incompetent. To think as the Newtonians do is to "have a very mean notion of the wisdom and power of God" ([1717] 1956, 12). Schleiermacher would pick up this same argument a century later[3], and it continues to motivate noninterventionists to this day.[4]

2.1.2 An inconsistent god

As we will discuss in Chapter 4, theists since the seventeenth century have widely believed that God set the laws of nature in place and continues to uphold them. Noninterventionists and nonviolationists argue that it would be inconsistent for God to intervene in nature and thereby violate the same laws he had previously ordained:

> The very notion of God as the faithful source of rationality and regularity in the created order appears to be undermined if one simultaneously wishes to depict his action as *both* sustaining the "laws of nature" that express his divine will for creation *and* at the same time intervening to act in ways abrogating these very laws – almost as if he had second thoughts about whether he can achieve his purposes in what he has created.
>
> (Peacocke 1993, 142)

If God had wanted some event to happen, he could have structured the laws to bring it about – à la Leibniz – or changed the initial conditions at creation. To implement and then break his[5] own laws would involve a kind of divine schizophrenia. Hence, God does not violate the decrees that we recognize as the laws of nature.

2.1.3 God-of-the-gaps

Newton's theory of gravitation is "universal" in the sense that it applies to every mass in the universe. Why then, Newton wondered, don't we observe stars colliding over long periods of time? After all, they attract each other. Why don't they move? His answer was that God acts in such a way to keep the stars in place (*Opticks*, Query 28). In time, of course, a naturalistic explanation was found and there was no need to posit divine action to account for the fixed stars or, as I mentioned earlier, to keep the solar system stable.[6]

Newton's explanation is an example of what is now called "God-of-the-gaps reasoning": When a given phenomenon does not seem possible according to our best theories, one infers that God is responsible, thus filling the gap in our understanding. The problem is that when science eventually closes the same gap with a naturalistic explanation, God is pushed out. Each time that God is eliminated in this way strengthens the atheistic conclusion that divine action is never needed to explain anything. "Science," the atheist assures us, "will plug all of the gaps in time." Nonviolationists believe this argument can best be undermined by avoiding gap-reasoning in the first place:

> Contemporary theologians, therefore, have been understandably reluctant to adopt an account of God's relation to the world that appeals to the incompleteness of scientific explanations. Any theological reliance upon gaps in our understanding of the natural order may look like a return to [a] discredited apologetic strategy.
>
> (Tracy 1995, 290)

In short, theists should not appeal to divine intervention to explain phenomena that they find surprising. Avoiding gap-arguments is one motivation behind both noninterventionism and nonviolationism.

2.1.4 Science

It is widely believed that, with the possible exception of quantum mechanics, science takes nature to be an unbroken chain of causes. Physical effects are always produced by physical causes. In other words, many believe that science has proved the *causal closure of the physical*: Physical events can only be caused by earlier physical events in conjunction with the laws of nature.[7] Divine intervention is problematic because it breaks the chain of causation.[8] This is not a new idea. German scholar David Friedrich Strauss in his *Life of Jesus* wrote, "All things are linked together by a chain of causes and effects, which suffer no interruption" (Brooke 1991, 270–71). Philip Clayton incorporates the God-of-the-gaps in his version of this objection:

> Physical science, it appears, leaves no place for divine action. To do science is generally to presuppose that the universe is a closed physical system, that interactions are regular and lawlike, that all causal histories can be traced, and that anomalies will ultimately have physical explanations. Unfortunately, the traditional way of asserting that God acts in the world conflicts with all four of these conditions. It presupposes that the universe is open, that God acts from time to time according to particular purposes, that the ultimate source and explanation of these actions is the divine will, and that no earthly account would ever suffice to explain God's intentions.
>
> (2008, 186)

Remaining in harmony with science is a key *desideratum* for most scholars working on divine action, and so science tacitly dictates the boundaries within which the discussion takes place. The models discussed in the following sections therefore take pains to avoid running afoul of science in any way.[9]

2.1.5 The problem of evil

If the arguments against intervention seem weightier the further we have gone, that is no mistake. We now arrive at the central concern. Many believe that if there are no limits to divine action, the problem of evil becomes an insurmountable objection to theism. If God simply chooses to intervene and stop some tragedies from occurring, why not more? Why not all? Here is theologian Thomas Oord:

> [Interventionists] typically believe God permits or allows evil because God has the kind of controlling power to prevent such evil. . . [But the] God who can violate the lawlike regularities of the universe *ought* to violate those regularities more often to make our lives better [italics added].
>
> (2015, 142)

It is common to say that God has the ability to prevent evil and yet has overarching reasons not to intervene. But once the door is opened to interventions, every case where God does not to prevent an identical evil becomes a challenge to God's goodness. Oord chooses instead to accept constraints on direct divine action within the course of history in order to explain human suffering.

There are similarities here to the standard free will defense. It begins with the premise that creatures with libertarian freedom have greater intrinsic value than automata or creatures with some lesser variety of free will. If so, God ordaining free will both adds to the intrinsic value of the universe and inevitably leads to those creatures choosing evil from time to time. While God has the ability to intervene and stop such choices, doing so would mean that the agent is no longer free. There is therefore an important reason for God not to do so. The value of libertarian freedom thereby becomes a kind of constraint on divine intervention. A well-known reply to this argument is that it only pertains to moral evil – the kind brought about by rational beings – but has nothing to say about natural evil: disease, disasters, and the like.

What if God likewise has principled reasons for not stepping in to prevent natural evil? Polkinghorne advances this line:

> I think the only possible solution lies in a variation of the free-will defense, applied to the whole created world. One might call it "the free-process defense." In his great act of creation I believe that God allows the physical world to be itself. . . . in that independence which is Love's gift of freedom to the one beloved . . . The cosmos is given the opportunity to be itself. . . . It is from that precariousness that natural *evil* arises.
> (2005, 77–78)

It is not the case that God chooses to aid some and withhold from others. God instead has overarching reasons for not intervening in order to prevent natural evil. The autonomy of nature has value analogous to libertarian freedom in persons. Some noninterventionists go so far as to claim that this solves the problem of evil.

These, then, are the main reasons given for rejecting interventionist divine action. None of them are decisive, in my view. Nonetheless, I would like to examine the current terrain before making any positive proposals of my own. Let's begin with the two main types of noninterventionism before moving on to nonviolationism.[10]

2.2 Thomism

While its roots are premodern, Thomism of some variety or other is still a live option. This is especially true of Catholic thinkers but not exclusively so. Like most noninterventionist models of divine action, this one begins with the relationship between God and nature (God–world).

The Thomist view of divine action rests on two categories of causation: primary and secondary. God is the primary cause in the sense that God is a necessary being, the sole uncaused cause. Everything else is secondary and contingent, depending on God for its existence. More precisely, God is not merely the first cause in the sense of, say, initiating the Big Bang, as the cosmological argument for the existence of God is so often presented in introductory philosophy courses. Rather, secondary causes depend on the primary cause synchronically. As Aquinas taught (*Summa Contra Gentiles*, 1.44), God could have created a physical reality with a temporally infinite past with no first sequential event, yet the entire timeline would still be contingent and dependent on God for its existence. God is "continually creating" in the upholding of all other contingent beings.

Nothing thus far is distinctively Thomistic. Most theists would agree up to this point. Under Thomism, secondary causes are properly thought of as the way in which God is acting in the world. God acts in and through secondary causes:

> [Consider] God's continuing creative action in the universe, conceived now more richly than simply as *just* divine existential conservancy. It is that a principal mode of God's activity in the world at the level of inanimate and nonpersonal beings is precisely through the underlying regularities, constraints, and relationships he/she has established in nature, and which we sometimes refer to as "the laws of nature." . . . The regularities, constraints, and relationships are as they are by God's allowance or choice – he/she works through the secondary causes of our world.
>
> (Stoeger 1995, 248)

The key to this account is that God does not intervene to act in nature. God instead works through the causal powers of natural entities.[11] For any given event in nature, there is both a primary and a secondary cause. While the natural sciences will only ever observe secondary causes, all events are nonetheless acts of God *qua* primary cause:

> When a primary and secondary cause act together, however, the effect belongs entirely to both. The influence of the primary cause does not diminish the action of the secondary cause, but enables it.
>
> When God acts as primary cause in a creature, the effect is not divided between them, but belongs wholly to both.
>
> (Dodds 2016, 192)

For any physical event, the question is never whether the cause was natural or supernatural. In virtually every case, the Thomistic view is that both are at work. While some will cite miracles as exceptions, others believe that even then God is working through secondary causes.[12]

Thomism has several virtues from a noninterventionist point of view. First, unlike Intelligent Design Theory, it does not contradict science. The natural sciences are the study of secondary causes. Since God works through the causal powers of contingent beings rather than overriding them, no observable events will be out-of-bounds from a scientific perspective. Second, there is no temptation for a God-of-the-gaps since only secondary causes are candidates to explain a scientific anomaly. Third, the problem of evil is diminished as compared to interventionism. God's action within nature is limited to the causal powers found in nature. God could therefore create new islands by working in and through the capacities of a volcano, but God could not directly intervene to stop a lava flow from destroying a house.

All theists should agree with Thomism that God is continuously involved with natural events in some way or other. This, again, is what distinguishes theism from deism. The question remains, however, as to what exactly God is doing. God acts "in and through" secondary causes, but what does that mean? In what sense does God make any sort of causal contribution?

There are two answers to this question, grounded in different understandings of the relation between primary and secondary causes. The first looks back to Aquinas's cosmological argument for the existence of God, specifically his "third way" (Aquinas 2006, *Summa Theologica* I, q.2, a.3). It is premised on the idea that each being relies on other contingent beings and conditions for its existence. The notion of reliance here is synchronic, rather than some sort of causal dependency backward in time. While it is true that I am a contingent being dependent on the prior existence of my parents, that diachronic dependence is a different matter. What we are talking about here is closer to the dependence of my desk on the existence of atoms: Take away the atoms and the desk ceases to be. Note that the atoms are likewise contingent beings, depending on their parts and other states of affairs, such as the cooling of the universe since the since the Big Bang. Aquinas rejected the idea that this sort of appeal to yet another level of contingent beings could go on forever. It cannot be turtles all the way down. Hence the need at some point for a noncontingent, necessary being at the ground floor of reality. All things continually depend on God.

This picture can then be extended to events. When contingent creatures act (secondary causes), they serve as intermediaries between whatever effect is brought about and God (primary cause):

> On this view, the changes of state from moment to moment that make up the history of the universe have as their proximate causes the interactions of creatures within the order of nature. These events can be regarded as acts of God, however, insofar as they result from a series of causal intermediaries that God has established.
>
> (Tracy 2009, 236)

Secondary causes in this view have an instrumental role in divine action. Primary causation is mediated by secondary causes:

> Divine Providence works through intermediaries. For God governs the lower through the higher, not from any impotence on his part, but from

the abundance of his goodness imparting to creatures also the dignity of causing.

(Aquinas 2006, *Summa Theologica* I, q.22, a.3)

And so God works by way of contingent creatures and does not act within nature apart from them. Some then emphasize the autonomy given to creation in that it has causal powers apart from God. As Edwards writes, "[At] the heart of this approach is the idea that God gives creatures independence and integrity, including the capacity to act as real causes. In this view, God consistently respects the proper autonomy of creation" (2010, 62).

The second approach denies that primary causation is in any way mediated by secondary causes. Freddoso stresses that primary causation is immediate and that every action in nature is due to both primary and secondary causes (1988, 77). The previous view, he says, takes primary causation to be little more than the "mere conservation" of secondary causes. Not surprisingly, Freddoso also cites Aquinas:

> Therefore God is the cause or the action of all things inasmuch as he gives them power to act and preserves them and applies them to action and inasmuch as by his power every other power acts. And when we add that God is his own power and that he is within each thing, not as a part of its essence, but as holding the thing in being, it follows that he operates immediately in every operation, without excluding the operation of the will and nature.
>
> (Aquinas 2011, *De Potentia*, q.3 q.7)

I do not know how to square this passage from *De Potentia* with the previous one from the *Summa*. One speaks of divine action as immediate; the other, as mediated. Under the former, it is difficult to understand what the causal contribution of God amounts to. If every event involves both primary and secondary causation, yet it appears that secondary causes are fully capable of bringing about effects on their own, what does primary causation do? As Ritchie suggests, it may be best to simply appeal to mystery (2017, 369). The primary/secondary relation is a metaphysical question that is beyond our grasp.

Well, perhaps. Ideally, though, an appeal to mystery occurs after a great deal of progress has been made on an issue. Whole books have been written on the problem of evil giving a variety of answers. If there is some remaining instance of evil left unaccounted for, one might say that there *is* a good reason for God allowing such events, but one can only know that reason from a God's-eye perspective. Fair enough. In this case, however, the mystery seems to be at the very heart of the matter. While primary causation is supposed to be an account of special divine action, the model rests squarely on the mystery. What does it mean to say that God *acts* in and through secondary causes? We don't know.

This approach to divine action is attractive to two groups. The first is made up of Catholic scholars who take a broadly Thomistic approach to metaphysics overall. They have theological reasons for preferring Thomism (or something in the neighborhood) and are simply applying it here to the question of divine action. This is not uncommon in philosophy. Take physicalism, the metaphysical view that everything that exists can ultimately be reduced to the entities of fundamental physics. If one believes that the arguments for physicalism are compelling, that person will reject mind-body dualism in the philosophy of mind, reject realism in ethics, reject theism in the philosophy of religion, and so on. One's metaphysical views ramify across the philosophical landscape. The same with Thomism.

A second group that might favor this approach are those who believe in causal powers, dispositions, and capacities to explain natural regularities.[13] These are the philosophical descendants of Aquinas's secondary causes. Many dispositionalists reject Thomism, but they believe that his overall approach regarding causation is better than the alternatives. For theistic metaphysicians of this stripe, then, the primary/secondary distinction among causes fits nicely with their program.[14]

In short, there are two main doors to a Thomist view of divine action, one theological (Thomism writ large) and one philosophical (causal powers and dispositions). But what if you don't find either attractive – no metaphysical inclination toward causal powers and no theological motivation to embrace Thomism?[15] Then you will likely be looking elsewhere for a model of special divine action. As I will argue in Chapters 4 and 5, medieval Aristotelianism was deliberately set aside to make room for more modern ideas, such as the laws of nature. That ship has sailed and there is no pressing need to call it back to port. This is not an argument that Thomists should stop what they are doing and get on board with a less antiquated view. Perhaps Thomism will yield something sufficiently powerful and explanatory to justify it. But that day has not yet come.

2.3 Panentheism

Panentheism leads to a second type of noninterventionism, one that denies the strict creation-creator demarcation between nature and God. The central metaphor used by most – but not all (Culp 2017, sec. 4) – panentheists is that the relation is like body to soul. God and nature are far more interrelated and less independent of each other than in classical theism.[16] Many deny creation *ex nihilo*. Others closer to classical theism would want to qualify these claims in various ways, all of which is to say that "panentheism" is not a precise term (Gregersen 2004).[17]

The main panentheist contribution to special divine action is that intervention is not a choice; it is a metaphysical impossibility. God and nature do not have the sort of relation whereby God could intervene. To push the metaphor, one's soul cannot intervene in one's body. Intervention becomes a category mistake. God cannot act on the universe "from the outside." The world is already "in" God, although cashing out this second metaphor is no easier than the first (Meister 2017, 8). In any case, the point is that interventionism is ruled out as a metaphysical constraint, not because it is wise or morally better not to do so. God cannot intervene any more than a necessary being can choose to no longer exist.

A closely related view is Oord's *essential kenosis* (2015). Here the metaphysical constraint is not due to the relation between God and nature (soul and body), but rather part of God's essence: It is God's nature to be in relation.[18] A crucial part of this relation is not controlling either persons or natural processes.[19] There is some similarity here to Polkinghorne's free-process thesis mentioned in section 2.1. The difference for Oord is that God's noninterference is not a matter of choice. Like other panentheists, Oord holds that God cannot intervene (2015, 94–5).

Panentheism avoids all the concerns theologians have about interventionism. There is no danger of running counter to science or positing God-of-the-gaps explanations since interventions are ruled out. There is no mystery for why God does not prevent evil. It is simply not possible for the panentheistic God to do so. God cannot override the free will of persons and God cannot intervene to prevent natural disasters.

For better or worse, panentheism has far more support within mainstream academic theology than elsewhere. If the medievals believed in the God-of-the-philosophers, panentheism is the God-of-the-theologians. While the process thought of Alfred North Whitehead is part of the recent history of philosophy, it had little lasting influence among analytic philosophers or the more recent movement toward analytic theology. For that matter, analytics have a similar lack of interest in Hegel and German Idealism.

Many contemporary Thomists and panentheists approach the question of divine action by way of the God–world relation. In other words, once we get the metaphysics straight, noninterventionism becomes the obvious right answer regarding divine action. This approach contrasts the search for a specific "causal-joint" between God and nature – the place where divine action first registers a difference in physical events. Many theologians now believe that focusing on the God–world relation is preferred and that the search for a causal-joint was the wrong way to address the question of divine action (Ritchie 2017, 361–2).

While I acknowledge the difficulty of the causal-joint question, this shift is not so much a different approach to divine action but rather a refusal of the question and a change in subject. There is a lot about what divine action *isn't* among these authors: It's not intervention. And their schemas employ a lot of suggestive metaphors and analogies: "in and through," "body to soul." But the *how*, the mechanics of divine action, is never addressed. Consider this passage from Oord: "For this reason, miracles are neither coercive interventions nor the result of natural causes alone. Miracles occur when creatures, organisms or entities of various size and complexity cooperate with God's initiating and empowering love" (2015, 200). While the principle of charity should be extended to authors (assuming the more informed and favorable reading over a lesser one) and all the more so to friends like Tom, I must confess that I have no idea what that means. What would it be for a brain tumor to cooperate? What does God initiating and empowering love *do*?

Evolution would seem to be an excellent test case. Panentheists and Thomists overwhelmingly favor some variety of theistic evolution. And many theistic evolutionists believe that God has somehow or other guided the evolutionary process. So, again, guided in what sense? Not like guiding a golf ball into the hole by nudging it from time to time. That would be an intervention. God's upholding the process is a necessary condition, but so is the existence of atoms. One would not want to say, however, that atoms guide evolution, photosynthesis, or other biological processes. If there is more to God's guidance, what is it?

One perfectly understandable answer is the deistic one: nothing. God doesn't do anything more. God creates the universe and that exhausts the degree to which God interacts with nature. Perhaps there is more in terms of God's guidance and motivating of persons. Nature, on the other hand, is left to its laws.

Few noninterventionists today are willing to bite that particular bullet. But instead of providing a different answer to the question, many simply change the subject to the God–world relation. That's fine, but unless one can say what God does on his side of the God–world relation that makes a *difference* on the other side, the question of special divine action has not been addressed.

While some accept this challenge and supplement the God–world relation with something more (see section 2.4), others believe that any direct answer would be an unhelpful retreat. "You are missing the point," I can imagine my interlocutor replying, "the only way to answer your question is to posit a causal-joint at which such guidance can take place. Noninterventionists are instead giving reasons for why God cannot be more involved in the natural order. Anything more opens the door to a hands-on, interventionist deity making the problem of evil insurmountable."

Let's say a bit more about the problem of evil, then, since it appears to be a key motivator in the turn away from causal-joint models. The core idea is that an active God makes the problem worse:

> If it is supposed that God has adequate reason to restrict divine action to a combination of ordinary action (in and through natural processes) and revelation (such as the Resurrection of Christ) then the problem of evil does not take on the same dimensions as it does when it is assumed that God might freely intervene in any sort of process at any time.
>
> (Russell 1995, 31)

One of the proposed strengths of God–world models is that they include principled limits on what God will do and that these limits help explain why God does not intervene to prevent evil. Some believe this self-limiting is rational and voluntary: God could intervene but has stronger, countervailing reasons not to. Panentheists take the self-limiting to be involuntary. The inconsistency between omnipotence, omniscience, omnibenevolence, and the existence of evil is broken by proposed metaphysical limitations on what God can do. Oord is explicit on this point: "[Why] doesn't a loving and powerful God prevent genuine evil? The essential kenosis model of providence offers one principal answer. . . . Let me state this answer simply: God *cannot* unilaterally prevent genuine evil" (2015, 110). It is God's metaphysical relation to nature that makes intervention impossible.

So why am I not a noninterventionist? Two reasons. First, it does not *solve* the problem of evil. While any universe with laws of nature will have natural evil (i.e., people will inevitably get in the way of nature's most powerful forces), it seems as if God could have arranged things so that the world had less. God could have made a universe without tobacco or with mosquitos that do not like human blood. God could have made us more genetically predisposed toward virtue without taking away free will. To be a solution to the problem of evil, noninterventionists would also have to argue that this is the best of all possible worlds – a doctrine that has few defenders these days.

The second reason is that I do not see this limiting of God as a strength of these models. Putting theological distance between God and nature is the failed philosophical strategy of Gnosticism. Let's be clear: No theologian mentioned here is a Gnostic. The Gnostics were not concerned with the problem of evil. For them, it was the "problem of matter." They did not believe that a spiritually perfect God would get his hands dirty through direct involvement with a material world. Yet Hebrew and Christian scriptures both seem to portray an interactive God, one who is undeniably the Creator. What to do? The solution was to place a buffer between God and nature, a lesser deity responsible for the world of matter. The Gnostic God did not create the material world and is therefore off the hook regarding the problem of matter. The theological price is a god who is removed from our physical reality.

This is both the general strategy and the price to be paid by panentheism and other God–world models in which the problem of evil is the central concern. God is not responsible for evil, they say, because there are metaphysical restrictions on what God can do in nature. The price is an attenuated view of omnipotence, where God is unable to respond to many of our prayers. In my view – and this may reflect a disciplinary bias different from that in (nonanalytic) theology – the price is too high. The models discussed thus far allow God far too little freedom to act.[20]

2.4 Pneumatological naturalism

The next proposal, which Ritchie calls *pneumatological naturalism* (2017, 374), comes from theologian Amos Yong and philosopher James K. A.

Smith. It is pneumatological insofar as the account focuses on God's Spirit, which is immanent throughout creation. Why Ritchie considers it a type of naturalism needs some explanation. Naturalism in philosophy is a descendant of *materialism*: Everything that exists is made of matter. This gave way in the twentieth century to *physicalism*: Everything that exists can ultimately be reduced to the entities of fundamental physics.[21] Naturalism expands this to include all the entities recognized by the natural sciences, not just physics. Hence, "theistic naturalism" sounds like an oxymoron to philosophers. Theism and naturalism have incompatible ontologies.

Theologians use the term somewhat differently, typically when the focus is on a holistic theology of nature with the God–world relation at its core (Ritchie 2017, 367). Theistic naturalists emphasize the unity of all reality, including God.[22]

To make things clear, "metaphysical naturalism" will refer here to the way philosophers use the term; "theological naturalism," to the theologian's version. Pneumatological naturalism is one type of theological naturalism.

Let's approach pneumatological naturalism *via negativa*. It rejects deism in that nature is not an autonomous "self-sufficient 'world' that runs on its own steam" (Smith 2010, 97). It is not an interventionist model, what Smith calls "naïve supernaturalism" (2010, 89), as intervention makes sense only given the false natural/supernatural bifurcation posited by deism (Smith 2008, 880). Pneumatological naturalism makes no appeal to secondary causes as intermediaries through which God acts. It is not panentheistic insofar as a strict creator-creation distinction is maintained.[23]

The central metaphor of pneumatological naturalism is that nature is infused with the Spirit. The very distinction between natural and supernatural wrongly implies that creation has a kind of autonomy. Instead, nature has no capacity to act apart from the Spirit working:

> The shape of this theological or participatory ontology is nonreductive and incarnational. It affirms that matter *as created* exceeds itself and *is* only insofar as it participates in or is suspended from the transcendent Creator, and it affirms that there is a significant sense in which the transcendent inheres in immanence.
>
> (Smith 2008, 889)

The unique aspect of this "participatory ontology" is that the Spirit sometimes changes nature's capacities.

Let's continue with Smith's version since his is the clearer of the two. One reason he rejects intervention is that he takes all natural events to be divine action. It just happens that most of these fall within the regularities we identify as laws of nature. At other times, the action of the Spirit produces unusual events – what we think of as miracles. Strictly speaking, there are no laws or independent powers "out there" in reality responsible for the regularity of events. Both the regularities and the miracles are part of God continuously acting:

> Because nature is always already inhabited by the Spirit, it is also primed for (not merely "open to") special or unique singularities; these will not be "antinature," because nature is not a discrete, autonomous entity. Rather, we can think of these "special" miraculous manifestations of the Spirit's presence in creation as more intense instances of the Spirit in creation – or as "sped-up" modes of the Spirit's more "regular" presences.
>
> (Smith 2010, 104)

From a God's-eye perspective, there is no difference between providence and special divine action – an idea that goes back at least as far as Newton (Davis 1996, 85). Our readiness to ascribe miracles to God's intervention is due to a tacit metaphysical naturalism on our part, seeing nature as fully autonomous.

Yong's view is harder to pin down. He speaks favorably of top-down causation and the input of information into nature (2011, 95), which will be discussed in the next section, but these do not seem to be central to his account. Like Smith, he rejects the uniformity of nature and the universality of law. The laws at work now need not be the same as those in the past or the future: "[The] laws of nature are amenable to the basic actions of God and sufficiently flexible so that they can be miraculously redeemed to usher in new patterns and habits of the coming world" (Yong 2011, 131).[24] Elsewhere, Yong embraces physicist George Ellis's idea that the laws of nature contain seldom-tapped ranges of freedom. Given the right conditions, "miraculous" events can unfold in a perfectly lawlike way. As Ellis suggests, perhaps some initial conditions involve "God-centered minds" to such a degree that these conditions are seldom met (1995, 386). While the various ideas mentioned are interesting, it isn't clear whether Yong is endorsing them or merely sketching proposals in the same conceptual neighborhood as his own.

In the end, Yong claims to opt for a view of law championed by C. S. Peirce, bringing the hope of greater clarity (2011, 120). Peirce scholars know this to be a false hope, however, given the notorious difficulty of interpreting his work on this topic. Many take Peircean laws to be nothing more than habits of our own minds projected onto reality (Burch 2017). That would make Peirce's view a type of Humeanism regarding law (see section 5.1) and would be similar to Smith's in the sense that the laws do not have their own ontology (Smith 2008, 891). While Yong's metaphysics never become clear, there is one idea he shares with Peirce: The laws of nature are not fixed but evolve over time. The eschatological laws of the kingdom of God are not the same as the current laws of nature. It is this lack of fixedness that allows for miracles. Miraculous events are governed by new laws that are temporarily active in the present age (Yong 2011, 128–30). Such laws will become the norm in the eschatological future.

Pneumatological naturalism has two advantages over the other accounts discussed thus far. First, it envisions a far more active God. Answers to prayer, miraculous healing, and more are accepted at face value rather than being written off or reinterpreted in some way. As Plantinga has correctly diagnosed, it is not natural science that mitigates against such things but rather metaphysical naturalism that is smuggled in under the supposed *imprimatur* of science (2011, ix–x). Smith likewise argues that the science and religion literature typically cedes too much to naturalism from the start (2008, 884–5).

Second, while other types of theological naturalism fail to say what exactly God does with respect to divine action, Yong and Smith have an answer: From time to time, God changes those regularities that we take to be laws of nature. Every causal regularity is due to God's manifest presence. When the particulars of that presence change, God brings about different events than what would have otherwise occurred.

While this is a step in the right direction in my view, it has not garnered much support. Before we get to the theological objections, philosophers of science would question whether one should take the laws of nature to be quite so plastic. The uniformity of nature, which says that the laws are invariant with respect to both time and space, is a metaphysical principle that has served science well for several centuries. Without it, astronomy and cosmology would be impossible. While astronomers could make observations, no calculations based on the behavior of distant objects could be trusted if those objects obey different laws. Cosmology itself would never have become a science, since all its models presuppose the uniformity of nature. Of course, Smith and Yong are probably not envisioning global changes in the laws, so perhaps the problem can be mitigated. If the changes are limited to a specific place for a short period, they would not interfere with science.

Another issue is that while their view is technically a type of nonviolationism, I doubt that others will find it to be a welcome addition. When nonviolationists discuss the value of not violating the laws of nature, they tacitly mean "the actual laws of nature as they stand." The idea that God might change the laws temporarily is not what they had in mind.

In addition, Yong and Smith seem to be committed to a form of *occasionalism*, whereby God is causally responsible for all physical events.[25] In their view, all events in nature, whether lawlike or miraculous, are the result of immediate divine action. It isn't clear whether they would consider that a defect, but they do not allude to this sort of meticulous control elsewhere. In any case, another objection comes close on its heels.

The flexibility in the laws because of God's mutable will that Smith and Yong describe makes the problem of evil worse. If every event in nature, both the commonplace and the miraculous, is a consequence of God's will,

God is responsible for all natural evils. The regularities that brought about the 2004 tsunami in the Indian Ocean were literally acts of God. And since, in their view, God changes the laws from time to time, God chose not to do so in this case.

This is a good place to point out the Scylla and Charybdis of special divine action. Scylla is deism, the ultimate hands-off theology. Charybdis is theological determinism, in which God directly causes all events. Both are distinctly enticing. The attractions of deism are first as a type of perfection, à la the Leibnizian clockmaker, and second as a diminishment of the problem of evil. The less involved God is or can be with physical reality, the less responsible God is. Moral evils are the choices of persons with free will. Natural evil is the outworking of the laws of nature. The deistic Creator is not involved. The attraction of a highly interactive, hands-on theology is that it fits more naturally with a biblical God who hears and responds to prayer. The strength of one is the weakness of the other. In my view, none of the proposals discussed thus far successfully navigate the dilemma. Thomism and panentheism introduce metaphysical constraints on divine action but run too close to deism in my view. There isn't much that God can do under these models. Pneumatological naturalism skirts the other extreme but must then accept the baggage that comes with occasionalism.

While the next two models are initially more promising, they also are devoured by Scylla for reasons that will require a deeper dive into the philosophy of science.

2.5 Emergence

Questions about reduction and emergence might seem like a change of subject here. Let's consider the underlying ideas before making the connection to divine action.

As different as they are, no one doubts that solids, liquids, and gases are composed of atoms. Even the relative warmth of the air in my office is explained in terms of the behavior of particles. This and many more successful explanations of macroscopic phenomena in terms of the microscopic have fueled reductionism in science – the principle that more fundamental explanations are almost always available at some lower level of physical reality. But like any good idea, this one can only be pushed so far. Many philosophers of science now doubt reductionism as an overarching approach to science.

Reductionism holds that everything is simpler in the small. Whether we are talking about a watch or the circulatory system, in order to understand the whole one must first discover the properties of its component parts. Examples can be drawn from each of the sciences. The closer one examines those success stories, however, the less compelling they become. While the temperature of the air can be explained in terms of the average kinetic energy of its molecules, thermodynamics has never been fully reduced to statistical mechanics. The direction of time, the role of probability, and some ineliminable idealizations remain controversial more than a century after this reduction was thought to have taken place. Instead of a consistent march showing how every entity is "really nothing but" its constituents, the sciences are more fragmented than ever. Greater knowledge of the micro does not always help in the macro, as Nobel Laureate Philip Anderson notes:

> The ability to reduce everything to simple fundamental laws does not imply the ability to start from those laws and reconstruct the universe. In fact, the more the elementary particle physicists tell us about the nature of the fundamental laws, the less relevance they seem to have to the very real problems of the rest of science, much less to those of society.
>
> (2008, 222)

Like all broad methodological approaches, reductionism has limits.

Emergentism is a direct challenge to reductionism. It says that the reason for the increasingly long list of failed reductions is that new entities, laws, properties, or causes can emerge from a base level. An exhaustive understanding of the base will inevitably be incomplete. "[At] each level of complexity entirely new properties appear, and the understanding of the new behaviors requires research which I think is as fundamental in its nature as any other" (Anderson 2008, 222). There is a corollary. Research in the sciences often takes place along different scales or levels: particle physics at one, organic chemistry at another, on through genetics, psychology, economics, etc.[26] Why does this division of labor work so well? Emergentists believe it is due to nature organizing itself along these levels. They are part of the structure of reality. Emergent higher levels bring into being novel, irreducible entities and processes that go beyond the capacities of the lower level base.

Consider some examples: 1) While chemistry emerges from quantum mechanics, it cannot be reduced to quantum mechanics. Not even the shape of molecules can be derived from physics alone. 2) Chaos theory, which will be discussed more fully in the next chapter, not only cannot be derived from quantum mechanics but also seems to be forbidden by quantum physics. Yet chaos is detectable in many observable systems. 3) The most widely used example is consciousness. A brain and a body are necessary for consciousness, but it is still a mystery how consciousness emerges from a working brain.[27] We might also put purposeful behavior here. One example that Polkinghorne has often used is the explanation for why a tea pot is boiling. A partial explanation can be given in terms of chemistry and phase changes, but the full explanation must include my intention to make some tea. Chemistry alone will never explain why there is water in the pot.

There are some general principles that can be derived from these examples. According to philosopher of physics Robert Batterman, emergence typically includes three things (2009). The first, as we have seen, is antireductionism: "The behavior of the emergent whole does not reduce to some function of the behavior of its components." The second is unpredictability: "The behavior of the emergent whole is unpredictable given knowledge of the nature of its parts." A modified Laplacian demon, with an exhaustive understanding of physics, would not thereby know biology.[28] The third is novelty: "The behavior of the emergent whole is completely different, new, and unexpected, given knowledge of the nature of its parts. In addition, there is often a demand that the emergent feature is not explainable by a theory of the nature of its parts."

Now things start getting more controversial. Most scientists and philosophers of science are willing to accept an epistemic version of emergence. They agree that, as a matter of scientific knowledge, the many branches of science will remain fragmented. Nature is too complex to fit all research into a neatly integrated, reductive hierarchy. Nonetheless, they believe that the limits of reduction are merely epistemic. If we were smarter as a species and able to apprehend how it all fits together, we would not need higher-level laws and nonfundamental science. Metaphysically speaking, they are physicalists: The only things that ultimately exist are matters of fundamental physics. They are emergentists insofar as they do not believe that the full reduction of any one branch of science to another will come to pass.

Some accept a stronger, ontological form of emergence. In this view, upper-level properties, causes, and laws are not merely irreplaceable tools for dealing with a complex world. They are irreducible and real. The emergent brings something metaphysically new to the fore.

> Strong emergence is a far more contentious position, in which it is asserted that the micro-level principles are quite simply inadequate to account for the system's behaviour as a whole. Strong emergence cannot succeed in systems that are causally closed at the microscopic level, because there is no room for additional principles to operate that are not already implicit in the lower-level rules. Thus a closed system of Newtonian particles cannot exhibit strongly emergent properties, as everything that can be said about the system is already contained in the micro-level dynamics (including the initial conditions).
>
> (Davies 2008, xii)

Under ontological emergence, the lower levels provide necessary conditions for the upper, but the lower does not determine the upper. As Davies says, this is a minority position. Why are scientists and philosophers of science less willing to take this step?

One reason is that both tend to be metaphysically squeamish, preferring to hedge when it comes to the ontological implications of science. Another is that ontological emergence is often paired with a still more controversial belief in downward causation, starting with the idea that natural causes are not restricted to their own level. Some have effects at higher levels; some have effects at lower levels. The first part is unproblematic. Some of the noise found in electronics (higher level) is ultimately due to energy changes in its constituent electrons (lower level). The expression of various genes (lower) causes changes that affect the entire circulatory system (higher). What about downward causation?

Consciousness is again a common example. Consider the causal chain starting with my intention to drink from a mug and ending with my hand, the mug, and its contents moving toward by mouth. My mental states (higher) are a key part of the sequence and are causally responsible for physical changes (lower). This is enough for many emergentists to embrace the idea of downward causation.

It is now a short step to a model of divine action. If both ontological emergence and downward causation are real, higher levels influence lower ones without violating the laws at either level. God might therefore influence nature at the highest level, bringing about change in a top-down fashion, all without breaking the laws of nature.

> If God interacts with the "world" at this supervenient level of totality, then he could be causatively effective in a "top-down" manner without abrogating the laws and regularities . . . that operate at the myriad sub-levels of existence that constitute that "world." Particular events could occur in the world and be what they are because God intends them to be so, without at any point any contravention of the laws of physics, biology, psychology, sociology, or whatever is the pertinent science for the level of description in question.
>
> (Peacocke 1993, 159)[29]

Peacocke tends to see downward causation in terms of the whole determining the behavior of its parts, but whole–part mereology is not the only way to think of the relation between levels. In any case, this proposal is nonviolationist insofar as God can bring about change in nature without breaking any laws.

The case for this model of divine action depends on the plausibility of ontological emergence and downward causation. Critics are not hard to find. Polkinghorne argues that what downward causation *is* remains unclear (1995, 151). Appealing to mental causation is no help given other vexing questions about free will and agency.

The main philosophical hurdle to emergence comes from philosopher Jaegwon Kim (2003). Consider a two-level diagram (Figure 2.1) for the relation between an emergent level and its base. Each of the four nodes represents the state of a system at its given level:

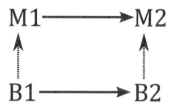

Figure 2.1 Levels diagram.

Emergentists generally affirm three claims:

(i)   **Causal efficacy.** B1 causes B2 and M1 causes M2. Causation along levels is real. This is represented by the horizontal arrows.
(ii) **Supervenience.** The emergent level depends on its base.[30] This is represented by the vertical arrows. Supervenience is a relatively weak type of dependence. In various places Kim says that the base level determines, necessitates, and "is (at least) nomologically sufficient" for the upper level (2003, 155–57).
(iii) **Irreducibility.** Supervenient properties are neither reducible to nor identical with their bases.

Since mental causation is such a prominent example, let M1 and M2 be mental states that supervene on brain states B1 and B2. Now consider a person in state M2 – say, the desire to take a drink. Why is this person in M2 at time t_2? There seem to be two equally good answers. The first is that the person was in M1 at t_1, which in turn caused M2. M1 could be the feeling of thirst. The feeling prompts the desire to take a drink. The second answer is that the person is in brain state B2 at t_2. Since B2 necessitates M2, if the person is in B2 at t_2, he or she will be in M2 at t_2 no matter what happened previously. The problem is that both answers seem to be sufficient for bringing about M2. One makes the other superfluous.

Moreover, the causal connection between B1 and B2 makes the upper-level one between M1 and M2 redundant. Since B1 causes B2 and B2 is sufficient for M2, there is no work left for M1 to do. "There is a tension between vertical determination and horizontal causation. In fact, vertical determination excludes horizontal causation" (Kim 2003, 153). In our example, this means that thirst in no way causes the desire to take a drink. Mental states do not bring about other mental states. If that doesn't seem too important in the case of thirst and desire, move the sequence forward a couple of steps. Typically, the desire to take a drink would bring about M3 the intention to get one, perhaps to move one's hand to lift a glass of water. But the causal link between

M2 and M3 is as redundant as any other at this level. One's intentions are causally inert. Again, all the real causal work is done one level down.

The problem does not stop there, however. There is nothing unique about mind–body supervenience. If biological properties supervene on chemical ones, biological causes are undermined in like fashion. Biological causes are redundant given the more fundamental chemical causes on which they depend. Having now set foot on the slippery slope, there doesn't seem to be anywhere to stop this "causal drainage" until it reaches the most fundamental level of physics. In other words, the only real causation in nature is at the lowest level, precisely as the reductionist had always claimed. This means that virtually every causal assertion ever made is strictly speaking false, since the only true causes are on the ground floor of physical reality. This is not the conclusion that emergentists were hoping for.

The upshot is that the metaphysics of ontological emergence has well-known problems, and anyone wanting to use emergence as part of a model of divine action inherits them all. Several proposals have been floated to avoid causal drainage. None of them are easy fixes.[31] Those wanting to employ emergence for divine action need to address this challenge. In my view, once the idea of levels has been reified, causal drainage is inevitable.

2.6 Quantum indeterminism

The most prominent type of nonviolationism is God working through quantum randomness. Chapter 3 is devoted to this model so this will be brief. The main idea is that quantum mechanics allows for indeterministic gaps through which God can act without violating the laws of nature. Its main proponents are Robert J. Russell, George Ellis, Thomas Tracy, and Nancey Murphy, although none hold exclusively to this model.[32] (Tracy also favors Thomistic primary/secondary causation (Tracy 2009, 235). Murphy appeals to downward causation and chaos theory.)

Why does this one warrant an entire chapter, especially when some see its popularity as being on the wane?[33] First, it remains the best-known nonviolationist approach. Few outside professional theology are attracted to panentheism. Interest in Thomism tends to be concentrated among Catholic scholars. Emergence has far wider support, but not as a type of divine action. In contrast, any acquaintance with the divine action literature includes the idea of God working through quantum randomness, even if the details remain murky.

Second, even though quantum mechanics does not play a central role for every science-and-religion scholar, many take it to be a necessary condition for nonviolationism.[34] Consider downward causation once again. Tracy argues that it requires indeterministic gaps in nature to be effective (1995, 305–6). Without such gaps, no sort of holistic influence exerted by God could make a difference at lower levels. The thinking here is similar to that in arguments for free will. Few libertarians have quantum mechanics as a centerpiece of their proposals, but they routinely point to the need for quantum random-ness to have broken the hold of determinism. Both arguments take some amount of indeterminism to be necessary for nature to have room for agent causation. On its standard interpretation, quantum mechanics fits the bill.

Third, the criticisms aimed at this model to date are almost entirely theological. I believe that the more serious problems arise from physics and philosophy of science. These will require a bit more space to explain (Chapter 3).

The debate about special divine action is puzzling at first. Why all the fuss over whether the Creator of the laws of nature can also set them aside? The short answer is that naïve interventionism has significant theological baggage. Once made clear, we can see why noninterventionist and nonviolationist models have proliferated.

Unfortunately, the proposals presented here fail to strike a balance between competing *desiderata*. They want to avoid both the impersonal God of deism and the capricious miracle worker of interventionism, all without running afoul of science or too quickly appealing to mystery. That is a tall order. Intuitions vary about how to weight these goals. No matter where one plants a flag, there will be a bevy of critics who lean the other way. The model that will unfold over the course of this book is no different. Nonetheless, there is a place on the conceptual map that no one has yet fully explored. After the next chapter, it will be clear why further exploration is needed.

Notes

1 Framing the issue of divine action in terms of the laws of nature begs some important questions, which will be dealt with in Chapters 4 and 5.
2 Which isn't to say that I agree with them. For the most part, I believe these arguments are weaker than they are often assumed to be. See (Koperski 2017) for more.
3 "But it is difficult to conceive, on the one side, how omnipotence is shown to be greater in the suspension of the interdependence of nature than its original immutable course which was no less divinely ordered. For, indeed, capacity to make a change in what has been ordained is only a merit in the ordainer, if a change is necessary, which again can only be the result of some imperfection in him or his work" (Schleiermacher [1830] 1928, 179).
4 See (Pollard 1958, 28–29).
5 I choose to use the traditional male pronoun throughout for God rather than creating a new one or using the inelegant s/he. Its use does not imply that God is male any more than the use of "calorie" entails the existence of caloric fluid.
6 By the final edition of his *Principia Mathematica*, however, Newton had himself rejected the need for this explanation. It was instead the vast distances between the stars that kept them from colliding.
7 This is a false assumption that will be taken up in section 6.5.
8 William Stoeger is one example:

> [The] laws of nature [do] not easily allow for divine intervention – at least not direct divine intervention – because that would involve an immaterial agent acting on or within a material context as a cause or a relationship like other material causes and relationships. This is not possible; if it were, either

energy and information would be added to a system spontaneously and mysteriously, contravening the conservation of energy (and we just do not have substantiated cases of that happening).

(1995, 244)

9 Philosopher James K. A. Smith, is an exception. For much of the theology/science dialogue, he says that

"science" is the primary authority and is the first to stipulate what could be theoretically acceptable. Theology then looks for places that remain "open" to theological intervention. After science has made first and preeminent claim to the territory, theology can then look for remaining corners of the realm where it can set up shop. The natural sciences, then, are taken to be "objective" arbiters of "the way things really are," and theology (and religious communities) is expected to modify and conform ("correlate") its beliefs and practices to the dispensations of the scientific magisterium. Failure to accede to these conditions of engagement entails refusal of admission to the "parlor," and being written off as a "fundamentalist."

(2010, 94)

10 The rest of the chapter follows the helpful taxonomy provided by Sarah Lane Ritchie (2017).
11 *Causal powers* is a technical term. See section 5.2 for more.
12 Stoeger believes that even miracles will involve the secondary causation:

"[An] apparent divine intervention on our behalf – a miracle – in answer to our prayers, for instance, a healing of a disease of paralysis which cannot be explained by contemporary medical science, does not of itself manifest the direct action of God, though it does manifest God's personal loving and life-giving action towards us. We always experience it through some intermediary datum or agent.

(1995, 251)

13 See section 5.2 for more.
14 Edwards is one example:

Why, then opt for the approach to divine action in which the Creator is thought of as acting through secondary causes? Fundamentally, I embrace this approach because it represents a foundational metaphysical understanding of the God-world relationship which is at the heart of the Christian tradition and which I find intellectually coherent and religiously meaningful. At its center is the idea that the Creator is present to all creatures, closer to them than they are to themselves, conferring existence and the capacity to act on every entity and every process.

(2010, 62)

15 As Russell puts it far more diplomatically, "In response, I would start by questioning the degree of authority which one needs to grant the Thomist framework which Dodds presupposes – and which I do not" (2019, 154).
16 Some would even say that God and nature are essentially interdependent (Gregersen 2004, 22).
17 More recently, the term is used by those merely denying traditional doctrines such as atemporality and impassibility (Meister 2017, 4–5), but that seems far too loose. Although the rejection of these two doctrines means that one cannot be an Augustinian or a Thomistic theist, panentheism is not the only alternative.
18 "According to essential kenosis, God is present throughout all creation, to every creature and entity, no matter how small or large. God is also always influential

in creation. To use philosophical language, essential kenosis says God is a necessary cause in all things" (Oord 2016). See also (Oord 2015, 130).

19 "Essential kenosis says that from the big bang, in the emergence of life, through evolutionary history, and ongoing today, God creates through uncontrolling love. This direct but uncontrolling divine action both gives to creatures and receives from them. Our loving God is personal and relational but never controlling" (Oord 2016).

20 Emergentism (section 2.5) is a middle ground insofar as several prominent panentheists also hold that view (Clayton 2006, 319; Peacocke 1993, 158–59).

21 These terms can also be used more narrowly. Theists who deny mind-body dualism describe their position as "physicalism," but only with respect to this issue.

22 Most also give science unquestioned authority in the science-religion dialogue, as they believe that theology ought never conflict with science, which is somehow or other allied to naturalism. Amos and Smith are exceptions to this.

23 Metaphysically, Smith does take panentheism to be a "close cousin" (2008, 882), although it isn't clear whether panentheists themselves would embrace the family resemblance.

24 Yong also quotes Steven D. Crain favorably in this passage:

> [Miracles] do not constitute an adjustment to creation, but an aspect of what the Apostle Paul calls the new creation. Indeed, that a miracle violates natural law is itself a sign indicating the depths to which sin spoils the integrity of the created order, for in the wake of sin, God re-creates that order to its very roots, all the way down to the natural laws that for so long had operated without interference.
>
> (Yong 2011, 90–91)

> Yong concludes, "In sum, the resurrection gives us good reason to question nomological universality, at least in the far-off future, and grants us insights into God's intentions to restructure (re-create) the laws of nature infected by sin" (91).

25 As we will see in Chapter 8, others have tried to paint me with that same brush (Larmer 2017).

26 While this is an intuitive way to introduce the topic, it is also oversimplified. Physics deals with phenomena at many different scales from quantum field theory through condensed matter physics and cosmology.

27 That way of putting it reflects a materialist view of mind and body, but some dualists agree that minds are emergent entities (Hasker 2001, 48:195). Even more traditional Christian dualists admit that the human person was created both mind and body and that the orthodox understanding of the afterlife is resurrection of the body, rather than Plato's immortality of the soul.

28 A Laplacian demon is a thought experiment in which an extreme intelligence knows both the laws of nature and the exact state of every particle in the universe at a given time. In a Newtonian world, such a being could predict the state of those particles arbitrarily far into the future. Since no event escapes the laws of nature and Laplacian demons do not suffer from our lack of information, they would have no trouble solving the relevant equations and thereby know the outcome of any future event.

29 See also Peacocke (2006), Gregersen (2006), and Clayton (2006).

30 Technically this is *strong supervenience*. This means that whatever correlations exist between the base properties and supervening properties also exist in every possible world where those properties could be found. In other words, the supervenience relation is modal. It is not something peculiar to our universe.

31 Many think the culprit lies in the horizontal arrows of Figure 2.1. In other words, perhaps a more sophisticated understanding of causation can break the

redundancy (Loewer 2002, Rueger 2004). Others point to the vertical arrows, arguing that it is the relation between levels that needs to be revised (Humphreys 1997). In my view, the problem begins with the notion that nature has strict levels (Koperski 2015, sec. 6.6).

32 Some will be surprised that John Polkinghorne is not on this list, but that is intentional. Polkinghorne does not hold this view. He instead believes that quantum mechanics and chaos theory are indicators of greater, undiscovered openness in nature through which God might continually act (Polkinghorne 1995, 154).

33 This is one of Ritchie's main points (2017), and it was also stressed by an anonymous reviewer of this manuscript for Routledge.

34 See (Polkinghorne 1995, 151). Russell also makes this clear:

> NIODA requires the possibility that the world of natural processes, at some or many levels of complexity, is causally incomplete: Here God may act non-miraculously to produce an event in nature which nature on its own would not have produced. In this way, the principle of sufficient reason (that for every effect there is a sufficient cause) is satisfied in some cases by the direct action of God even though in an overwhelming number of cases it is satisfied by natural causes.
>
> (2019, 139–40)

Works cited

Anderson, Philip W. 2008. "More Is Different: Broken Symmetry and the Nature of the Hierarchical Structure of Science." In *Emergence: Contemporary Readings in Philosophy and Science*, edited by M. Bedau and P. Humphreys, 221–29. Cambridge: MIT Press.

Aquinas, Thomas. 2006. *Christian Theology*. Translated by Thomas Gilby. Paperback reissue. *Summa Theologica*. Cambridge: Cambridge University Press.

———. 2011. *Thomas Aquinas in Translation*. Translated by S. C. Selner-Wright. Washington, DC: Catholic University of America Press.

Batterman, Robert W. 2009. "Emergence in Physics." In *Routledge Encyclopedia of Philosophy*, edited by Edward Craig. London: Routledge.

Brooke, John Hedley. 1991. *Science and Religion: Some Historical Perspectives*. Cambridge: Cambridge University Press.

Burch, Robert. 2017. "Charles Sanders Peirce." In *Stanford Encyclopedia of Philosophy*, edited by Edward N. Zalta, 2017th ed. https://plato.stanford.edu/archives/fall2017/entries/peirce/.

Clayton, Philip. 2006. "Emergence from Quantum Physics to Religion: A Critical Appraisal." In *The Re-Emergence of Emergence*, edited by Philip Clayton and Paul Davies, 303–22. Oxford: Oxford University Press.

———. 2008. *Adventures in the Spirit: God, World, Divine Action*. Edited by Zachary R. Simpson. Minneapolis: Fortress Press.

Culp, John. 2017. "Panentheism." In *Stanford Encyclopedia of Philosophy*, edited by Edward N. Zalta. https://plato.stanford.edu/archives/sum2017/entries/panentheism/.

Davies, Paul. 2008. "Preface." In *The Re-Emergence of Emergence: The Emergentist Hypothesis from Science to Religion*, edited by Philip Clayton and Paul Davies, i–xiv. Oxford: Oxford University Press.

Davis, Edward B. 1996. "Newton's Rejection of the 'Newtonian World View': The Role of Divine Will in Newton's Natural Philosophy." In *Facets of Faith and*

Science: The Role of Beliefs in the Natural Sciences, edited by Jitse M. van der Meer, 3:75–96. Lanham: University Press of America.

Dodds, Michael J. 2016. *Unlocking Divine Action: Contemporary Science and Thomas Aquinas*. Washington, DC: Catholic University of America Press.

Edwards, Denis. 2010. *How God Acts: Creation, Redemption, and Special Divine Action*. Theology and the Sciences. Minneapolis, MN: Fortress Press.

Ellis, George F. R. 1995. "Ordinary and Extraordinary Divine Action." In *Chaos and Complexity: Scientific Perspectives on Divine Action*, edited by Robert J. Russell, 359–95. Berkeley, CA: Center for Theology and the Natural Sciences.

Freddoso, Alfred J. 1988. "Medieval Aristotelianism and the Case against Secondary Causation in Nature." In *Divine and Human Action: Essays in the Metaphysics of Theism*, edited by Thomas V. Morris, 74–118. Ithaca: Cornell University Press.

Gregersen, Niels Henrik. 2004. "Three Varieties of Panentheism." In *In Whom We Live and Move and Have Our Being: Panentheistic Reflections on God's Presence in a Scientific World*, edited by Philip Clayton and Niels Henrik Gregersen, 19–35. Grand Rapids: Eerdmans.

———. 2006. "Emergence: What Is at Stake for Religious Reflection?" In *The Re-Emergence of Emergence*, edited by Philip Clayton and Paul Davies, 279–302. Oxford: Oxford University Press.

Hasker, William. 2001. *The Emergent Self*. Vol. 48. Cornell Studies in the Philosophy of Religion. Ithaca: Cornell University Press.

Humphreys, Paul. 1997. "How Properties Emerge." *Philosophy of Science* 64 (1): 1–17.

Janiak, Andrew. 2016. "Newton's Philosophy." In *Stanford Encyclopedia of Philosophy*, edited by Edward N. Zalta. https://plato.stanford.edu/archives/win2016/entries/newton-philosophy.

Kim, Jaegwon. 2003. "Blocking Causal Drainage and Other Maintenance Chores with Mental Causation." *Philosophy and Phenomenological Research* 67 (1): 151–76.

Koperski, Jeffrey. 2015. *The Physics of Theism: God, Physics, and the Philosophy of Science*. Chichester, UK: Wiley-Blackwell.

———. 2017. "Divine Action." In *Dictionary of Christianity and Science: The Definitive Reference for the Intersection of Christian Faith and Contemporary Science*, edited by Paul Copan, Tremper Longman, Christopher L. Reese, and Michael G. Strauss, 1:186–88. Grand Rapids: Zondervan.

Larmer, Robert. 2017. "Decretalism and the Laws of Nature: A Response to Jeffrey Koperski." *Philosophia Christi* 19 (2): 439–47.

Leibniz, Gottfried W., and Samuel Clarke. (1717) 1956. *The Leibniz-Clarke Correspondence: Together with Extracts from Newton's Principia and Optics*. Edited by H. G. Alexander. Manchester: Manchester University Press.

Loewer, Barry. 2002. "Comments on Jaegwon Kim's Mind and the Physical World." *Philosophy and Phenomenological Research* 65 (3): 655–62.

Meister, Chad. 2017. "Ancient and Contemporary Expressions of Panentheism." *Philosophy Compass* 12 (9). https://doi.org/10.1111/phc3.12436.

Oord, Thomas Jay. 2015. *The Uncontrolling Love of God: An Open and Relational Account of Providence*. Downers Grove: InterVarsity Press.

————. 2016. "Divine Action as Uncontrolling Love." *BioLogos*. https:// biologos.org/blogs/jim-stump-faith-and-science-seeking-understanding/ divine-action-as-uncontrolling-love.

Peacocke, Arthur. 1993. *Theology for a Scientific Age: Being and Becoming—Natural, Divine and Human*. 2nd ed. Minneapolis, MN: SCM Press.

————. 2006. "Emergence, Mind, and Divine Action: The Hierarchy of the Sciences in Relation to the Human Mind-Brain-Body." In *The Re-Emergence of Emergence*, edited by Philip Clayton and Paul Davies, 257–78. Oxford: Oxford University Press.

Plantinga, Alvin. 2011. *Where the Conflict Really Lies: Science, Religion, and Naturalism*. Oxford: Oxford University Press.

Polkinghorne, John. 1995. "The Metaphysics of Divine Action." In *Chaos and Complexity: Scientific Perspectives on Divine Action*, edited by Robert J. Russell, Nancey Murphy, and Arthur R. Peacocke, 147–56. Berkeley: Center for Theology and the Natural Sciences.

————. 2005. *Science and Providence: God's Interaction with the World*. Templeton Foundation Press ed. Philadelphia: Templeton Foundation Press.

Pollard, William G. 1958. *Chance and Providence: God's Action in a World Governed by Scientific Law*. New York: Charles Scribner's Sons.

Ritchie, Sarah Lane. 2017. "Dancing Around the Causal Joint: Challenging the Theological Turn in Divine Action Theories." *Zygon* 52 (2): 361–79. https://doi.org/10.1111/zygo.12336.

Rueger, Alexander. 2004. "Reduction, Autonomy, and Causal Exclusion among Physical Properties." *Synthese* 139 (1): 1–21.

Russell, Robert J. 1995. "Introduction." In *Chaos and Complexity: Scientific Perspectives on Divine Action*, edited by Robert J. Russell, Nancey Murphy, and Arthur R. Peacocke, 1–31. Scientific Perspectives on Divine Action. Berkeley: Center for Theology and the Natural Sciences.

————. 2019. "What We've Learned from Quantum Mechanics About Non-Interventionist Objective Divine Action in Nature—and What Are Its Remaining Challenges?" In *God's Providence and Randomness in Nature: Scientific and Theological Perspectives*, edited by Robert J. Russell and Joshua M. Moritz. West Conshohocken: Templeton Foundation Press.

Schleiermacher, Friedrich. (1830) 1928. *The Christian Faith*. Edited by H. R. Mackintosh and James S. Stewart. Edinburgh: T. & T. Clark.

Smith, James K. A. 2008. "Is the Universe Open for Surprise? Pentecostal Ontology and the Spirit of Naturalism." *Zygon* 43 (4): 879–96. https://doi.org/10.1111/ j.1467-9744.2008.00966.x.

————. 2010. *Thinking in Tongues: Pentecostal Contributions to Christian Philosophy*. Pentecostal Manifestos. Grand Rapids: Eerdmans.

Stoeger, William. 1995. "Describing God's Action in the World in Light of Scientific Knowledge of Reality." In *Chaos and Complexity: Scientific Perspectives on Divine Action*, edited by Robert J. Russell, Nancey Murphy, and Arthur R. Peacocke, 239–61. Berkeley, CA: Center for Theology and the Natural Sciences.

Tracy, Thomas F. 1995. "Particular Providence and the God of the Gaps." In *Chaos and Complexity: Scientific Perspectives on Divine Action*, edited by R. J. Russell,

N. Murphy, and A. R. Peacocke, 291–324. Berkeley, CA: Center for Theology and the Natural Sciences.

———. 2009. "Creation, Providence and Quantum Chance." In *Philosophy, Science and Divine Action*, edited by F. LeRon Shults, Nancey C. Murphy, and Robert J. Russell, 227–61. Philosophical Studies in Science and Religion. Leiden: Brill.

Yong, Amos. 2011. *The Spirit of Creation: Modern Science and Divine Action in the Pentecostal-Charismatic Imagination*. Pentecostal Manifestos. Grand Rapids: Eerdmans.

3 Nonviolation, quantum mechanics, and chaos

If you have heard of only one nonviolationist proposal, it will likely be the idea of God working through quantum mechanics. While its popularity seems to have peaked, critics of this model focus almost exclusively on theological matters.[1] Less well-known are challenges posed by physics and the philosophy of science. In the end, what I call *divine quantum determination* suffers the same fate as most of the proposals discussed in Chapter 2, leaving far too little room in which God can act.[2] There is not much daylight between this type of hands-on nonviolationism and the hands-off noninterventionism it tries to avoid.

As a note to the reader, this is the most technical chapter in the book. It can be skipped if the idea of God working through quantum indeterminism holds no interest.

3.1 Divine quantum determination

3.1.1 Indeterminism and randomness

Quantum mechanics forced physicists to reconsider the role of randomness in nature. To see why, let's distinguish two types of randomness.[3] Epistemic randomness is what we (typically) find in classical mechanics. Games of chance use dice because only the probability of a given roll can be known in advance. But that isn't entirely true. A physicist with enough information about the linear and angular momentum of the dice, the coefficient of friction of the table, and a handful of other variables could predict the outcome with certainty. However, the dice end up, they *had* to have that result given the conditions and the laws of nature. To say this is a random event is merely a reflection of our ignorance. We don't have the relevant information and could not solve the equations quickly enough even if we did. In a practical sense then, one cannot predict the outcome of this "random" event even though it is just as determined by the laws of nature as the motion of a clock.

The physicist Pierre-Simon Laplace extended this idea to the entire universe. As a thought experiment, he considered a superintelligence that knew the laws of nature and the precise state of all the particles in the universe at a particular instant. A so-called Laplacian demon could then calculate the state of the universe at any future time. Solving this set of equations is beyond the means of any computer, but there is nothing about the mathematics to prevent it in principle. To a Laplacian demon in a Newtonian world, there would be no such thing as epistemic randomness and no need to resort to probabilities. Any given event would happen (or not) with absolute certainty.[4]

What about a Laplacian demon in a quantum world? That's an entirely different matter. Some events are indeterministic under the standard interpretation of quantum mechanics.[5] Indeterminism produces a type of randomness that is not merely due to a lack of knowledge. Consider the radioactive decay of a specific uranium-232 atom. Such events are not physically determined by any prior cause. As far as nature is concerned, there is only a probability that a decay event will occur at any given time. A uranium atom has a 50 percent chance of decaying any time in the next 70 years. There is no hidden physics that triggers radioactive decay – no tiny fuse that determines when this event will happen. A Laplacian demon could only calculate the chance of such a decay at any point in time.

This ontological randomness is not the most important and not nearly the most bizarre feature of the quantum world. Nor is quantum mechanics completely random. Schrödinger's equation is deterministic and in some ways more restrictive than classical mechanics. Ontological randomness is found in one set of quantum events, what are misleadingly called "measurements."

Schrödinger's cat remains one of the best thought experiments to illustrate. In one version, a cat is in a small, opaque room with a flask of poison gas. The flask is rigged to a device that will smash the glass if a photon detector is triggered. There is also a precision light source aimed toward a partially silvered mirror. Half the light will be reflected and half will pass through, like mirrored sunglasses. The mirror is angled toward the detector. When the test begins, a single photon is fired from the light source. There seem to be two options. The photon will either pass through the half-silvered mirror, the experiment is over, and the cat lives, or the photon will be reflected, thus triggering the detector, releasing the gas, and killing the cat. That's all clear enough. Whence the controversy?

The problem is that according to Schrödinger's equation, the photon does not take one path or the other. In some sense the photon takes both paths – the one allowing the cat to live *and* the one releasing the poison. Both final states, cat-dead and cat-alive, happily coexist in the quantum state described by the wavefunction, the mathematical entity that evolves over time according to Schrödinger's equation. However, we never observe the quantum state that captures both cat-dead and cat-alive. As soon as a measurement is taken, the wavefunction collapses and we are left with a live cat or a dead one. The state prior to collapse, where two or more definite possibilities are held suspended at the same time, is unobservable. Nonetheless there are good theoretical and experimental reasons to believe that this *superposition* state exists prior to measurement.

The outcomes in this particular scenario are intentionally limited, and if things are prepared correctly, there is a 50 percent chance of observing a dead cat and a 50 percent chance of observing a live one. Under the standard interpretation of quantum mechanics, the outcome is ontologically random. Not even a Laplacian demon could predict which result would occur.

A longstanding question is, What counts as a measurement? The term itself connotes something that humans do. We measure all sorts of things to gain information. In that sense, there is no measurement in the Schrödinger's cat scenario until a person looks inside to see the result. In principle the cat could remain in a superposition state indefinitely if no one looks inside.

Others have thought that measurement is a conscious act, one that animals could engage in as well. If so, the cat would be sufficient. The wavefunction would collapse at the instant the cat might hear the breaking of the glass flask.

The majority view today is that any sort of irreversible process is sufficient for a quantum measurement.[6] In the cat example, the point at which the photon either triggers the detector or impacts the wall constitutes a collapse of the wavefunction. Consciousness is not required. Hence, superposition states emerge and collapse continually throughout the universe, each time constituting an ontologically random event.

We can now complete the picture. Under divine quantum determination, God can influence the collapsing wavefunction in such a way as to get the outcome that he wants from among the ontologically random possibilities. If God wants Schrödinger's cat to live, he can bring about that outcome without violating any laws, since there is some objective probability that it would happen. God merely chooses from among the ontologically random, physically possible outcomes, making one of them actual. And since nature is, at its root, quantum mechanical, God can influence the physical world without breaking the laws of nature:

> Nature may provide the necessary conditions for a specific quantum event to occur, but the actual quantum event happens without nature providing a sufficient cause. . . . That means that if quantum physics is correct [we can interpret it as implying that] there can never be a complete scientific explanation of just why specific quantum events happen as they do. . . . When a quantum event occurs it occurs by God's direct action.
>
> (Russell 2008, 157)

By "quantum event" Russell means a collapse of the wavefunction under the standard von Neumann–Dirac axioms.

Note that the orthodox interpretation of quantum mechanics – now misleadingly called the "Copenhagen interpretation" – is not the only one with ontologically random events. One that is popular among philosophers of science is the Ghirardi-Rimini-Weber (GRW) or "spontaneous collapse" view (Lewis 2016, 50–55). For our purposes, the only important difference is that wavefunction collapse does not require measurements of any kind under GRW. Instead, each wavefunction is overwhelming likely to quickly and spontaneously collapse within every macroscopic object.

Other interpretations are deterministic and do not support ontological randomness. We will discuss those at the end of this chapter. Such interpretations are incompatible with divine quantum determination. Some might think it unwise for a theological program to take a stand on an unresolved scientific question. I agree with Del Ratzsch (2001), however, that it is a virtue to put one's view "in empirical harm's way" (98). Too much of metaphysics and theology is insulated from any sort of disconfirmation.

The limitations of divine quantum determination explained in the following section are matters of physics and the philosophy of science, not theology. What they show is that quantum mechanics provides too little freedom in which God can act. It does not support the hands-on theology that its proponents had hoped for.

3.1.2 The amplification problem

The rest of the chapter explores different facets of one idea: What goes on at the quantum level stays at the quantum level, at least when we are talking about those random collapse-events through which God is supposed to act. Unless those events can be amplified into the macroscopic realm, there isn't much that God can do with them. This is not news to proponents of quantum determination:

> [I]ndeterministic chance at the quantum level would need to make a difference in the way events unfold in the world. Chance will be irrelevant to history if its effects, when taken together in probabilistic patterns, disappear altogether into wider deterministic regularities. It is commonly said that this is the case with quantum indeterminacies, since the statistical patterns of these events give rise to the deterministic structures of macroscopic processes.
>
> (Tracy 1995, 317)

While there are many indeterministic quantum events, they rarely have anything to do with the realm of our experience. For God to effectively influence nature by way of quantum mechanics, these events must be amplified.

There are two good examples of the kind of mechanisms that are needed. One involves the electrochemical nature of the mammalian eye:

> In some species the eye can detect individual photons falling on the retina. The photon is absorbed by a molecule of rhodopsin, eventually

resulting in a nervous impulse coming out of the opposite end of the cell with an energy at least a million times that contained in the original photon.

(Ellis 2001, 260)

There is also the case of genetic mutation and evolution:

A second example has been presented by Ian Percival, who states that "DNA responds to quantum events, as when mutations are produced by single photons, with consequences that may be macroscopic – leukemia for example." In this case the amplifier is the developmental process by which the information in DNA is read out in the course of the organism's developmental history. . . . Indeed, mutations caused by cosmic rays may well have played a significant role in evolutionary history.

(Ellis 2001, 260)

This is a type of theistic evolution, albeit one with critics (Clayton 1998, 18). Quantum events can cause genetic mutations, which in turn affect the evolution of a species.[7]

While these are legitimate cases of amplification, they exhaust the store of good examples. I agree that eyesight and point mutations in DNA-based organisms are significant, and perhaps some nonviolationists might be content with this. In my view, more is needed. There is a large gap between a mechanism-for-theistic-evolution on one hand and a robust-model-of-divine-action on the other. Advocates of quantum determination hope that the program can be broadened, although most agree that the amplification problem remains largely unsolved.

With that in mind, I am going to argue for a surprisingly strong thesis: In light of current physics, the amplification problem cannot be solved. Not only are amplification mechanisms hard to find but the physics between scales also puts obstacles in the way. In other words, nature is predisposed to block the amplification of indeterministic quantum events.

To see why, recall a central idea from section 2.5: the notion of levels. Reductionists claim that high-level laws and phenomena can be reduced to lower-level ones, at least in principle. Emergentists are betting that this reduction will fail. Both sides agree that natural causes tend to run along their own level. The level of causes and laws that biochemists study, for example, is distinct from the level of those that botanists study.

Something that was not discussed earlier is that there are many levels at which phenomena are blind to perturbations at smaller scales. Changes of state at the more fundamental level have an undetectable effect at higher levels. There are firebreaks between some levels of reality such that small changes, including quantum changes, cannot influence the goings-on at the next level up. Higher level phenomena with this sort of insulation from quantum effects are what Nobel Laureate physicist

Robert Laughlin refers to as "protectorates." A quantum protectorate is "a stable state of matter whose generic low-energy properties are determined by a higher organizing principle and nothing else" (Laughlin and Pines 2000, 29). More generally, a protectorate is a domain of physics whose behavior is independent of the microdetails found at smaller scales (Batterman 2010, 1034).

Let's be clear that no one is challenging the fact that nature is quantum mechanical at its foundation. The argument of this chapter is not some sort of antirealist rejection of quantum theory. The entire structure of the periodic table depends to one degree or another on quantum mechanics. But quantum mechanics is far more than those random collapse events that divine quantum determination requires. Many physicists who surely believe in quantum mechanics don't believe in the collapse of the wavefunction. The issue here is whether those peculiar and somewhat questionable events can make their way into the realm of our experience. For the most part, the answer is that they cannot.

3.1.3 Two quick solutions

Perhaps this is not such a difficult problem to overcome after all. While quantum events are surely small and undetectable, so are individual atoms. But of course when enough atoms are put together, they form macroscopic wholes. Doesn't this same principle apply to quantum events? This is Murphy's solution, here in the context of Schrödinger's cat:

> [Russell] would argue that the important fact that has been overlooked here is the extent to which the general character of the entire macroscopic world is a function of the character of quantum events. Putting it playfully, he points out that *the whole cat is constituted by quantum events*!
>
> We can imagine in a straightforward way God's effect on the quantum event that the experimental apparatus is designed to isolate; we cannot so easily imagine the cumulative effect of God's action on the innumerable quantum events that constitute the cat's existence. Yet this latter is equally the realm of divine action. . . . The picture presented is straightforward: the behavior of the parts (quantum events) determines the behavior of the whole (macroscopic events). Every material object is therefore subject to quantum determination. Just as a sufficient accumulation of snowflakes can eventually produce an avalanche, God's determination of a massive number of quantum events can have observable effects.
>
> (Murphy 1995, 356–7)

This sort of part-whole inference is completely intuitive. Why isn't this a solution to the amplification problem?

Let's consider a better analogy. Say that you are standing on a bluff look-ing out over Lake Michigan. A teenager on the beach far below is trying to throw rocks onto the observation deck where you are. He can throw as many rocks as he wants, but unless he can impart sufficient kinetic energy, none of the rocks will reach the deck. How many attempts the boy makes is irrelevant. There is no sense in which the sheer number of throws cumula-tively allows one of the rocks to reach the bluff.

This is why Murphy's mereological intuitions fail here. Events need not accumulate like atoms. To solve the amplification problem, one must intro-duce mechanisms that allow quantum events to cross an energetic threshold. The number of events is irrelevant.

Let's consider a second solution. Many point to the ways in which quan-tum mechanics is important for macroscopic physics.

> [Besides] the fictional "Schrodinger's cat," other examples of macro-scopic quantum effects (suitable for divine exploitation) are Bose-Einstein condensates, lasers, SQUIDs (superconducting quantum interference devices) and the millions of field-effect transistors in your nearby computer. Quantum effects are far from impotent in the macro-world.
>
> (McDermid 2008a, 163–4)

There are without question examples of macroscopic quantum mechanical phenomena. There are two reasons why they do not constitute an answer to the amplification problem.

First, like Schrödinger's cat, these examples involve a high degree of engi-neering. They are not phenomena one finds in everyday experience; hence, they will be limited in terms of divine action. Perhaps there are examples in nature. Photosynthesis might be one. Let's assume that it is, even though it remains controversial (Ball 2018). If photosynthesis involves quantum superposition, clearly quantum effects are all around us.

There is an important ambiguity to note here about "quantum effects." No one is denying that modern physics is thoroughly quantum mechani-cal. The very stability of atoms – and thereby every macroscopic entity – depends on it. But that is not the issue. Recall the only source of ontological randomness in quantum mechanics that matters here: the collapse of the wavefunction.[8] Those are the only quantum events that are relevant for this model of divine action. Do these examples involve wavefunction collapse? There is an easy test to find out. Ask whether the deterministic interpreta-tions of quantum mechanics deny any of these phenomena. If not – i.e., if those interpretations also allow for lasers, SQUIDS, etc. – these examples do not involve collapse events or ontological randomness. The answer is that Bohmian mechanics, the Everettian interpretation, and more can all account for these phenomena. If they could not, there would be no contro-versy involving the interpretation of quantum mechanics. This means that these examples do not require a collapse of the wavefunction and so do not count as counterexamples to the amplification problem. We will have to look elsewhere.

One area that initially seemed promising was chaos theory.

3.2 Chaos as amplifier

Chaos theory has been called the third great theory of the twentieth century, along with quantum mechanics and the general theory of relativity. If that seems like naïve enthusiasm, consider a quote from a physics textbook: "Arguably the most broad based revolution in the worldview of science in the twentieth century will be associated with chaotic dynamics" (Rasband 1990, 1). While things have not turned out quite so grandly, chaos has been a fruitful area of research in physics and elsewhere.

3.2.1 A brief tutorial on chaos

Chaos theory isn't a theory *of* anything in particular the way, say, fluid mechanics has a clear subject matter. Chaos is instead part of a large area of mathematical science known as *dynamical systems theory*. A "system" in this context could be a simple pendulum, chemicals in a mixing chamber, or a dripping faucet. When the system can be described by means of a differential equation, the state of the system is given by the values of the variables in the equation at a given time.

Until the 1970s, most of the work done in dynamical systems theory had dealt with linear equations, which are both extremely useful and relatively well-behaved. Nonlinear models, on the other hand, are often intractable. Engineers often had no choice but to replace nonlinear equations with linear ones that closely mimic their behavior. Things began to change in the computer age. Many nonlinear equations whose solutions were analytically out of reach could now be simulated on a computer.

The most important property of chaotic systems is *sensitive dependence on initial conditions* (SDIC). If a system displays SDIC, the future states of the system change dramatically given an arbitrarily small change in initial conditions. This notion of small changes having large consequences is what is often called "the butterfly effect." The idea is that if the earth's atmosphere is subject to SDIC, a butterfly flapping its wings in Japan today might be sufficient to change the weather in Miami sometime next year from what would have been a sunny day into a hurricane.

A useful way of understanding this starts with a *phase space*, a geometrical representation of the state and evolution of a system. Each point in the space represents a possible state of the entire system, no matter how many particles or parts are involved. As the system evolves over time, the state point changes, carving a trajectory through the phase space. Trajectories in the space represent a system's possible evolution from different initial conditions. Most real-world systems are dissipative, meaning they have some amount of friction, electrical resistance, or other sort of loss. In those systems, *attractors* will develop in their phase spaces.[9] An attractor is a set of points toward which neighboring trajectories flow. Once a system state enters the basin of attraction, it inevitably moves to the attractor and remains there unless the system is perturbed. Figure 3.1 is the simplest example, a *point attractor*. The system evolves to one particular state regardless of the initial conditions (within the basin of attraction). This would represent something like the coin funnels often found at shopping malls. Figure 3.2 is a *limit cycle*, an attractor for systems such as a clock pendulum. No matter how the pendulum starts, the clock's mechanism ensures a regular, periodic motion will ensue.

The presence of a *strange attractor*, such as Figure 3.3, entails that the system is chaotic and displays SDIC, which means that minute changes of state can dramatically change the way that system will evolve in the future. The slightest perturbation, even a single flap of a butterfly's wings, moves

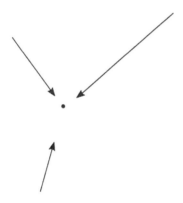

Figure 3.1 Nonchaotic point attractor.

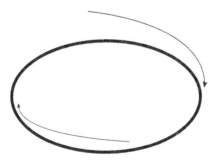

Figure 3.2 Nonchaotic limit cycle.

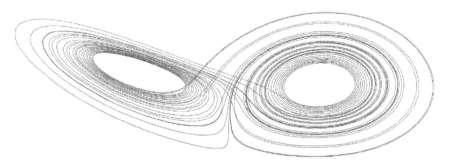

Figure 3.3 Lorenz Mask.

the system from one state trajectory to another. Once on a neighboring trajectory within a strange attraction, the new time evolution of the system will diverge exponentially fast from what it would have been.

How might this help solve the amplification problem? Consider the butterfly effect again, but this time at the quantum level. Jason Colwell gives a good example. God, he says, can choose

> the position of an electron at one time while preserving its probability density function through His pattern of choices over all time. The electron's position at that moment could influence the motion of one, then several air molecules. This would soon affect the flow of a tiny region of air. Amplified through chaos, this could cause a significant meteorological event after more time had elapsed. God, being omniscient, sees all the intricate workings of chaotic systems. He knows where tiny changes would have huge effects later on. This enables Him to act providentially in many situations to produce a desired result.
>
> (Colwell 2000, 135; quoted in Saunders 2002, 186)

Divine quantum determination causes a state change at the quantum level. In a chaotic system, such a change produces a shift in the system's state trajectory, dramatically altering its evolution. Since chaos is found in many macroscopic systems, God can effectively govern their evolution through quantum events, all within the dictates of nonviolationism. And so it seemed that the amplification problem had been solved, at least for chaotic systems.

The story, however, does not end there. Polkinghorne calls this wedding of chaos to quantum determination "the hybrid scheme" (1996, 37).[10] There are reasons why he and other physicist-theologians do not use it to solve the amplification problem.

3.2.2 *Not enough chaos*

First, there is not as much dynamical chaos in the world as popular accounts imply. It's true that chaos has been discovered throughout the natural sciences – moons, convection cells, predator-prey models, etc. The scientific journals in the 1980s and 90s had no end of new examples. In a sense, then, chaos is all around us, which is good news for advocates of the hybrid scheme. The bad news is that chaos is far less prevalent than it might appear.

3.2.2.1 *The math*

Optimism about the ubiquity of chaos in nature was grounded in part by a simple mathematical argument. As we have seen, chaos lives in the realm of nonlinear differential equations. Without question, nonlinear models far outnumber linear ones.[11] While the latter are more tractable, they are often based on idealizations that do not hold in reality. (Recall those frictionless planes in freshman physics.) Hence a realistic model of a given system in nature is far more likely to be nonlinear and chaotic than linear. As Karl Popper observed, the world is filled with clouds, not clocks (1973, 213–15). Linearity is the exception.

As simple as this argument is, there is an equally simple flaw. Nonlinearity is a necessary but not sufficient condition for chaos. Most nonlinear models do not exhibit chaos.[12] The prevalence of nonlinear systems in the space of differential equations does not by itself indicate that nature is mostly chaotic.

3.2.2.2 *Signal and noise*

As David Ruelle, one of the fathers of modern chaos theory, has noted, chaos is a lot like noise: There can be a little or there can be a lot (1994). To say that a system is chaotic does not entail that the overall behavior of the system is completely unpredictable. Healthy heartbeats are chaotic. But what does that mean? Heartbeats are mostly regular and predictable.

In most real-world examples, the chaotic part of a system's dynamics is negligible on most scales. Often the effect of chaos is so small that it requires precise equipment and lots of data to detect. So yes, there is chaos in nature, but not that much of it, relatively speaking.

3.2.2.3 *Stable boundary conditions*

Philosopher Peter Smith points out another restriction on SDIC in nature. He argues that the presence of chaos in dynamical systems presupposes other sorts of stability to get off the ground. Consider the first published example of chaos in nature. In 1963 meteorologist Edward Lorenz proposed a rough mathematical model for the behavior of convection cells in the atmosphere. Computer simulations of this model unexpectedly revealed SDIC. This is the basis of the claim that our weather is chaotic. Smith quotes a typical conclusion based on this research:

> Lorenz realized that his equations weren't behaving the way a traditionally-minded mathematician would expect. Lorenz coined his famous phrase: "butterfly effect." The flapping of a single butterfly's wing today produces a tiny change in the state of the atmosphere. Over a period of time, what the atmosphere actually does diverges from what it would have done. So, in a month's time, a tornado that would have devastated the Indonesian coast doesn't happen. Or maybe one that wasn't going to happen, does.
>
> (Stewart 1989, 141)

Smith then points to a crucial oversight in the exposition of Lorenz's discovery, one that is common in the popular literature:

> Even if we ignore for the moment the empirical short-comings of the Lorenz model, how on earth are *tornadoes* supposed to get into the story? The model was intended to describe the behaviour inside one of a series of parallel horizontal convection rolls: and it actually counts *against* butterfly-sized causes producing tornado-like effects. For the model assumes that the large-scale pattern of rolls, laid side by side like so many felled logs, remains entirely stable: the chaotic behaviour is local, as the rolls change their rotation-speeds in never repeating patterns. . . . [S]o long as we are still working within the Lorenz paradigm, there is no destructive break-up of the rolls, no wildly accelerating convection, and hence certainly no tornadoes!
>
> (1998, 67)

The presence of chaos in a given atmospheric phenomenon does not imply SDIC in global weather patterns. Lorenz's model presupposes a stable layer of convection cells. A butterfly's wings would perturb the random-looking rotation within a cell, but this limited effect is a far cry from stormfronts and tornadoes. Assuming the model is realistic,[13] there is some meteorological phenomenon that displays SDIC. However, this fact does not support the kind of broad extrapolation one generally sees in discussions about chaos and the weather.

The upshot for the amplification problem is that the mere presence of chaos in a physical system might not amount to much. The Lorenz model provides no justification for the claim that a butterfly outside my window – let alone quantum effects – can change the weather in Asia. Chaos at the level of Lorenzian convection is restricted and has little effect on global weather patterns. The moral is the same as with the heartbeat example: The presence of chaos may have no effect on the global evolution of the system in which it is found.

3.2.2.4 *Models and modeling*

Let's now consider what it means to say that chaos has been "discovered" in some phenomenon. To do so, we need to be a bit more precise. Let *dynamical systems* refer to real world objects with identifiable states that change over time. *Dynamical models*, usually sets of differential equations, are used to describe their behavior. *Phase spaces*, like those containing attractors in Figures 3.1, 3.2, and 3.3, are geometrical representations of the possible evolutions of those equations.

With that distinction in mind, Ruelle raises a new objection:

> Many published papers give the superficial impression that they deal with real physical, biological or economic systems, while in reality they present only computer studies of models. By "real system" I mean a system in, say, astronomy, mechanics, physics, geophysics, chemistry, biology or economics with a time evolution that one wants to investigate. Computer study of a model is an important method of investigation, but the results can only be as good as the model.
>
> (1994, 26)

If a poor model behaves chaotically, there is little reason to expect chaos in the subject of the model. Nonetheless, when casual readers see a title such as "Chaotic Behaviour in the Solar System" (Wisdom 1987), they would likely infer that chaos has been detected in the motion of nearby celestial bodies. That is not the case. Instead, the paper describes a dynamical model for one such body, namely, Hyperion, one of Saturn's moons. When the equations are solved with the help a computer, the output indicates chaos. However, this does not seem to be a discovery in the ordinary sense of the word; rather, it is the prediction of a computer simulation. Exploring the behavior of the mathematics is different from discovering a new species of moth. The existence of chaotic behavior in the solar system still seems to be an open question. Smith's summation of the problem is correct:

> Why should I accept that, because a mathematical *model* has a certain feature, then the *physical world* has a corresponding feature? Discussions of chaos typically blur over the issue here by sliding in an indisciplined way between talking of dynamical systems *qua* physical phenomena and talking of systems *qua* mathematical constructs.
>
> (1990, 255)

One must bridge the gap from the dynamical equations to the dynamical system they are intended to model.[14] Smith has argued that this cannot be done for the models of interest here (1998, 39).

3.2.2.5 *The quantum suppression of chaos*

Perhaps the best-known reason not to rely on chaos as a solution to the amplification problem is the so-called *problem of quantum chaos*. It starts with the fact that one cannot predict the onset of classical chaos using quantum mechanics alone. This is not surprising. As we saw in section 2.5, one of the arguments for emergentism is the impossibility of deriving the properties of macroscopic objects simply by looking at their microscopic constituents. However, one does expect the laws governing the constituents to *permit* what is observed at the macroscopic level. Not being able to predict phenomenon *P* from textbook theory *T* is one thing. That *P* appears to be impossible given the truth of *T* is another. Geneticists may not be able to tell that a DNA sample came from a specific albatross, but we would expect genetic analysis to show that the sample could possibly have come from a bird. If DNA testing is trustworthy, it ought not *disallow* the possibility that the sample came from an albatross when we know that it did. If that were the case, it would present a clear challenge to the theory and procedures used in genetic testing.

This scenario has a close analogue in the relation between quantum mechanics and classical chaos. The more fundamental, microscopic theory disallows what is observed in larger, classical systems, an effect physicist Michael Berry calls "the quantum suppression of classical chaos" (1987). One way to understand it starts with the idea that strange attractors have a fractal structure. Under classical mechanics, this infinite structure within a phase space is merely unusual. Matters are different in quantum mechanics, as mathematician Ian Stewart explains: "Classical chaos involves fractal attractors, that is, structure on all scales. But in quantum mechanics . . . structure does not exist on a scale smaller than Planck's constant. So quantum effects smooth out the fine detail so necessary of true chaos" (1989, 295).[15] True fractals have structure at all scales. Intuitively, no matter how closely one "zoomed in" on Figure 3.3, there would still be trajectories running through every region of phase space on the attractor. But from a quantum mechanical point of view, perfectly precise phase space trajectories are idealizations. At some scale, state points and trajectories are no longer physically meaningful. If fractal structure is a necessary condition for chaos, quantum mechanics makes classical chaos impossible.[16]

Direct answers to the problem have largely been abandoned, although work continues on finding correlations between the quantum and the classical realms in the presence of chaos. With no clear resolution to the quantum suppression of chaos, the so-called hybrid project between chaos and quantum mechanics was dropped by the main proponents of divine quantum determination.[17]

These then are the reasons why chaos theory did not solve the amplification problem. But things get worse. Not only does nature contain less SDIC than the popular literature implies but in many ways there is also extreme *insensitivity* to small changes. Examples like gene mutation and the mammalian eye (section 3.1.2) are the exceptions, not the rule. Even within physics alone, systems more often block the influence of lower levels, rather than amplifying them.

3.3 Dynamical systems theory

Section 3.2.1 follows an unfortunate tendency in explanations of chaos, rushing through the less interesting parts of dynamical systems theory to get to SDIC and strange attractors. We now need to consider the rest of the terrain more closely. As we saw, strange attractors are only one member of a family of attracting sets in dissipative systems. Among the simplest are point attractors (Figure 3.1) and limit cycles (Figure 3.2). There are also torus-shaped attractors and many more at higher dimensions. The technical literature contains a menagerie of attracting and repelling sets, most of which have nothing to do with chaos. There are also nondissipative systems, which do not have attractors of any kind.

In the vast family of systems described by ordinary differential equations and represented by phase spaces, strange attractors are relatively rare. Even those dynamical models that produce chaos must have their parameters tuned to the "chaotic regime." The models that produce chaos can just as readily display nonchaotic behavior. But with nonchaotic attractors, there is no SDIC. No matter what the initial conditions are within the basin of attraction, the system will inevitably fall into the attractor, producing the same evolution as any other starting point.

Consider three pendulum-clocks hung on a wall, all at rest. Now start the pendulums swinging one by one. Most likely, the three will be out of phase with one another: One pendulum will reach its highest point when the others are somewhere else in their arcs. As Dutch physicist Christiaan Huygens noted in the seventeenth century, the three clocks will become synchronized with one another, a phenomenon now known as *entrainment*. So long as each pendulum is lifted far enough to get the mechanism started, the clocks will either come to have the same phase or be exactly 180 degrees out of phase with the others. A phase space used to describe this evolution contains a limit cycle. Every set of initial conditions – the starting angles of the pendulums – eventually produces the same periodic behavior. Notice that this is the opposite of SDIC. Small changes in the initial conditions of this system have no effect on its long-term behavior. Regardless of how the clocks are started, entrainment ensures that they will become synchronized. This is the characteristic behavior of nonchaotic attractors. Small changes matter only in the transient of most dissipative systems, not in their steady state evolution.

From the point of view of divine quantum determination, this is disappointing news. Not only did chaos not solve the amplification problem but dynamical systems theory also made it worse. Nonchaotic attractors erase microfluctuations. Small-scale changes of state make no difference to the long-term evolution of the system. Since nonchaotic models are more prevalent than their chaotic cousins, for most dissipative dynamical systems, any change of state that God might make at the quantum level will have no measurable effect on the final state of the system.

3.4 Continuum mechanics

Terms like "chaos theory" and "strange attractors" were perfectly suited for popular science writers. Not so for the physics of bending beams and fluids. It's sometimes difficult to even know where continuum mechanics fits as a field of study. Taking matter to be a continuum is contrary to treating it as discrete and atomic. As philosopher Bertrand Russell (reportedly) once put it, the difference is between thinking of nature deep down as a pail of sand as opposed to a bucket of molasses. The molasses camp believed that matter at the most fundamental level is smooshed out and continuous. But why consider the continuum view at all? Everyone since Newton has believed in atoms, right?

Actually, atomism was still in doubt until the twentieth century. Ernst Mach argued that the idea was nothing but a useful fiction. Ostwald and the energeticist movement hoped to reduce molecules to energy (Harman 1982, 146–7). Still others, like Lorentz, believed that electromagnetism might form the ground floor of physical reality (Harman 1982, 151). Classical physics developed along various fronts with conflicting and sometimes false views about the nature of matter. Happily, both the continuum and the atom approaches were equally useful, as Poincaré observed:

> In most questions the analyst assumes, at the beginning of his calculations, either that matter is continuous, or the reverse, that it is formed of atoms. In either case, his results would have been the same. On the atomic supposition he has a little more difficulty in obtaining them – that is all.

> ([1905] 1952, 152)

At a certain level, it doesn't matter whether nature is atomic or continuous.

Now, how can that be? It doesn't matter! How can the right answer not matter? Answering that question reveals another example where small-scale changes fail to influence the behavior of a system, thereby compounding the amplification problem.

Poincaré was referring to two ways to derive the Navier-Stokes equations, which are the central laws of classical fluid mechanics.[18] One of these treats matter as either atoms or a collection of point particles.[19] The other takes matter to be a true continuum, like a field. On the continuum view, there are no atoms. Many nineteenth-century physicists believed that the continuum approach would prove to be the more realistic one. The surprise is that both approaches yield the same equations for the behavior of macroscopic fluids. Truesdell explains what Poincaré had in mind:

> Continuum physics stands in no contradiction with structural [i.e., molecular] theories, since the equations expressing its general principles may be identified with equations of exactly the same form in sufficiently general statistical mechanics. . . . Long experience with molecular theories shows that quantities such as stress and heat flux are quite insensitive to molecular structure: Very different, apparently almost contradictory hypotheses of structure and definitions of gross variables based upon them, lead to the same equations for continua.
>
> (1984, 55)

The true microscopic nature of a fluid is irrelevant. This is one of many examples where physics employs – to borrow a phrase from Mark Wilson – the "effacement of the small." Engineers could as easily work with molecules, continua, point particles, or Leibnizian monads. The same macroequations can be derived from either a particle or true continuum base.

Let's get into the weeds a bit to see how continuum mechanics relates micro- to macroscales. Start with a tiny volume element within a solid (Figure 3.4). If the element experiences a contact force on one side, the force will stretch it away from equilibrium. This stretching (strain) produces a force (stress) that tries to bring the element back into equilibrium. This new force impinges on the next volume element, which induces a strain, and so on down the line.[20]

The stresses and strains on the volume elements encode all the causally relevant information about small-scale interactions in the body. But volume elements are still far above the scale of atoms. This is the effacement of the small. The physics of stress and strain relations is indifferent to whether the microlevel is a composition of atoms or a true continuum. Yes, atoms exist, but their interactions are irrelevant at the smallest scale recognized by continuum models. This means that the observable behavior of such a system is largely independent of events at the level of its microconstituents.

In other words, the macrosolid is an emergent protectorate (section 3.1.2). Atomic-scale events are absorbed within the volume element and prevented from having any causal influence on the whole. Nothing in quantum mechanics changes this fact.

Let's consider two objections. One might say, "Well, we don't believe in *classical* continuum mechanics anymore. We now know that the world is atomic and quantum mechanical, so we can safely ignore these examples."

Several things should be noted. Continuum mechanics describes observable systems like beams and fluids. It offers not false models of subatomic

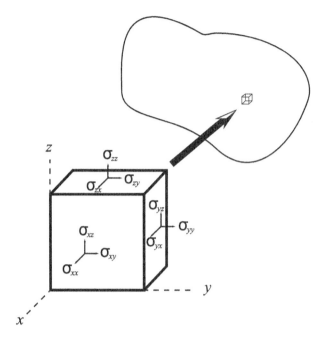

Figure 3.4 Stress on a volume element.

physics but rather accurate descriptions of the behavior of gross matter. As Truesdell puts it, "Molecular hypotheses have come and gone, but the phenomenological equations of D'Alembert, Euler, and Cauchy remain exact as at the day of their discovery, exempt from fashion" (Truesdell 1984, 55n5). Computer simulations now confirm this (Bishop 2008). Again, while such systems depend on unobservable stresses and volume elements, those are far above the scale of fundamental physics. From both a theoretical and an experimental point of view, smaller scales are irrelevant, including the goings-on in quantum mechanics.

Second, the complaint might be that continuum mechanics idealizes microcausal relations and ought not be treated as a guide. The question of atomic composition versus continuum has been resolved. Hence, any realistic treatment of these systems must involve atoms, not the stress on homogeneous volume elements.

If the problem here is the use of idealizations, this criticism reaches into all areas of physics, not just continuum mechanics. Idealizations are employed no matter how far one drills down. Even quantum field theory suffers "the same kind of flaw exhibited by continuum hydrodynamics." Rather than dismissing quantum field theory, one should hold that "if our foundational theories can provide answers to questions about what there is in the world and what it is like, then non-foundational theories can do likewise, notwithstanding their having similar flaws" (Teller 2004, 440). The use of idealizations is not itself a problem, but the failure to spot artifacts generated by those idealizations is. If continuum mechanics asserted that matter were truly a continuum all the way down, that would be an error. As we have seen, however, "continuum physics presumes *nothing* regarding the [fundamental] structure of matter" (Truesdell 1984, 54).

Because of the effacement of the small, events at the microlevel make no observable difference to the behavior of a flexible body or fluid – the exact opposite of what one would hope in trying to solve the amplification problem. Proponents of divine quantum determination are looking for ways in which microchanges can influence the macro. In continuum mechanics, that typically cannot happen.

The common theme running through the last sections of this chapter is that physics blocks small-scale changes from having macroscopic effects. Let's consider one last example from the fastest-growing area of research today.

3.5 Condensed matter

The extraordinary scope of condensed matter physics makes it hard to characterize. It includes exotic creations such as superfluids and graphene, as well as the mathematics of phase transitions. One defining feature is that condensed matter involves many interacting degrees of freedom, which is the very thing that makes these systems difficult to study. There are too many moving parts to know which are causally relevant.

One intriguing discovery is the degree to which unrelated systems exhibit the same properties. Many fluids with completely different chemical compositions behave identically. More surprising is that phase transitions in liquids work according to the same mathematics as magnets. The transition from liquid to vapor mirrors changes found in electromagnetic materials.[21] Fluids are obviously quite different from magnets. How is it that the two, which seem to have no relation whatsoever, obey the same sorts of mathematics? Physicists want to know.

One set of mathematical tools in particular has helped tame the complexity of condensed matter systems: *renormalization group theory*. The details are technical, but we need at least a minimal description to draw any conclusions. Recall that strange attractors are creatures of phase space rather than physical space. Physics relies on all sorts of abstract mathematical spaces to bridge the equations to the phenomena. Renormalization group theory uses a space of Hamiltonians. A Hamiltonian is a mathematical description of a system's degrees of freedom and the influence of external fields. In many areas of physics, finding a Hamiltonian is the key to describing a system's behavior. Historically, this is what made condensed matter research too difficult to pursue. Such systems involve so many parts that a realistic Hamiltonian quickly becomes mathematically intractable. The trick of renormalization is to move from a Hamiltonian of the actual system of interest to a Hamiltonian that behaves in the same way but with fewer degrees of freedom (Batterman 2002, 39–41). While not a perfect analogy, the idea is somewhat similar to engineering textbooks in which a three-dimensional wheel is restricted to two dimensions. Engineering students can effectively deal with the simplified model, but allowing the wheel to wobble a bit along a third dimension would be far more difficult. Renormalization group analysis likewise boils the physics down to the properties that caus-ally dominate the behavior of a system, stripping away the noise.

With a renormalized Hamiltonian in hand, the causally relevant proper-ties of a system become clear. What we find is that systems in condensed matter physics also exhibit the effacement of the small. The interactions among the constituents of these systems are not responsible for how the system behaves. What matters are mid-scale properties like dimension and symmetry, as Morrison explains:

> [T]he framework provided by [renormalization group theory] . . . has shown that while emergent phenomena, especially the "universal" phe-nomena in condensed matter physics are certainly composed of micro constituents [like atoms], they are nevertheless largely insensitive to changes in their microphysical base.
>
> (2012, 142)

This is similar to philosopher Batterman's assessment:

> [Renormalization analysis reveals] a class of macrostates of various sys-tems at the scale of everyday objects (fluids) that are essentially decou-pled or independent of their microdetails. The renormalization group explanation provides principled physical reasons (reasons grounded in the physics and mathematics of systems in the thermodynamic limit) for ignoring details about the microstructure of the constituents of the fluids.
>
> (2010, 1037)

It's that decoupling from microstructure and the autonomy of the macro-scale that Laughlin and Pines had in mind when they coined the term "quan-tum protectorate." A quantum protectorate is a stable state of matter whose behavior is independent of events at the quantum scale.[22] They are found throughout condensed matter research.[23]

3.6 Application: what it means

The research discussed in the previous three sections covers a vast range of applied physics. What the examples have in common is macroscale insensitivity to changes at lower levels. In terms of divine action, this insensitivity and autonomy make the amplification problem considerably worse. In the presence of a protectorate, the state of the macrosystem is largely immune to changes of state in its components at the quantum level. Protectorates prevent changes at the quantum scale from bubbling up into the macro. This means that the amplification problem is not merely something that the quantum determination program will solve in the fullness of time. Nature has firewalls in place that keep random events at the quantum level from influencing the realm of our everyday experience. In light of current physics, the amplification problem cannot be solved in a system with a protectorate. Given the prevalence of systems mentioned in this chapter, the unhappy consequence is that if God governs the universe by way of quantum randomness alone, we are left with something close to deism.

Perhaps this is overstated. As one referee objected, I have already acknowledged that amplifications occur. Photons in the mammalian eye are amplified. Gene mutation is another possible mechanism. When discussing fluid mechanics, I might also have mentioned turbulence, the fluid counterpart to chaos. A fluid in a state of turbulence does exhibit sensitive dependence on initial conditions. All told, the more balanced conclusion may be that divine quantum determination faces more obstacles than those that have been recognized, but it is not physically impossible.

While my argument would be stronger if I had shown that amplification of quantum events were impossible, that objection misses the point. The amplification problem cannot be solved by way of exceptions. Divine quantum determination becomes less plausible as a model of divine action if one must resort to special cases to keep it alive. Consider an analogy. Say that your favorite football team has a weak offense. Ultimately, they need to find a way to score more points. It does not solve the problem to point out that they do, in fact, score now and then. Similarly, nonviolationists who look to quantum mechanics realize that they need to find still more ways in which quantum events can be amplified in order for quantum determination to serve as a robust mechanism for divine action. That is the amplification problem briefly stated. What we have seen is that nature imposes barriers that make it extremely difficult for random quantum events to influence the world of our experience. To solve the problem, nonviolationists must find more avenues for this to occur in. It is not enough merely to say that, despite the barriers posed by protectorates, amplification might happen on occasion.

Divine quantum determination is most plausible when the focus is on quantum mechanics alone. In my view, it is no longer viable given *everything* we know in physics. Protectorates constitute a major challenge for anyone looking to quantum events as a significant mechanism for divine action.

One might look to future developments in physics to offer a solution, but current trends do not offer much hope. If anything, physics and the philosophy of science point toward the eventual rejection of ontological randomness in quantum mechanics.

3.7 *Contra* ontological randomness

A necessary condition for divine quantum determination is the collapse of the wavefunction. While collapse interpretations of quantum mechanics remain the majority view, deterministic noncollapse alternatives continue to gain popularity among both physicists and philosophers of physics. If current trends continue, one of these will likely become the majority view among experts in the second half of this century.

3.7.1 *Bohmian mechanics*

My prediction does not refer to Bohmian mechanics, but since this is the best-known deterministic interpretation of quantum mechanics, let's start there. A more accurate name is de Broglie–Bohm theory, since Bohm in essence rediscovered what de Broglie had pioneered in 1927 (Goldstein 2017, sec. 3). In Bohm's view, particles do not sometimes appear particle-like and other times wavelike. Particles instead always have a precise position in space. In the two-slit experiment, for example, the particle goes through one or the other slit, but never both. That doesn't mean that we can discover which slit or the precise position of the particle, since Heisenberg uncertainty still applies. But in this interpretation the uncertainty principle is merely epistemic – a limitation on knowledge.

If fundamental physics is particle-based, how can we account for wave-like phenomena, including the two-slit experiment just mentioned? The answer is that Bohm posits a new, unobservable entity: the pilot wave.[24] This is the entity that is governed by Schrödinger's equation and described by a mathematical wavefunction. It is this wave that goes through both slits in the two-slit experiment, constructively and destructively interferes with itself, and, ultimately, directs the motion of particles.

With this dual ontology, there is no sense in which particles take on wave-like properties and then collapse back into particles. Both pilot waves and particles are always present. This means that there is no collapse of the wavefunction and therefore no introduction of ontologically random quantum events. Determinism is restored. A Laplacian demon with direct access to both the state of the particles and the pilot wave at an instant in time could calculate the future with precision.

From the point of view of the bench scientist, however, nothing has changed. We are still able to make only probabilistic predictions about where the particle will strike in the two-slit experiment, about the prospects for Schrödinger's cat, etc.[25] It is widely agreed that the orthodox and Bohmian interpretations are empirically equivalent. No experiment can be run that confirms one and disconfirms the other.

That is not to say, as Russell emphasizes (2009, 366), that an intuitive Newtonian world is thereby reinstated. Bohmian mechanics is highly nonlocal, meaning that causes in one place produce effects at a distance without intermediate steps in between. Bohmian mechanics still contains a lot of odd quantum phenomena, just not as many as the standard interpretation.

Why then has Bohm's view failed to attract many advocates? To physicists, the theory seems *ad hoc* – in Polkinghorne's words, "too clever by half" (personal communication). It looks as if someone had started with orthodox quantum mechanics and then added an equation and some bits of ontology to make the theory seem more classical, all of which is more or less correct. As a bit of counterfactual history, one wonders what would have happened if Bohmian mechanics had somehow been presented in 1924. Would a pilot wave theory now be "orthodox quantum mechanics" and our textbook view be the odd, empirically equivalent formulation that physicists know about but widely reject? ("It rejects determinism! It requires the wavefunction to in some sense *collapse!*") In that possible world, divine quantum determination would never have been considered a viable option.

The fact remains that indeterministic collapse interpretations remain far more popular than Bohmian mechanics. The more serious challenge to orthodoxy is next.

3.7.2 *The many-worlds interpretation*

To introduce the Everettian many-worlds view, let's first go back to Schrödinger's cat. In the standard example, there is a superposition state in which the cat is in some sense both alive and dead prior to "measurement." Superposition is entailed by the mathematics, although we never observe these states, only their effects. Measurement triggers the collapse of the wavefunction, destroying superposition, and the cat becomes either fully dead or fully alive.

Wavefunction reduction has always been something of an embarrassment to physics. Schrödinger's equation does all the heavy lifting, only to be replaced by this mysterious collapse during measurements. Many interpretations of quantum mechanics aim to remove collapse events from the picture, including Hugh Everett's relative state approach (1957). While it isn't clear whether Everett himself thought that his view had metaphysical ramifications, it is clear that Bryce DeWitt did. The name "many-worlds" traces back to DeWitt's way of making sense of Everett's PhD thesis. According to DeWitt, if a collapse had occurred under the standard interpretation, separate universes would have come into existence (1970). Each possible outcome of a measurement happens in its own universe. An individual universe or "world" has definite classical-looking outcomes. For Schrödinger's cat, there is one world with a live cat and another world with a dead cat. The key is that the wavefunction never collapses. All the possible outcomes it encodes become actual in their own worlds.

DeWitt's many-worlds was never a popular option among physicists or philosophers. It eliminates the mystery of measurement and collapse but does so only by a massive expansion of ontology. Even in terms of conservation of energy, many questioned how an imperceivable quantum event brings about the creation of whole universes. This seemed to be one of those proposals that, had a philosopher brought it to the table rather than a physicist, would have been wholly derided in the science community.

In recent years, all this has changed. A group of Oxford University physicists and philosophers has remade the Everettian program (Deutsch 1997; Saunders 2010; Wallace 2012). In their view, there is only one universe, and there is only one wavefunction for that universe, which evolves according to Schrödinger's equation. Within this one complex wavefunction, there are "branches" that do not interact. The "many-worlds" are in reality many branches of the single global wavefunction which never collapses. From the point of view of people within each branch, the world looks quasiclassical (e.g., cat dead in one branch, cat alive in another).[26]

While moving from literal universes to branches might seem like a slight conceptual change, there is another advantage to this approach. Those mysterious measurements are also eliminated. Wallace instead appeals to chaos and decoherence (2012, 69–74). First consider the standard explanation of why our experience is so classical rather than quantum mechanical: In a macro-object composed of many atoms, the wavefunction "bunches up" and becomes concentrated in "wavepackets." Mathematically, these wavepackets behave much like their classical counterparts: trajectories through phase spaces. As long as wavepackets remain compact, the macro-realm looks mostly classical.

Chaos makes that story untenable. In a chaotic system, a wavepacket will disperse exponentially fast. Among other things, this means that superposition states, like Schrödinger's cat being both dead and alive, should have observable effects. If this breakdown of the wavepacket started today for an object the size of Hyperion, Saturn's chaotically tumbling moon, Hyperion would no longer have a precise position in space after four years (Wallace 2012, 74).

The standard (von Neumann–Dirac) approach appeals to measurements to solve this problem. When we observe Hyperion through a telescope, a measurement is made and the wavefunction collapses. More recently, physicists have come to believe that neither a consciousness nor a detector is needed to trigger a collapse. They start with the idea that no system is ever completely isolated from its environment. Gravity, photons, and more interact with nearly everything. The interaction of a quantum system with its environment in itself counts as a type of measurement. This continual interaction suppresses nonclassical states, what is technically known as *decoherence*. This, Wallace argues, is the reason we do not observe the effects of superposition in chaotic systems. Oddly, Schrödinger's cat situations occur only in idealized, isolated systems.

There is one last step in the Oxford-style Everettian story. Decoherence helps explain why quantum weirdness is generally so well hidden, but it does not determine which classical state one will observe. Decoherence explains why we never see the cat-dead-and-cat-alive state, but it does not say which of the two possibilities one will observe.

Everett's many-worlds is the last piece of the puzzle. Once decoherence has suppressed the nonclassical parts of the universal wavefunction, it branches, with each branch containing one of the possible classical outcomes – again, cat-dead in one, cat-alive in another, all within the single, universal wavefunction. From each observer's standpoint within a given branch, virtually all phenomena have determinate outcomes. Thus, Oxford-style Everettianism accounts for our classical-looking experience, all without either a collapse of the wavefunction or ontologically random events. The many-worlds interpretation is deterministic.

For decades, Bohmian mechanics and many-worlds were little more than abstract alternatives to the Copenhagen interpretation. Proponents of divine quantum determination have never taken them as serious threats to ontological randomness. That is still true for Bohmian mechanics, which never gained many adherents. The Oxford many-worlds approach is a different beast. If its current popularity continues to grow, it will be the majority view in decades to come. Such a change would undermine any model of divine action that presupposes ontological randomness at the quantum level.

In so many ways then, the future does not bode well for divine quantum determination. A new model of divine action is needed, one that will survive if physics reestablishes determinism. Rather than jump into the mix of views described in Chapter 2, I intend to start with the foundations. If the key nonviolationist worry is that divine action cannot involve breaking the laws of nature, we need to consider the notion of law more carefully.

Notes

1 Nicholas Saunders's (2002) was especially influential. It remains one of the best books written from a noninterventionist perspective regarding nonviolationism.
2 Divine quantum determination is essentially the same as Russell's quantum mechanical noninterventionist objective divine action (QM-NIODA) and Plantinga's divine collapse-causation (2008, 393). While QM-NIODA is Russell's primary model of divine action, he believes that other approaches will likely be needed in order to form a complete account.
3 Most philosophers of science do not like this terminology, even though it is now common. The real issue is not randomness *per se* but rather indeterminism. Randomness is an epistemic notion found in many areas of science. Determinism and indeterminism are matters of physics and metaphysics. I have chosen to acquiesce and use "randomness" here rather than trying to force a terminological change.
4 As we will see in Chapter 6, this is an oversimplified view of classical mechanics.
5 While the "standard" or "orthodox" interpretation of quantum mechanics is often called the "Copenhagen interpretation," that is not quite correct. The

Copenhagen approach is properly that of Niels Bohr, who for the most part was an antirealist about the quantum realm. He believed that quantum mechanics provides the correct probabilities for macroscopic observations but does not describe the nature of the microworld. The realist approach to uniquely quantum phenomena such as superposition, entanglement, and the collapse of the wavefunction traces back to the von Neumann–Dirac formulation of quantum mechanics. For an excellent history of quantum theory that makes this clear, see (Becker 2018).

6 Russell explicitly endorses this understanding of measurements (2008, 166). Such a definition also captures vacuum fluctuations – e.g., when an excited atom spontaneously transitions into a lower energy state and emits a photon. See (Svozil 2018, sec. 14).

7 Russell takes this to be highly significant insofar as it refutes the idea that evolution is in conflict with theism and intrinsically atheistic (2008, chap. 6). Others argue that directed evolution is not compatible with neo-Darwinism, whether there is a violation of natural law or not. Darwinian mutations are random precisely in that "they do not occur according to the needs of their possessors" (Ruse 2012, 623). If God caused mutations to ensure that humans evolve, it would be nonrandom and hence non-Darwinian. As Ruse points out, when Darwin's friend and supporter Asa Gray first proposed a version of theistic evolution, Darwin argued that it was incompatible with his theory. Contrary to this, Russell believes that as long as mutations continue to appear random from a biologist's point of view, God could still arrange them to bring about a particular outcome.

8 Quantum vacuum fluctuations are also ontologically random but extraordinarily brief. Those fluctuations related to radiation were discussed in the previous subsection.

9 Chaos can also be defined for conservative (nondissipative) systems (Tabor 1989, chap. 4). I choose the more familiar dissipative systems for ease of exposition.

10 For more, see (Clayton 1997, 196), (Murphy 1995, 349–49), (Tracy 1995, 317–18).

11 In essence, the idea is similar to the set-theoretic truth that there are far more real numbers than there are whole numbers. If the cardinality of whole numbers is , the cardinality of reals is .

12 Many nonlinear models are one- or two-dimensional, which are mathematically incapable of instantiating chaotic dynamics. Even for possibly chaotic systems governed by ordinary differential equations, there are parameters that can put the system into either a chaotic or a nonchaotic regime. Experimentalists often have to "tune" these parameters in order for a given system to exhibit chaos. For more on the relation of parameter space to the so-called "routes to chaos," see (Ott 1993, chaps. 2, 8).

13 Which it almost certainly is not. The mathematical simplifications used in order to derive the Lorenz model are extreme. In fact, the partial differential equations Lorenz started with are not themselves chaotic! See (Lichtenberg and Lieberman 1983, 446).

14 Engineering professor Francis Moon, an influential voice in the development of chaos theory, put it this way:

> In the rush to explain chaotic dynamics in physical systems, there is a temptation to propose mathematical models that emulate the classic chaos paradigms more than the actual physics of the system. This could be forgiven in the early days of discovery and exploration in the subject. But, as the field of nonlinear dynamics matures, more accountability for both the mathematical and *physical* principles underlying the phenomena must be required. The

connection between physical laws (e.g., Newton's laws and Maxwell's equations) and mathematical models should eventually become transparent if the new explanations of chaotic phenomena are to be accepted.

(1987, 106)

15 See also (Hobbs 1991, 159).

16 A second, more precise way to understand the problem starts with *quasiperiodicity*, a distinct category of dynamical behavior from chaos. If a system displays quasiperiodic behavior, it cannot, at the same time, be chaotic. Chaos is a full step beyond quasiperiodicity *vis-à-vis* complexity of motion. Unlike the ordinary differential equations that govern the behavior of classical chaotic systems, Schrödinger's equation can only evolve periodically or quasiperiodically. Quantum systems cannot reach higher levels of dynamic complexity (Jensen 1992).

17 Nancey Murphy (1995) is a notable exception, although Russell takes her use of chaos as merely a suggestion rather than a firm solution to the amplification problem (private discussion). While John Polkinghorne coined the term "hybrid project," he never held such a view, nor did he endorse divine quantum determination itself. He believes instead that chaos and quantum mechanics point to some undiscovered openness in nature through which God might continually input information. See (Silva 2012) for more. Kirk McDermid appeals to chaos in his discussion of special divine action, but for different reasons (2008b). In his view, the presence of chaos would provide God more options in a fully deterministic universe since the precise initial conditions God might choose become crucial to the evolution of the entire system. The problems raised in the next section apply to this sort of chaos-based proposal.

18 Technically, these are nonlinear, partial differential equations, which means they are beyond our ability to solve in most instances. It isn't yet known whether unique solutions for the equations *exist* except for some special cases.

19 Other than Boscovich, few thought that matter consisted of point particles – true mathematical points, not atoms.

20 In solids, the mathematics of stress and strain are captured by *constitutive relations* – more precisely, how the stress tensor σ is related to the strain ε. In undergraduate texts, these are reduced to simple vectors or scalar quantities.

21 They share the same *critical exponents*, which describe a shift in phase (Batterman 2010, 1035). The phase transition is between ferromagnetic (below the critical point temperature when dipoles align) and paramagnetic (above the critical point temperature when they are naturally disordered but will line up under the influence of a magnetic field).

22 Laughlin earned the Nobel Prize in 1998 for his research on the fractional quantum Hall effect, which exhibits this sort of independence.

23 Independence and autonomy are important themes in the emergence literature. As we discussed in section 2.5, emergent phenomena often behave in ways that are largely independent of their subvenient base. This independence blocks the reduction of higher-level entities and laws to their small-scale constituents. For our purposes, the thing to notice is that this same autonomy insulates many macroscopic systems from changes at smaller scales. Examples of emergence expand the family of protectorates.

24 This is an interesting claim in itself. The pilot wave is a perfectly legitimate physical entity that is fundamentally undetectable, and not merely because it is too small to be seen.

25 The Born rule for converting a mathematical wavefunction into probabilities still holds (Lewis 2016, 56).

26 How do Oxford-style many-worlds avoid the conservation of energy problem mentioned in the previous paragraph? The difference is ontological. All that

exists in this account is one wavefunction, which is taken to be an actually existing entity, not merely a mathematical description of something. That single, universal wavefunction never collapses and never literally splits into different worlds, thus avoiding any problem with conservation of energy.

Works cited

Ball, Philip. 2018. "Is Photosynthesis Quantum-Ish?" *Physics World*. April 10, 2018. https://physicsworld.com/a/is-photosynthesis-quantum-ish/.

Batterman, Robert W. 2002. *The Devil in the Details: Asymptotic Reasoning in Explanation, Reduction, and Emergence*. Oxford: Oxford University Press.

———. 2010. "Emergence, Singularities, and Symmetry Breaking." *Foundations of Physics* 41 (6): 1031–50. https://doi.org/10.1007/s10701-010-9493-4.

Becker, Adam. 2018. *What Is Real? The Unfinished Quest for the Meaning of Quantum Physics*. New York: Basic Books.

Berry, Michael. 1987. "Quantum Chaology." In *Dynamical Chaos*, edited by M. V. Berry, I. C. Percival, and N. O. Weiss, 183–98. Princeton, NJ: Princeton University Press.

Bishop, Robert C. 2008. "Downward Causation in Fluid Convection." *Synthese* 160 (2): 229–48. https://doi.org/10.1007/s11229-006-9112-2.

Clayton, Philip. 1997. *God and Contemporary Science*. Edinburgh: Edinburgh University Press.

———. 1998. "Metaphysics Can Be a Harsh Mistress." *CTNS Bulletin*, Philosophical studies in science and religion 18 (1): 15–19.

Colwell, Jason. 2000. "Chaos and Providence." *International Journal for Philosophy of Religion* 48 (3): 131–38.

Deutsch, David. 1997. *The Fabric of Reality: The Science of Parallel Universes and Its Implications*. New York: Allen Lane.

DeWitt, B. S. M. 1970. "Quantum Mechanics and Reality." *Physics Today* 23 (9): 30–35.

Ellis, George F. R. 2001. "Quantum Theory and the Macroscopic World." In *Quantum Mechanics: Scientific Perspectives on Divine Action*, edited by Robert J. Russell, Kirk Wegter-McNelly, and John Polkinghorne, 259–91. Berkeley, CA: Center for Theology and the Natural Sciences.

Everett, Hugh. 1957. "'Relative State' Formulation of Quantum Mechanics." *Reviews of Modern Physics* 29: 454–62.

Goldstein, Sheldon. 2017. "Bohmian Mechanics." In *Stanford Encyclopedia of Philosophy*, edited by Edward N. Zalta. https://plato.stanford.edu/archives/sum2017/entries/qm-bohm/.

Harman, P. M. 1982. *Energy, Force and Matter: The Conceptual Development of Nineteenth-Century Physics*. Cambridge: Cambridge University Press.

Hobbs, Jesse. 1991. "Chaos and Indeterminism." *Canadian Journal of Philosophy* 21 (2): 141–64. https://doi.org/10.1080/00455091.1991.10717241.

Jensen, Roderick V. 1992. "Quantum Chaos." *Nature* 355 (6358): 311–18. https://doi.org/10.1038/355311a0.

Laughlin, Robert B., and David Pines. 2000. "The Theory of Everything." *Proceedings of the National Academy of Sciences of the United States of America* 97 (1): 28–31.

Lewis, Peter J. 2016. *Quantum Ontology: A Guide to the Metaphysics of Quantum Mechanics*. New York: Oxford University Press.

Lichtenberg, A. J., and M. A. Lieberman. 1983. *Regular and Chaotic Dynamics*. New York: Springer.

McDermid, Kirk. 2008a. "A Reply to Robert Larmer." *Religious Studies* 44 (2): 161–64. https://doi.org/10.1017/S0034412507009286.

———. 2008b. "Miracles: Metaphysics, Physics, and Physicalism." *Religious Studies* 44 (2): 125–47. https://doi.org/10.1017/S0034412507009262.

Moon, Francis C. 1987. *Chaotic Vibrations: An Introduction for Applied Scientists and Engineers*. New York: Wiley.

Morrison, Margaret. 2012. "Emergent Physics and Micro-Ontology." *Philosophy of Science* 79 (1): 141–66.

Murphy, Nancey. 1995. "Divine Action in the Natural Order: Buridan's Ass and Schrödinger's Cat." In *Chaos and Complexity: Scientific Perspectives on Divine Action*, edited by Robert J. Russell, Nancey Murphy, and Arthur R. Peacocke, 325–57. Berkeley, CA: Center for Theology and the Natural Sciences.

Ott, Edward. 1993. *Chaos in Dynamical Systems*. Cambridge: Cambridge University Press.

Plantinga, Alvin. 2008. "What Is 'Intervention'?" *Theology and Science* 6 (4): 369–401. https://doi.org/10.1080/14746700802396106.

Poincaré, Henri. (1905) 1952. *Science and Hypothesis*. Translated by W. J. Greenstreet. New York: Dover.

Polkinghorne, John. 1996. *Scientists as Theologians: A Comparison of the Writings of Ian Barbour, Arthur Peacocke and John Polkinghorne*. London: SPCK.

Popper, Karl. 1973. *Objective Knowledge: An Evolutionary Approach*. Clarendon Press.

Rasband, S. Neil. 1990. *Chaotic Dynamics of Nonlinear Systems*. New York: Wiley.

Ratzsch, Del. 2001. *Nature, Design, and Science*. Albany: SUNY Press.

Ruelle, David. 1994. "Where Can One Hope to Profitably Apply the Ideas of Chaos?" *Physics Today* 47 (7): 24–30.

Ruse, Michael. 2012. "How Not to Solve the Science-Religion Conflict." *The Philosophical Quarterly* 62 (248): 620–25. https://doi.org/10.1111/j.1467-9213.2012.00066.x.

Russell, Robert J. 2008. *Cosmology: From Alpha to Omega*. Minneapolis: Fortress Press.

———. 2009. "Divine Action and Quantum Mechanics: A Fresh Assessment." In *Philosophy, Science and Divine Action*, edited by F. LeRon Shults, Nancey C. Murphy, and Robert J. Russell, 351–403. Leiden: Brill.

Saunders, Nicholas. 2002. *Divine Action and Modern Science*. Cambridge: Cambridge University Press.

Saunders, Simon. 2010. "Many Worlds? An Introduction." In *Many Worlds? Everett, Quantum Theory, and Reality*, edited by Simon Saunders, Jonathan Barrett, Adrian Kent, and David Wallace, 1–49. Oxford: Oxford University Press.

Silva, Ignacio. 2012. "John Polkinghorne on Divine Action: A Coherent Theological Evolution." *Science & Christian Belief* 24: 19–30.

Smith, Peter. 1990. "The Butterfly Effect." *Proceedings of the Aristotelian Society* 91: 247–67.

———. 1998. *Explaining Chaos*. Cambridge: Cambridge University Press.

Stewart, Ian. 1989. *Does God Play Dice? The Mathematics of Chaos*. Cambridge: Blackwell.

Svozil, Karl. 2018. *Physical (A)Causality*. Fundamental Theories of Physics. Cham: Springer International Publishing. https://doi.org/10.1007/978-3-319-70815-7.

Tabor, Michael. 1989. *Chaos and Integrability in Nonlinear Dynamics: An Intro-duction.* New York: Wiley.

Teller, Paul. 2004. "How We Dapple the World*." *Philosophy of Science* 71 (4): 425–47. https://doi.org/10.1086/423625.

Tracy, Thomas F. 1995. "Particular Providence and the God of the Gaps." In *Chaos and Complexity: Scientific Perspectives on Divine Action*, edited by R. J. Russell, N. Murphy, and A. R. Peacocke, 291–324. Berkeley, CA: Center for Theology and the Natural Sciences.

Truesdell, Clifford. 1984. *An Idiot's Fugitive Essays on Science: Methods, Criticism, Training, Circumstances.* New York: Springer-Verlag.

Wallace, David. 2012. *The Emergent Multiverse: Quantum Theory According to the Everett Interpretation.* Oxford: Oxford University Press.

Wisdom, J. 1987. "Chaotic Behaviour in the Solar System." *Proceedings of the Royal Society of London. Series A, Mathematical and Physical Sciences* 413 (1844): 109–29.

4 A brief history of the laws of nature

That nature works in predictable ways is not a new discovery. Prescientific folk knew perfectly well about the phases of the moon, the change of seasons, and the behavior of tides. But why are these events stable and recurring while others seem so random?

The gods were one answer. It was more or less in their job description to keep nature running on schedule. For Plato, it was instead the *forms*. On his view, a triangle drawn on the board, as well as every triangle anyone has seen, in only an imperfect instantiation of triangularity itself. The limited justice found in a Greek city-state was likewise a rough copy of the form of justice. Plato taught that justice, goodness, mathematical objects, and more have their own kind of perfect, abstract existence – more "real" in a sense than the realm of our own experience.

Plato explains how the forms come to be instantiated in the material world in the *Timaeus*. Like many other ancient creation stories, it involves a divine person of sorts, although one who is far more limited than a monotheistic Creator. Plato's Demiurge is a divine craftsman. As such, he is unable to create matter any more than a sculptor is able to create a piece of marble. Fortunately, matter itself already exists in Plato's story, albeit in a state of disordered chaos. Once the Demiurge wishes to mold the chaos into an orderly cosmos, his choices are limited. He is not an omnipotent designer able to do whatever he wants; instead, he is limited to the unchanging principles of order found in the forms. They alone contain the blueprints the Craftsman can use. Euclidean geometry was not one option among many, for example. There is only one set of mathematical truths. While Plato seemed to consider this no more than a "likely story" (Zeyl 2014, sec. 4), the *Timaeus* gives one explanation for how the immutable forms bring order to the realm of our experience.

Aristotle rejected Plato's timeless realm of abstract objects. That metaphysical niche, he taught, was occupied instead by *essences / substantial forms*. Aristotle believed that every substance, like a given horse, is a combination of essence and matter. Essences provide structure and uniformity to nature. No horses will be reptiles. No triangles will ever have more than three sides. Unless impeded, rocks always fall. Fire always rises. But there is no platonic realm in which essences exist that is in some sense more real than the material world. Essences are present within physical substances. This was the metaphysical system developed by Thomas Aquinas and others in the thirteenth century.

The early modern era introduced a rival explanation for this orderliness: laws of nature. While a longstanding "natural law" tradition in ethics goes back to the Stoics, it took Descartes to unambiguously apply the idea to physics (Garber 2013, n. 7).[1] This was no incremental change, as philosopher Eric Watkins notes:

> By placing laws at the foundation of scientific inquiry (in the broader context of the Scientific Revolution), modern thinkers redefined the order of nature, which had previously been conceived of (by medieval thinkers such as Aquinas, Scotus, Ockham, and Maimonides) as based on the natures and causal powers of finite substances.
>
> (2013, xxvi)

This fundamental shift from essences and substantial forms to laws of nature is sometimes obscured since both approaches are still live options in metaphysics. (More on that in Chapter 5.) In terms of the history and the philosophy of science, however, the change was dramatic, having ramifications for divine freedom, empiricism, and divine action. These are the issues considered in this chapter, beginning with the turn from medieval Aristotelianism. The appendix discusses the surprising relevance of this material to the controversy over the theory of intelligent design.

4.1 From essences to laws of nature

There were three principal reasons for the rejection of Aristotelian metaphysics. First, essences came to be seen as hopelessly obscure. Robert Boyle went as far as to call them unintelligible (Anstey 2002, 23–24), and Pierre Gassendi argued that even if substantial forms existed, they would be useless in science since we do not have epistemic access to them (Fisher 2014). Newton agreed:

> Such occult Qualities put a stop to the Improvement of natural Philosophy, and therefore of late Years have been rejected. To tell us that every Species of Things is endow'd with an occult specifick Quality by which it acts and produces manifest Effects, is to tell us nothing.
>
> (*Opticks*, Query 31)

While Newton is sometimes credited – or in some circles vilified – for overthrowing Aristotelian-Thomism, that debate had long since been decided in Britain. Newton's starting point was the mechanical philosophy of Descartes, not Aquinas.

A second anti-Aristotelian argument goes back to the thirteenth century. Many Muslim, Jewish, and Christian thinkers argued that such a metaphysic would limit God in unacceptable ways (Oakley 1961, 438). If a thing's essence were immutable, not even an omnipotent being would be able to change it. This worry reached a high-water mark with the Condemnation of 1277, in which the bishop of Paris restricted the teaching of, among other things, Aristotelian doctrines about divine freedom.

A final argument is the most important of the three in understanding the move to laws. If substantial forms were responsible for the order and stability of nature, they would be the proximate governors of the cosmos and God would be a step removed. But why would an omnipotent creator need the help of intermediaries to govern nature? One of the pillars of seventeenth-century mechanical philosophy was that God needs no such help. This argument will be discussed more fully in section 4.2.

In my view, the dramatic nature of this change is unappreciated because of our anachronistic use of "laws." Many resist the claim that Greco-Roman philosophers did not believe that there were laws of nature. "Aristotle clearly believed in an orderly cosmos and the regularities of nature," I hear in reply, "how can you say that he didn't believe in the laws of nature?" The answer has already been discussed. Aristotle believed in substantial forms, not laws. The notion of a law of nature is an early modern innovation that is now so familiar that we use it as a placeholder for any form of universal order. As such, it obscures the metaphysical shift at work in the 1600s. The change is not lost on philosophers still working within the Aristotelian-Thomist tradition, however. For them, the abandonment of essences in favor of laws is the source of a great many evils in the centuries that follow.

Let's now consider how theology influenced this change.

4.2 Theological voluntarism and the rejection of intermediaries

One of the great debates in late medieval philosophy was between *voluntarism* and *intellectualism*. The former says that God can freely do whatever he wants and is not restricted by his own essence; the latter, that God makes choices based on reason and his essential goodness.[2]

As a matter of moral philosophy, the voluntarist grabs the second horn of the Euthyphro dilemma: x is good because God has commanded it, and how God chooses is primarily a matter of will. The intellectualist believes instead that God commands what he does because God is perfectly good and rational. Brian Leftow contrasts Aquinas, the intellectualist, with Duns Scotus, the voluntarist:

> For Aquinas, all ten Commandments are necessary moral truths, which God sees and proclaims. For Scotus, necessarily, loving God is right and hating him wrong. . . . All other acts, though naturally good or bad

(perfecting or destroying our nature), are right or wrong contingently, because God commands or prohibits them.

(1998)

Under intellectualism, God's commands can give insight into his nature since he will direct us to do only what is in accord with divine goodness and perfect rationality. For the voluntarist, in contrast, no such inference is possible. There is no such thing as ethical right or wrong until God commands it. Voluntarism thus rejects any link between ethics and God's nature. Moreover, it is impossible to infer what God would command in this or that circumstance since those choices are in no way constrained or dictated by God's essential goodness. Ethical truth must be revealed.

These ideas reemerged in the seventeenth century, but as a matter of natural philosophy rather than ethics, specifically regarding laws. The laws of nature, the new voluntarists believed, need not be what they are: "[The] laws of motion . . . did not necessarily spring from the nature of matter, but depended upon the will of the divine author of things" (Boyle 1725, 2:245). God had many options from which to choose, and the actual choice of laws was arbitrary – a matter of will rather than reason or goodness. This presents an epistemic problem, however. Whatever decisions God has made by fiat alone cannot be inferred from theological first principles. In the next section, we will consider how this motivated an empirical approach to the question of laws. Let's first consider another important theme that emerged from voluntarism: the rejection of intermediaries between God and nature.

As I mentioned earlier, one of the standard arguments for the early modern shift away from Aristotle was the obscurity and the unobservability of substantial forms. A less-appreciated point is that they constituted an unnecessary intermediary between God and nature. Consider philosopher John Milton's take on Descartes:

> God governs the world, not by means of intermediaries of any kind, but directly, by regulating the motion of every single body, however tiny and unimportant. In physics, God not only gives an impulse to matter at the beginning but also conserves this impulse by means of exactly the same action as that which first created it. Indeed, according to Descartes the difference between creation and conservation is nothing more than a difference of reason, made by our minds but not found in reality. Because God acts directly on matter everywhere, all the intermediaries proposed by the various schools of Greek philosophy and absorbed into the world-picture of the Middle Ages and Renaissance are to be discarded without exception.

(1981, 193)

In short, God needs no occult entities to govern nature for him, whether Aristotelian essences or Neoplatonic alternatives, such as a world-soul or

Nature itself (Henry 2009, 93). In the latter case, the Cambridge Platonists often used locutions such as "the spirit of nature" for a reification that is responsible for physical events. Historian Peter Harrison describes Ralph Cudworth as believing that

> since inanimate matter cannot literally "obey" laws of nature prom-ulgated by God, there must be some intermediate agent that can, and that is the efficient cause for every effect of the laws: "Wherefore the *Divine Law* and *Command*, by which the things of Nature are adminis-tred, must be conceived to be the Real Appointment of some *Energetick Effectual* and *Operative Cause* for the Production of every Effect." And that agent is nothing other than a spiritual, plastic nature.
>
> (2013, 140)

Boyle would have none of it, rejecting both the Aristotelianism still entrenched in much of Europe and this homegrown Neoplatonism. Both metaphysical systems stood in the way of God's direct and unmediated governance:

> [N]ature is not to be looked on, as a distinct or separate agent, but as a rule, or rather a system of rules, according to which these agents and the bodies they work on, are, by the great Author of things, determined to act and suffer.
>
> (Boyle [1686] 1996, 106)

The same ideas are echoed by those natural philosophers associated with Newton:

> Isaac Barrow: "God uses no other means, instruments or applications in these productions, than his bare word or command."
>
> (1885, 303; quoted in Harrison 2002, 68).

> Samuel Clarke: "The course of nature, truly and properly speaking, is nothing else but the will of God producing certain effects in a contin-ued, regular, constant, and uniform manner; which course or manner of acting, being in every moment perfectly arbitrary, is as easy to be altered at any time as to be preserved."
>
> (1738, 2:698)

> William Whiston:[3] Gravity is simply God's "general, immechanical, immediate power."
>
> (1717, 111)

Arguments for the rejection of intermediaries even worked their way into the teaching of influential ministers.[4]

Rather than Nature itself or the intrinsic teleology of substances, the orderliness of the cosmos was thought to be imposed by its Creator God as "a system of rules" (Boyle) or as Newton put it, *principia* (principles). The more common term was "law of nature." Here we see Richard Bentley bringing together divine will, immediate divine action, and law in the first Boyle Lecture:

> all the powers of mechanism are entirely dependent on the Deity. . . . Gravity, the great basis of all mechanism, is not itself mechanical, but the immediate *fiat* and finger of God, and the execution of divine law.
>
> (Harrison 2013, 141)

Similar language can be found in an earlier letter from Newton to Bentley (25 Feb 1693).

The rejection of medieval occult entities in favor of laws had two important consequences: First, it removed the main reason for avoiding experiments. From an Aristotelian point of view, to understand the essence of a thing meant to understand its natural, unhindered behavior. The natural motion of rocks and other bits of matter, they held, is toward the center of the earth. This is confirmed by every rock lifted off the ground and then released. I can force a rock on my desk to slide across the top by pushing it with my hand, but as soon as my hand is removed, it stops. This, it was thought, proves that horizontal motion is contrary to its nature. *Violent motion* can be imposed on a substance, but such behavior is contrary to its nature and so was thought to have limited value. Only natural motion could reveal internal, teleological dispositions.[5] But that is not the sort of motion thought to be involved in experiments. Dropping a ball allowed it to behave naturally, but rolling that same ball down an inclined plane interfered with what, in a sense, it wants to do. Experiments with moving parts always involved some measure of violent motion, but forcing a substance to behave contrary to its nature could shed no light on its essential properties.

The conceptual shift from substantial forms to laws removed the distinction between violent and natural motion. The early moderns believed that all physical events are matters of law, whether they are observed in the wild or they are produced by artificial experiments.

That is often considered the end of the story of how the new experimental philosophy began. But there was a second, less well-known motivation – one that is more controversial.

4.3 From voluntarism to empiricism

Intellectualists believed that we know God's nature, at least in part, which allows us to make inferences about how God would act. An infinitely powerful, wise, and good deity would tend to do some things and refrain from others. This doesn't mean that one could deduce every decision that God has made. But when it came to the necessary truths of logic and mathematics, God could not have done anything differently. It made sense, then, to talk about thinking God's thoughts after him, at least in these cases.

The early modern voluntarists believed instead that the first principles of natural philosophy were contingent on God's choices, or at least far more so than intellectualists believed. Descartes argued that not even logic and mathematics were necessary truths. While nearly everyone thought Descartes's voluntarism was too extreme, voluntarists agreed there was one choice that was wholly contingent: the laws of nature.

This presents a problem, however. While reason might lead from Euclid's axioms to the theorems of geometry, there would be no comparable way to determine the laws of nature that God had chosen. No amount of theology or philosophy could bridge this inferential gap. God's choices were free, and reason alone cannot discern them. As Boyle emphasized, the problem is made even worse given the wide range of means available to God to produce a given outcome:

> For as an artificer can set all the wheels of a clock a going, as well with springs as with weights; and may with violence discharge a bullet out of the barrel of a gun, not only by means of gunpowder, but of compressed air, and even of a spring: so the same effects may be produced by diverse causes different from one another; and it will oftentimes be very difficult, if not impossible, for our dim reasons to discern surely, which of these several ways, whereby it is possible for nature to produce the same phaenomena, she has really made use of to exhibit them.
>
> ([1772], II, 45; quoted in Davis 1984, 171–2)

With such a range of options available, none of which logical or metaphysical necessities, the actual choices God had made could not be known *a priori*.

How then could science proceed? There were laws, but God had not revealed their content. (Descartes was an exception to this, as we will see.) One answer was made clear by mathematician Roger Cotes in his preface of Newton's *Principia*:

> Surely, this World – so beautifully diversified in all its forms and motions – could not have arisen except from the perfectly free will of God, who provides and governs all things. From this source, then, have all the laws that are called laws of nature come, in which many traces of the highest wisdom and counsel certainly appear, but no traces of necessity. *Accordingly we should not seek these laws by using untrustworthy conjectures, but learn them by observing and experimenting* [emphasis added].
>
> ([1687] 1962)

Only empirical data could provide knowledge of the laws, and then only imperfectly. For Cotes and others, voluntarism provided a second theological motivation for empiricism.[6] Armchair philosophy cannot determine the laws of nature, but observation and experiments can – an argument with roots at least as far back as Ockham.[7]

For Boyle, Newton, Barrow, Whiston, Cotes, Bentley, and Newton's surrogate in the debate with Leibniz, Samuel Clarke, the underlying argument is a dilemma: (i) the laws of nature are either necessary or contingent, (ii) if they are necessary truths, they can be known a *priori*, at least in part, (iii) if they are contingent upon God's free choice, then they can only be known a *posteriori*, (iv) the laws are not necessary, therefore, (v) observations and experiments are our only recourse. Voluntarism was thus one motivation for empiricism – another case in which theology positively influenced science.[8] Watkins sums up what is now the standard view:

> [Newton's] followers, such as Clarke, were more forthcoming, expressing skepticism that Newton's laws could be directly deduced from the divine order, since they held that human experience and especially the distinctive kind of experience gained through experimentation is essential to their discovery and justification.
>
> (2013, xxvii)

One prominent scholar who disputes the voluntarism-to-empiricism thesis is Peter Harrison. He makes his case by first reaching further back, to the Augustinian-Platonism of Kepler:

> Geometry, which before the origin of things was coeternal with the divine mind and is God himself (for what could there be in God which would not be God himself?), supplied God with patterns for the creation of the world, and passed over to Man along with the image of God.
>
> ([1619] 1997, 304)

> [As one might ask,] you do not hope to be able to give the reason for the number of planets, do you? This worry has been resolved, with the help of God, not badly. Geometrical reasons are co-eternal with God.
>
> ([1621] 1952, 863)

The "co-eternality" of geometry means that Kepler was not a voluntarist. He believed that mathematics was fixed, necessary, and beyond God's control (Henry 2009, n. 46). Kepler's Platonism famously led him to model the Copernican orbits of the planets by nesting them within the five perfect solids: the cube, tetrahedron, octahedron, icosahedron, and dodecahedron. He was forced to abandon this *a priori* approach in the face of Tycho Brahe's detailed observations (Di Liscia 2017, sec. 3), but the idea was completely reasonable given his assumptions about the nature of geometry.

Galileo also believed that if one could see things from a God's-eye perspective, we would understand that scientific truths are just as necessary as mathematical ones and "that it would be impossible for them to take place in any other manner. For such is the property and condition of things which are natural and true" ([1632] 1953, 424). If the fundamental mathematical truths of science were discovered, their implications would be derived with all the certainty of a Euclidean theorem. That, however, would remain an unreachable ideal (Davis 1984, 47). While Descartes trusted in clear and distinct ideas as indicators of truth, Galileo was more pessimistic, believing that God had given us only a limited ability to comprehend mathematics and to see how it applied to nature.[9]

This gap was clearest in cases of underdetermination, where different mathematical models fit the data equally well. For example, the systems of Ptolemy, Copernicus, and Tycho Brahe all "save the appearances," i.e., they yield correct predictions. They could not, of course, all be true. Matthew Hale argued that reason alone could not resolve the underdetermination in astronomy and that more would be needed (Harrison 2013, 135).[10]

Here, then, is the key to Harrison's argument. It was not voluntarism that motivated the demand for more data, he says, but our own limited rational abilities, which resulted from the fallenness of humanity (2007, 43). Galileo was an experimentalist, but voluntarism had no part to play. Experiments were instead a forced necessity to find the correct mathematical relations behind the phenomena.

Harrison also rightly argues that voluntarism did not inevitably lead to empiricism. Unlike Kepler, Descartes did not believe that the principles of logic and mathematics were necessary truths; rather, he believed they were dependent on God's choice in the matter. Such hypervoluntarism was rare. Few would agree that the "mathematical truths . . . were established by God and totally depend on him just like all the other creatures" ("Letter to Mersenne," quoted in Harrison 2002, 65). Descartes did not worry that God would change his mind, however, given divine perfection and immutability.[11]

Descartes was famously a continental rationalist, not an empiricist. How then does that fit with his voluntarism about mathematics and laws? If such things were not necessary truths, how would they be discovered? His answer was that some laws – principally the laws of motion – could be known *a priori* by way of noting the clear and distinct ideas that God had placed into our minds. A perfect God would not deceive us (*Meditations* III.38). Writing about the laws of nature, Descartes says, "The knowledge of these truths is so natural to our souls that we cannot but judge them infallible when we conceive them distinctly." ([1667] 1985, 97). And so voluntarism, even of this extreme type, did not lead to empiricism about fundamental laws and first principles.

Harrison's conclusion, then, is that empiricism has no logical relation to voluntarism. There were empiricists who were not voluntarists, voluntarists who were rationalists, and some early modern natural philosophers who were neither empiricists nor voluntarists. One is neither necessary nor sufficient for the other. While there was indeed a theological motivation for empiricism on Harrison's view, it was lapsarianism – the fall of humankind – rather than voluntarism.

While philosophers and scientists should be wary of disagreeing with Peter Harrison on matters of history, I believe that John Henry is correct: One can accept all of Harrison's counterexamples and still conclude that the new experimental philosophy was motivated in part by voluntarism (2009). Rather than rejecting the voluntarism-to-empiricism thesis, we should see their relation as something other than logical entailment.

Descartes himself provides evidence for both sides. While Harrison focuses on his *a priori* approach, notice what Descartes says about other physical truths, such as the size of particles in the universe:

> Since there are countless different configurations which God might have instituted here, experience alone must teach us which configurations he actually selected in preference to the rest. We are thus free to make any assumption on these matters with the sole proviso that all the consequences of our assumption must agree with our experience.
>
> ([1644] 1988, 256)

So, while there is only one set of fundamental laws governing the motion of all particles, which, according to Descartes, can be known *a priori*, there are many different systems in which those laws can be implemented. Only observation can reveal which one God has chosen.

The motivation behind empiricism is not an either-or prospect – either voluntarism or postlapsarian limitations. We can agree with Harrison that (i) there is more to the story of the rise of empiricism than voluntarism and that (ii) voluntarism is neither necessary nor sufficient for its rise. The link was nonetheless an increasingly important idea through the seventeenth century, especially in British natural philosophy (Davis 1984, 32–33).

4.4 Laws, voluntarism, and special divine action

Let's briefly consider how these matters relate to the question of divine action. Noninterventionism can trace its roots directly through Descartes and Leibniz. Descartes' God created and sustained the universe. More precisely, God conserved the same quantity of motion in the universe at all times. His absolute immutability ensured that whatever laws God had ordained would never be changed. Beyond that, Descartes had little use for divine action. Even in terms of creation, he thought that the world could have arisen from Chaos by way of the laws of nature and nothing else (Descartes [1667] 1985, chap. 6). He further believed that miracles performed in the course of history could impede the progress of science (Davis 1984, 90).

Many objected that the Cartesian system was far too self-contained. Newton was concerned that it would lead to atheism (Davis 1996, 79–80), and indeed it was soon exploited by atheists and later by the deist movement (Brooke 1991, 140).

Leibniz's system was at the same time intellectualist and non-Aristotelian. Rather than the free choices envisioned by the British voluntarists, Leibniz held that all divine decisions were made in accordance with the Principle of Sufficient Reason. Any sort of intervention in history, he argued, would be the mark of an imperfect God:

> If active force should diminish in the universe by the natural laws which God has established, so that there should be need for him to give a new impression in order to restore that force, like an artist's mending the imperfections of his machine, the disorder would not only be with respect to us but also with respect to God himself. He might have prevented it.
>
> (Leibniz and Clarke [1717] 1956, 29)

If things weren't going the way God wanted, instead of having to intervene and redirect events, God could have "taken better measures to avoid such an inconvenience, and therefore, indeed, he has actually done it" ([1717] 1956, 29). As we saw in Chapter 1, this intuition still motivates noninterventionism.

Clarke defended the Newtonian position that an active God is in no way a defective one (Leibniz and Clarke [1717] 1956, 34, 113, 117–18). Having rejected both Aristotelian and Neoplatonic intermediaries in favor of God's direct governance, Clarke argued that the laws are nothing more than patterns within the events dictated by divine will:

> With regard to God. . . [there are] no powers of nature at all, that can do any thing of themselves, (as weights and springs work of themselves with regard to men); but the wisdom and foresight of God, consist . . . in contriving at once, what his power and government is continually putting in actual execution.
>
> (Leibniz and Clarke [1717] 1956, 23)

> What men commonly call the course of nature . . . is nothing else but the will of God producing certain effects in a continued, constant, and uniform manner.
>
> (Clarke [1750] 1998, 149)

This was a common view at the time. It is not the case that God (i) set the laws in place at creation and then (ii) decided to intervene at some latter point in time. Instead, miracles, which are by definition outside readily observed regularities, are no different in terms of God's mode of activity

(Harrison 2013, 144). When unusual events occur, especially those with religious implications, we call it a "miracle," but from a God's-eye perspective there is nothing *sui generis* about such an event. For Clarke, the distinction between law and miracle is a matter of our ignorance, not metaphysics.[12] Both the observed regularities and the miraculous are matters of divine will.

For better or worse, the view that the laws of nature were simply God's decrees soon gave way to the reified version more common today (Brooke 1992). If a phenomenon is explained by way of natural law, many infer that there will be no need to appeal to God, thus setting the two in opposition to each other. Such a dichotomy would have been quite puzzling to those who first used the notion of laws to describe nature.

Scholars have paid a great deal of attention to the seventeenth century, and for good reason. The beginning of the modern era brought about changes that are underappreciated except by specialists in the field. And it is only within the most recent generation of scholars that the role of theism has been fully understood. Theological beliefs were not merely artifacts of a more religious climate; they were instead deeply integrated into the metaphysics and the epistemology of the early moderns, including those whom we anachronistically call "scientists."

4.5 Appendix: voluntarism and intelligent design theory

Let's return now to the present day. The issues discussed in this chapter are surprisingly helpful in understanding the controversy over intelligent design (ID) theory. To see why, consider what philosophers of science call the "explanatory virtues," those *desiderata* that make for a good scientific theory. These include empirical adequacy and fitting within what is already known. The two virtues of interest here are successful predictions and fruitfulness. The first is clear enough. We expect good theories to not only explain what we already know but also to yield predictions that, if successful, will further confirm the theory. Fruitfulness is the capacity of a theory to open new avenues of scientific research. Einstein's theory of general relativity was a fantastic achievement in and of itself. But once coupled with Edwin Hubble's observations, it soon led to Georges Lemaître's expanding universe and what we now call Big Bang cosmology. Contrast this with the rival steady-state model, of which few have heard because it was essentially a dead-end, the opposite of fruitfulness.

While there are books filled with criticisms of ID, some fair and some not, two longstanding problems are a lack of predictive success and fruitfulness. The ID "movement" had hundreds of scientists at one time and has, in fact, produced a small number of peer-reviewed papers. But with so much support and effort, why haven't ID advocates been able to produce more? One possible answer is that the theory is false. But let's grant for the moment ID's main hypothesis: The evolution of sentient creatures was overwhelming unlikely without the intervention of an intelligence. Most supporters have their money on God but acknowledge that the evidence cannot point to the specific designer in question. One would think that if such a proposal is true, it will lead to successful research.

From what we have discussed in this chapter, I think it is safe to say that while Descartes and Leibniz would have opposed ID on noninterventionist grounds, Newton and Clarke would have been friendlier toward it. Descartes' God was deemed so passive that he was charged with atheism in his own lifetime. And Leibniz would surely invoke his infinite clockmaker as an argument against the need for special divine action postcreation. Newton thought otherwise. As Clarke articulates his position, Newton saw no reason why Leibniz would want

> to exclude God's actual government of the world, and to allow his providence to act no further than . . . to let all things do only what they would do of themselves by mere mechanism.
>
> (Leibniz and Clarke [1717] 1956, 117–18)

In other words, the action of an intelligent designer in the course of history was not beyond the pale.

Nonetheless, Newtonians would also have pointed to some significant hurdles for ID to become a thriving research program. The issue, once again, is voluntarism. There was no sense in which God had to choose any set of laws of nature or the mechanisms that would obey those laws. With so many options and no direct revelation about what God had ordained, the only way to discover the laws and physical mechanisms involved was observation and experiments. Consider the quote from Roger Cotes again:

> Surely, this World . . . could not have arisen except from the perfectly free will of God. . . . From this source, then, have all the laws . . . come, in which many traces of the highest wisdom and counsel certainly appear, but no traces of necessity. Accordingly we should not seek these laws by using untrustworthy conjectures, but learn them by observing and experimenting.
>
> ([1687] 1962)

Natural philosophers could not predict how an omnipotent, omniscience being would create the world unless God had in some way revealed it. (The Cartesians believed that God had done so, but that part of their program quickly came under fire.) With the rejection of a *priori* knowledge of regarding physics, the only alternative was empiricism.

Consider what this means for ID. To make successful predictions, its theorists would have to do what many early moderns thought was impossible: rationally infer how God chooses to act in nature. Our inability to do so was one of the main arguments against intellectualism. Given God's freedom to choose and the array of options from which to choose, there was no getting around experimental science to discover the selections that were made. This is presumably why theistic scientists through 1800s tended to point to the elegance of the laws themselves as the best evidence of a Designer.

We could imagine, then, what a modern-day Cotes or Clarke would have to say about ID. While clearly God *might* intervene to produce irreducibly complex systems, there was no way to predict whether this would actually be the case or how prevalent such systems would be. The fact that God has so many options available makes it nearly impossible to know in advance how divine interventions – if there are any – might manifest themselves. If the success of a research program hinges on such knowledge, it will be no surprise that progress is limited.

So, while the British voluntarists would be sympathetic to the basic ideas, they would cite philosophical and theological reasons for why ID research will prove to be difficult if not impossible. Nothing prevents discoveries that might point back to design, such as cosmological fine-tuning, but these will tend to be surprises rather than successful predictions. As such, it is hard to imagine a fruitful research program based on the detection of design.

Notes

1 Some argue that Roger Bacon and Robert Grosseteste deserve more credit for the initial movement in the direction of laws (Kedar and Hon 2017). For other premodern uses of law, see (Van Dyck 2018).
2 For more on the contrasts between the two, see (Henry 2009, 79–82).
3 Barrow and Whiston were the holders of the Lucasian Chair at Cambridge immediately before (Barrow) and after (Whiston) Newton.
4 For example, the Puritan Cotton Mather:

> [There] is no such thing as an universal Soul, animating the vast system of the World, [as] according to Plato; nor any substantial Forms [as] according to Aristotle. . . . These unintelligent Beings are derogatory from the Wisdom and Power of the great God, who can easily govern the Machine He could create, by more direct Methods than employing such subservient divinities. . . . It is now plain from the most evident principles, that the great God . . . has the springs of this immense machine, and all the several parts of it, in his own Hand.
>
> (Mather 1721, 87–88)

5 In other words, only natural motion could reveal Aristotelian final causes, which could then help reveal a formal cause.
6 The first, as we noted earlier, was the rejection Aristotelian intermediaries and the distinction between natural and violent motion.
7 Historian Francis Oakley makes this point:

> [We] can in no way deduce the order of the world by any a priori reasoning, for, being completely dependent upon the divine choice, it corresponds to no necessity and can be discovered only by an examination of what is *de facto*. Thus, from Ockham's fundamental insistence upon the omnipotence and freedom of God follows, not only his ethical and legal voluntarism, but also his empiricism.
>
> (1961, 442)

8 For others arguing for this conclusion, see, Oakley (1961), Davis (1999), and Henry (2009). Many look back to Foster (1934) as one of the first articulators of this view, although most believe that Foster too quickly drew apologetic conclusions from the historical record.
9 Interestingly, Galileo did not call these mathematical principles "laws,"

> [but] spoke of them as *theorems* or *propositions* or *rules*. It is significant that the only reference to physical laws in all of Galileo's writings comes in a letter to his pupil Benedetto Castelli, the most important parts of which were later incorporated almost without change in the more well-known *Letter to the Grand Duchess Christina*. . . . In both letters he described nature as "the most observant executrix of the orders of God, obeying the laws *(leggi)* imposed on her" (34). The theological context and lack of scientific content of these phrases is significant. The idea of laws of nature was a theological inheritance quite foreign to the Archimedean paradigms Galileo followed in the formal exposition of his mechanics.
>
> (Milton 1981, 181)

10 Galileo also recognized many such cases of underdetermination but thought that one could create new data by way of experiments. As Davis notes, however, Galileo sometimes relied on reason when an experiment would have been the wiser choice (1984, 61–62).
11 The reasoning here is similar to that of the medieval distinction between what God might ordain *potentia absoluta* as opposed to *potentia ordinata*. In God's absolute power, mathematics and law could have been different. But having ordained such laws, an immutable God will not change them. Note that Harrison disputes whether these doctrines had any direct influence on the early moderns (2002, 13).
12 A point emphasized by Yenter and Vailati (2014, sec. 4.4).

Works cited

Anstey, Peter R. 2002. *The Philosophy of Robert Boyle*. Routledge Studies in Seventeenth-Century Philosophy. London: Routledge.

Barrow, Isaac. 1885. "Maker of Heaven and Earth (Sermon XII)." In *Theological Works*. Vol. 2. Cambridge: Cambridge University Press.

Boyle, Robert. 1725. *The Philosophical Works of the Honourable Robert Boyle Esq: Abridged, Methodized, and Disposed Under the General Heads of Physics, Statics, Pneumatics, Natural History, Chymistry, and Medicine*. Edited by Peter Shaw. Vol. 2. London: W. and J. Innys.

———. (1686) 1996. *A Free Enquiry into the Vulgarly Received Notion of Nature*. Edited by Edward B. Davis and Michael Cyril William Hunter. Cambridge Texts in the History of Philosophy. Cambridge: Cambridge University Press.

Brooke, John Hedley. 1991. *Science and Religion: Some Historical Perspectives*. Cambridge: Cambridge University Press.

———. 1992. "Natural Law in the Natural Sciences: The Origins of Modern Atheism?" *Science & Christian Belief* 4 (2): 83–103.

Clarke, Samuel. 1738. *Works, Containing Sermons on Several Subjects*. Vol. 2. London: John and Paul Knapton.

———. (1750) 1998. *A Demonstration of the Being and Attributes of God and Other Writings*. Edited by Ezio Vailati. Cambridge Texts in the History of Philosophy. Cambridge: Cambridge University Press.

Cotes, Roger. (1687) 1962. "Preface to Newton's Principia." In *Principia Mathematica*, edited by Florian Cajori, translated by Andrew Motte. Vol. 1. Berkeley: University of California Press.

Davis, Edward B. 1984. "Creation, Contingency, and Early Modern Science: The Impact of Voluntaristic Theology on Seventeenth Century Natural Philosophy." Doctoral dissertation, Bloomington: Indiana University.

————. 1996. "Newton's Rejection of the 'Newtonian World View': The Role of Divine Will in Newton's Natural Philosophy." In *Facets of Faith and Science: The Role of Beliefs in the Natural Sciences*, edited by Jitse M. van der Meer, 3:75–96. Lanham: University Press of America.

————. 1999. "Christianity and Early Modern Science: The Foster Thesis Reconsidered." In *Evangelicals and Science in Historical Perspective*, edited by D. N. Livingstone, D. G. Hart, and M. A. Noll, 75–95. New York: Oxford University Press.

Descartes, René. (1667) 1985. "The World." In *The Philosophical Writings of Descartes*, translated by J. Cottingham, R. Stoothoff, and D. Murdoch. Vol. 1. Cambridge: Cambridge University Press.

————. (1644) 1988. "Principles of Philosophy." In *Descartes: Selected Philosophical Writings*, translated by John Cottingham, Robert Stoothoff, and Dugald Murdoch, 1:177–291. Cambridge: Cambridge University Press.

Di Liscia, Daniel A. 2017. "Johannes Kepler." In *Stanford Encyclopedia of Philosophy*, edited by Edward N. Zalta. https://plato.stanford.edu/archives/fall2017/entries/kepler/.

Fisher, Paul. 2014. "Pierre Gassendi." In *Stanford Encyclopedia of Philosophy*, edited by Edward N. Zalta. http://plato.stanford.edu/archives/spr2014/entries/gassendi/.

Foster, M. B. 1934. "The Christian Doctrine of Creation and the Rise of Modern Natural Science." *Mind* 43 (172): 446–68.

Galilei, Galileo. (1632) 1953. *Dialogue Concerning the Two Chief World Systems, Ptolemaic & Copernican*. Translated by Stillman Drake. Berkeley, CA: University of California Press.

Garber, Daniel. 2013. "God, Laws, and the Order of Nature: Descartes and Leibniz, Hobbes and Spinoza." In *The Divine Order, the Human Order, and the Order of Nature: Historical Perspectives*, edited by Eric Watkins, 45–66. New York: Oxford University Press.

Harrison, Peter. 2002. "Voluntarism and Early Modern Science." *History of Science* (40): 63–89.

————. 2007. *The Fall of Man and the Foundations of Science*. Cambridge, UK: Cambridge University Press.

————. 2013. "Laws of Nature in Seventeenth-Century England: From Cambridge Platonism to Newtonianism." In *The Divine Order, the Human Order, and the Order of Nature: Historical Perspectives*, edited by Eric Watkins, 127–48. New York: Oxford University Press.

Henry, John. 2009. "Voluntarist Theology at the Origins of Modern Science: A Response to Peter Harrison." *History of Science* 47 (1): 79–113.

Kedar, Yael, and Giora Hon. 2017. " 'Natures' and 'Laws': The Making of the Concept of Law of Nature—Robert Grosseteste (c. 1168–1253) and Roger Bacon (1214/1220–1292)." *Studies in History and Philosophy of Science Part A* 61 (February): 21–31. https://doi.org/10.1016/j.shpsa.2016.12.001.

Kepler, Johannes. (1621) 1952. "Epitome of Copernican Astronomy, Book IV." In *Great Books of the Western World*, translated by Charles Glenn Wallis, 16:845–960. Chicago: Encyclopedia Britannica.

———. (1619) 1997. *The Harmony of the World*. Translated by E. J. Aiton, A. M. Duncan, and J. V. Field. Philadelphia: American Philosophical Society.

Leftow, Brian. 1998. "Voluntarism." In *Routledge Encyclopedia of Philosophy*, edited by E. Craig. London: Routledge.

Leibniz, Gottfried W., and Samuel Clarke. (1717) 1956. *The Leibniz-Clarke Correspondence: Together with Extracts from Newton's Principia and Optics*. Edited by H. G. Alexander. Manchester: Manchester University Press.

Mather, Cotton. 1721. *The Christian Philosopher: A Collection of the Best Discoveries in Nature, with Religious Improvements*. London: Eman. Matthews.

Milton, John R. 1981. "The Origin and Development of the Concept of the 'Laws of Nature.'" *European Journal of Sociology/Archives Européennes de Sociologie/Europäisches Archiv Für Soziologie* 22 (2): 173–95.

Oakley, Francis. 1961. "Christian Theology and the Newtonian Science: The Rise of the Concept of the Laws of Nature." *Church History* 30 (4): 433–57. https://doi.org/10.2307/3161219.

Van Dyck, Maarten. 2018. "Law, Renaissance Idea of Natural." In *Encyclopedia of Renaissance Philosophy*, edited by Marco Sgarbi, 1–7. Cham: Springer International Publishing. https://doi.org/10.1007/978-3-319-02848-4_71-1.

Watkins, Eric, ed. 2013. *The Divine Order, the Human Order, and the Order of Nature: Historical Perspectives*. New York: Oxford University Press.

Whiston, William. 1717. *Astronomical Principles of Religion, Natural and Reveal'd*. London: J. Senex, and W. Taylor.

Yenter, Timothy, and Ezio Vailati. 2014. "Samuel Clarke." In *Stanford Encyclopedia of Philosophy*, edited by Edward N. Zalta. http://plato.stanford.edu/archives/spr2014/entries/clarke/.

Zeyl, Donald. 2014. "Plato's Timaeus." In *Stanford Encyclopedia of Philosophy*, edited by Edward N. Zalta. https://plato.stanford.edu/archives/spr2014/entries/plato-timaeus/.

5 Philosophy of science and the laws of nature

Chapter 4 dealt with the history of law as a concept in science. We now turn to its place in the modern philosophical landscape. In one sense, the laws of nature are so familiar that further analysis seems unnecessary. Every freshman knows about Newton's laws and has at least heard of a few more. While there is consensus about the *content* of many laws of nature, there is much less agreement about the *nature* of the laws themselves.

There are four main approaches in the philosophy of science literature to understanding laws: First, there are those who deflate laws down to either mere regularities between events or statements about those events. These are called "Humean" laws, after David Hume, insofar as they avoid metaphysics as much as possible. Second, there are those who take the causal powers, dispositions, or capacities of things as fundamental and laws as derivative descriptions of their effects. Laws are not responsible for the regularities in nature, they say, the causal powers of substances are. The third is the least familiar as it relies on counterfactuals and possible worlds. Laws in this view are grounded in the stability of particular counterfactual claims. Finally, there are those who take laws themselves to be a fundamental category within metaphysics.

While critiquing these approaches is a useful exercise, that is not the sole purpose here. Noninterventionists and nonviolationists argue that God does not violate the laws of nature, but what a "violation" amounts to crucially depends on what the laws are. The problem of divine action looks different and in some cases dissolves completely under a given interpretation of law. In the end, I will side with the non-Humeans and argue for a metaphysically robust view, although one that does not rely on causal powers and dispositions. In fact, I believe that British early moderns, such as Boyle and Newton, largely had it right: The laws are regularities within the decrees of God for nature.

5.1 Humean laws

Most philosophers of science prefer metaphysically lean options when it comes to laws. Humeans believe in occurrent events, such as when a system evolves from one state to another, but they reject the idea that either causes or laws in some sense govern reality. Unlike the other positions discussed in this chapter, the Humean takes laws to be special types of statements. Coulomb's law, for example, is itself a law of nature, not merely our attempt to describe some sort of mind-independent power that exists in nature. This will become clearer as we go.

5.1.1 Regularity theory

An older Humean view is *regularity theory*. It says that while events sometimes occur in perfectly regular ways, there are no laws or causes over and above those events. For Hume, causation was a psychological projection. We see a regularity in nature – two states of affairs, one consistently followed by the other – and then impose a connection between the two. But our projection of causation has no more reality to it than that of the attempt to see Orion among a group of stars. Regularity theorists further argue that empirical science does not need anything more than occurrent events. Scientists do not care about metaphysics. They discover useful regularities and refer to some of them as laws. End of story.

Well, perhaps, but what about uninstantiated regularities? Look at the largest elements on the periodic table. Those at the bottom are unstable and cannot be found outside highly engineered physics labs. Was there no fact-of-the-matter, no physical truth, about the behavior of livermorium before it was created? This sort of Humean must say "no" since there had been no regularity of actually occurring events to ground any law covering livermorium. That element was outside the laws of nature during its first instant after being created. While not a *reductio*, this is an unwelcome implication for an interpretation of laws. Presumably those physicists in the lab were looking to discover the laws of livermorium, not create them.

Moreover, most laws in physics cover a range of parameter values, many of which never occur in the real world. Take a common distinction in cosmology. It could be that our universe is closed, meaning that eventually space-time will recollapse into a singularity – a Big Crunch. The more likely scenario is that the universe is open and will continue expanding forever. The reason physicists can talk coherently about open versus closed universes is that both are governed by one set of laws, Einstein's equation for general relativity.[1] The difference between the two has to do with the amount of mass-energy in the universe.

For regularity theorists, this literally makes no sense since the laws are just the regularities in this universe. There are no events that ground the truth of regularities in other possible universes. There are no laws that transcend events. According to regularity theory, then, much of what physicists have to say about cosmology is, strictly speaking, false. It seems to me that if a philosophical view is being promoted as the one that best fits science, that view ought not entail that most physicists are wrong.

Another well-known criticism of regularity theory is that it cannot distinguish those regularities that are actual laws from mere accidental generalizations. We want to be able to say that "all particles with mass have gravitational attraction" is a law but that "all of my children are male" is not. The problem is that both claims have the same logical structure. Call the first claim L for law and the second G for mere generalization. Why is L a law but not G? The regularity theorist says that there must be something that sets L apart, a special feature of those generalizations that count as laws. And whatever that something is, it must be free of untoward metaphysics. Fred Dretske considers five candidates (1977, 251–52):

(1) High degree of confirmation;
(2) Wide acceptance (well-established in the relevant community);
(3) Explanatory potential (can be used to explain its instances);
(4) Deductive integration (within a larger system of statements);
(5) Predictive success.

Each of these has been invoked as a characteristic that mere universal generalizations lack but that laws have. (4) is associated with a second Humean proposal, so let's ignore that one for now.

The rest are problematic. (3) confuses logical entailment with explanation. Both G and L entail their instances, but neither explains anything. L provides no insight into the relation between mass and gravity. That sort of work will be done by a related theory, not by the law itself. There is no doubt that (1) and (2) apply to L and not to G, but as Dretske points out, they are both epistemic notions having to do with what we or some group of experts believes. If (1) or (2) is a necessary condition for laws, we will not be able to say that the laws of nature are the same now as they were a millennium ago, since what astronomers believed then is not what they currently believe. If we define laws in a way that depends on our knowledge, the laws of nature will obviously change over time. Instead, we think of laws as being stable and independent of what we believe. The laws of nature are not a function of the sometimes-fickle state of scientific knowledge, which depends on what has and has not been discovered.

What about (5), then? Laws allow for successful predictions, but mere generalizations can easily fail to hold in the future. While it is true that every person to walk on the moon has been male, that generalization will be false once a female astronaut lands there, and so it cannot be a law. But why think that L will remain true, come what may? This is one instance of the famous problem of induction. Just because all bits of matter that we have examined gravitationally attract one another, how can we be sure that all unexamined future bits of matter will continue to do so? More generally, why do we think the pattern of (i) observations to (ii) inductive generalization to (iii) successful prediction will continue to be useful? Of course, it has worked well so far, but the appeal to past success is a well-known circular answer to the question. If what one is worried about is that the future might not continue to resemble the past, appealing to the previous successes of induction will not help. Why think that this past success will continue into the future? Why think, in other words, that nature will continue to be uniform?

The rival accounts of laws yet to be discussed have their own answers to this question, but they involve more robust metaphysics than the Humean empiricist will allow. The regularity theorist, again, believes that laws are merely descriptions of actual events. There is no necessary connection between those events that makes one follow the other, no sense in which masses must attract. It simply is the case that *L*. Non-Humeans argue that uniformity of nature as more than a happy coincidence requires some metaphysical principle that ensures nature will not go off the rails in the future. They disagree, however, about what sort of metaphysics plays this role.

5.1.2 Best systems

These problems explain why most Humeans today are not regularity theorists. A second approach looks to plane geometry and Euclid's axioms as a model. Say that we had a complete index of scientific truths – what Helen Beebee calls "God's Big Book of Facts" (2004, 253). That's an unattainable goal, but let's accept it as an idealization. Such an unwieldy compilation could presumably be organized so that detailed, narrow facts might be derived from more general ones. Say we organize these truths into a deductive system that would allow us to derive as many facts as possible from a set of axioms. In a best systems or Mill-Ramsey-Lewis (MRL) approach, the laws of nature are those generalizations that would appear either as axioms or as theorems in the systems with the best combination of content and simplicity (Lewis 1973b, 73). Run-of-the-mill occurrent facts would then be derivable from the laws plus a description of the context, in much the way physics students apply Newton's laws to different circumstances. This is (4) on Dretske's list. The *something more* that sets laws apart from mere universal generalizations is that only the former serve as axioms for the body of scientific knowledge.

Consider some points in favor of MRL. It allows that today's textbook laws might be wrong since they may not survive in the best deductive system in the future. MRL also supports the idea of undiscovered laws since the best system might be something other than what we currently have in hand. At the same time, textbook laws can provisionally be considered laws since they might be retained as axioms or theorems. These virtues explain why some version of the best systems approach seems to be favored by philosophers of science.

This appreciation is not shared by philosophers of religion or metaphysicians. To see why, consider a distinction that's been at the periphery throughout this section: laws and law-statements. Law-statements are what one finds in physics and chemistry classrooms – something one could point to on a whiteboard, like the ideal gas law. The laws themselves, if there are any, are the actual laws of nature that scientists are trying to discover. Laws cannot be wrong; they are whatever they happen to be. Law-statements, on the other hand, are descriptions of laws. If a law-statement is true, it is a law of nature that is its truth-maker. So, while gravity has been at work since before Earth existed, Newton's equation that describes it has only been around a few hundred years. Humeans will argue that this way of putting things begs the question since it assumes there are laws of nature over and above natural events themselves. Even so, there is still a distinction between laws and law-statements. Humeans do not believe that the former exist.

Here, then, is a key point: When Lewis says that laws are theorems in a deductive system, he really means law-statements. They can be written on a piece of paper. The best systems approach, like all Humean accounts of law, is not a theory about the laws of nature. It is a theory about law-statements, specifically which generalizations should be given the honorific "law." This comports with Humean assumptions since they do not believe there are such things as laws themselves. Critics, on the other hand, reject the deflation of laws to mere law-statements. They point again to the problem of induction and the need to explain the uniformity of nature. Law-statements cannot ensure that nature will not deviate in nonlawlike ways in the future.[2]

5.1.3 *Humean laws and divine action*

It is mildly surprisingly, then, that there are theologians and theistic philosophers who hold a Humean view of laws. This is unusual insofar as Humeans tend to be empiricists who favor a small ontology, typically one without God.[3] Nonetheless, there is a certain appeal to this approach when it comes to divine action.

The regularity theorist's laws are merely observed correlations between events. No further metaphysical commitment is required. If correct, nonviolationist worries about God possibly violating the laws of nature will simply be misplaced. No one needs to be concerned that disease might kill all the unicorns because there are no unicorns. Likewise, God cannot break the laws since there literally is no *thing* to be broken. The arguments in favor of nonviolationism discussed in Chapter 2 are largely nullified. There can be no tension within God's will since there was no point at which God brought the laws into existence and so no later time at which God chose to contravene them. At most, special divine action amounts to God doing something contrary to our expectations.

Much the same can be said under the best-systems/MRL approach. For there to be MRL laws, there would first have to be a set of true sentences that could be formed into a deductive system. Without knowledge of scientific facts in hand, there can be no laws for MRL. Hence, there literally were no laws in this view before life evolved, just as there was no such thing as grammar or rules of etiquette. Nor are there any necessary connections or causal relations between events that God could even possibly override. "Breaking a law of nature" under MRL just means that God does something contrary to what we would have expected based on what we know (i.e., based on the best deductive system of scientific knowledge). But that doesn't seem to be the sort of thing that nonviolationists are worried about. Terms such as "violation" and "breaking" indicate something more significant than God acting in a way contrary to our fallible expectations.

Humean laws have some appeal to theists trying to address challenges to special divine action. The question is whether one is willing to accept the other problems that come along with such a view. For those who cannot abide by Hume's impoverished metaphysic, the next option proves to be far more popular.

5.2 Dispositions and causal powers

The question that all non-Humeans are trying to answer is this: If laws govern events, *how* do they do so? What is the nature of this guidance? Dispositionalists do not believe that the stripped-down ontology of Humean laws provides an answer. They argue that something must *account* for the uniformity of nature, rather than accepting it as a matter of experience. But dispositionalists reject the nomological realist answer, which takes laws as fundamental, preferring an appeal to the causal powers, capacities, and dispositions of entities.[4] Laws have a lesser standing, metaphysically speaking, if they have any standing at all.

Consider molecular salt (NaCl). The molecules have several dispositions, such as dissolving when observable quantities are placed in water and attracting other bits of matter by way of gravitation. But note that it is not the law of universal gravitation that is responsible for this attraction. In this view, objects with mass have the disposition to attract each other in a particular way. More precisely,

> [Mass] is a disposition that manifests itself in the mutual attraction of massy objects. The presence of another mass m' acts as a stimulus on m (and conversely) for the manifestation of the disposition in terms of a mutual acceleration. As soon as there are at least two massive objects in a world, that disposition is triggered. It is essential for the property of gravitational mass to manifest itself in the mutual attraction of the objects that instantiate this property. That's what gravitational mass *is* – the property that makes objects accelerate in a certain manner.
>
> (Dorato and Esfeld 2016, 410)

Dispositions are the active powers in nature. Laws are epiphenomenal in this approach, as the underlying dispositions do all the metaphysical work. Law-statements, then, are merely convenient summaries of the behavior governed by those dispositions. If it sounds something like the Aristotelianism discussed in the previous chapter, it is. Dispositionalism is the philosophical descendant of Aristotelian natures.

Dispositionalists also allow for modal truths and truth-makers – which is, metaphysically, a bridge too far for Humeans. They believe that dispositions are responsible for true counterfactuals. For example, the truth-maker for "if you were to raise the temperature of a piece of paper to 246°C, it would ignite" is the disposition of the paper to burn (Mumford 2004, chap. 1). Humeans, in contrast, do not believe that law-statements need metaphysical truth-makers – a belief that sets their position apart from the others explained in this chapter.

This view has a number of strengths and prominent supporters, including metaphysician Stephen Mumford (2004) and philosopher Nancy Cartwright (1989). Nonetheless, many philosophers of science are suspicious of this approach, even those who are not Humeans.

5.2.1 Critique

One reason for this is that dispositions tend to be thing-centered: substances, in a technical sense. A substance is an entity in which properties and causal powers reside according to the dispositionalist. However, many important physical properties are not embedded in material objects (Wilson 2006, 261), center of mass, for example. This is a sometimes-measurable attribute – not merely something that can be calculated, like average height – yet there need be no object that exists at the center of mass of a system. The center of mass of our solar system is often thousands of miles from the sun. In what does this dispositional property reside when its location is empty space?[5] As Jerry Fodor once put it, "Nothing cramps one's causal powers like not existing" (2010, 121).

A second reason is based on the history of science. Dispositionalism represents a return to a more Aristotelian framework. But isn't such a move at least a bit odd given that medieval versions had to be set aside for the scientific revolution to proceed? As we saw in Chapter 4, substantial forms were intentionally displaced by a law-centric approach. When natural philosophers began thinking in these terms, they realized that God could have ordained many different sets of laws. Without direct revelation about these choices, the only way to discover them was empirical investigation and experiments. The point is that the shift from Aristotelian essences to laws spurred the development of empiricism in science – no small matter.

Not only did natural philosophers believe that laws exist but they also found them! We often call this era the "scientific revolution" because physics and chemistry thrived under this new philosophical foundation. If dispositionalism were right all along, why would their be the need to dismiss it in order to make such progress? Modern-day dispositionalists try to show that history never *disproved* their view and that, strictly speaking, all the law-based discoveries were compatible with their metaphysics. I agree, and that would be important if one were already a dispositionalist. But if one comes to the question philosophically and theologically neutral about the primacy of dispositions versus laws, the history of science will seem to strongly favor the latter. But this is not the most important problem.

The main concern among philosophers of physics is that the appeal to causal powers is not only "hopelessly vague" (Smith 2002, 252), it is a step backward in terms of understanding. There are many aspects of modern physics that are now taken for granted, like the difference between force, energy, and momentum. But in the history of science, these were all hard-won distinctions. They involved heated disputes among the followers of Leibniz and Newton, both of whom had empirical support of some kind or another.[6] Today, things are far clearer. Instead of force *simpliciter* there are contact forces, special force laws, and fundamental forces. There are not just laws but entire families of differential equations, all developed with an eye toward helping understand the underlying physics. Why, then, would philosophers now want to retreat to the far less precise notion of dispositions or causal powers? This seems to muddy the same waters it took centuries to clear up within classical mechanics. Del Ratzsch expresses it this way:

> Although this view has a number of attractions . . ., it is still seriously incomplete as an analysis until we know what sort of animal a dispositional property is. The attractiveness which this very fuzziness may permit may dissipate along with the fuzziness when we try to sharpen the picture up a bit.
>
> (1987, 386)

Causal powers and dispositions are perhaps more intuitive than alternative approaches to law, but those prescientific notions lack precision. That is not a knock-down argument, nor is there one to be found. But it does explain why most philosophers of physics have not gravitated toward dispositionalism.

Before moving on, note that the rejection of *causal powers* does not mean that the idea of *causation* is thereby banned from science. While "cause" is a highly ambiguous notion, it is often still useful. When those ambiguities are cashed out, however, one is never left with an irreducible disposition or a causal power.

5.2.2 Dispositionalism and divine action

Dispositionalism is non-Humean. It does not avoid metaphysics at all costs, although laws take a backseat to the more fundamental notions of causal powers/capacities/dispositions. It is the latter that are responsible for the nomic regularities in nature. As such, nonviolationist worries about God breaking his own laws are diminished. God did not decree any *laws* in this view; God created things with causal powers. What we call laws are epiphenomenal. Some theistic dispositionalists see special divine action as merely an alteration of the circumstances under which a given set of causal powers acts, working with nature's capacities rather than suspending them. Hence dispositionalism allows for divine action without breaking any laws.

On the other hand, if "altering circumstances" allows for too limited a range of activity on God's part, one can argue that God changes the causal powers themselves, at least for a time:

> [The] only thing God has to do in order to bring about a particular effect is to change temporarily the dispositions of the natural kind(s) that will constitute the state of affairs that God's special act of intervention intends to bring about.
>
> (Göcke 2015, 223)

Such a change need only affect causal powers locally. Even an event like the parting of the Red Sea could be explained by God changing the dispositions of the water molecules involved.

Nonetheless, such a move will not likely soothe every concern about divine action. Noninterventionists will still complain that these activities go far beyond the creating and sustaining of the universe and are therefore theologically out of bounds. Some nonviolationists will be more sympathetic since no laws of nature are violated. Others will reject it, I suspect, since law-claims could be easily translated into disposition-claims. In Göcke's proposal, for example, while no laws are violated, God is still overriding the natural capacities of objects. Some nonviolationists will surely argue that, having ordained the causal powers of nature, God would not later disrupt their guidance of natural processes. In other words, divine action is a violation if it interferes with those processes, regardless of whether the processes are grounded in laws or dispositions.[7]

5.3 Counterfactuals and possible worlds

As an interpretation of laws, this will be the least familiar to nonphilosophers. While originally developed as a way to understand possibility and necessity, the notion of a *possible world* soon ramified across analytic philosophy. "World" here does not mean planet or even universe. A possible world is an entire timeline for a universe. One possible world is a reality nearly identical to our own, with the exception that I am currently wearing a red shirt rather than a blue one. That world is said to be "nearby" in the sense that that one change has little effect on other events. A more distant possible world is one in which the United States never entered World

War I. That, presumably, would have had wide-ranging consequences. One (infamous) position in this literature is *modal realism*, which says that the possible worlds are not merely abstract ideas – rather, they actually exist. Its foremost proponent was David Lewis:

> I believe, and so do you, that things could have been different in count- less ways. But what does this mean? . . . I believe that things could have been different in countless ways; I believe permissible paraphrases of what I believe; taking the paraphrase at its face value, I therefore believe in the existence of entities that might be called "ways things could have been." I prefer to call them "possible worlds."
>
> (1973b, 84)

As we have seen, Lewis did not appeal to possible worlds in his account of laws. (MRL reduces laws to law-statements within a deductive system of scientific knowledge.) Counterfactuals, the contrary truths found in other possible worlds, are instead used in Lewis's analysis of causation. He argued that causal relations are a type of counterfactual dependence, and counterfactual dependence can be explained in terms of the structure of possible words (Lewis 1973a). In its simplest form, an event B caus- ally depends on event A when the following is true: If A were to occur, B would occur, and if A were not to occur, B would not occur. The truth of these conditionals depends on the relative closeness of possible worlds. Hence, for Lewis, possible words are more fundamental than causation or laws.

Presently, the main proponent of a counterfactual approach to law is phi- losopher Marc Lange (2009). To start, we should note that counterfactuals are famously context-dependent. Consider the counterfactual situation in which Caesar were in command in the Korean War. Which of the following would be true?

(1) If Caesar were in command during the Korean War, he would have used nuclear weapons.
(2) If Caesar were in command during the Korean War, he would have used catapults.

Lewis argued that the right answer depends on the context of the ques- tion. There is no context-free fact-of-the-matter about which is correct. According to Lange, however, law-statements are different. Laws are stable regardless of context. This explains why "all of my pets are dogs" is a mere accidental generalization. It is not counterfactually stable:

(3) If each of my pets had canine mothers, all my pets would be dogs. (true)
(4) If my wife brought home a cat today, all my pets would be dogs. (false)

However,

(5) If each of my pets had canine mothers, protons would be positively charged. (true)
(6) If my wife brought home a cat today, protons would be positively charged. (true)

The consequents in (5) and (6) are insensitive to changes in context. Lange's claim is that laws display this sort of counterfactual stability, come what may. More precisely, law-statements are grounded in counterfactual sentences exhibiting this sort of stability.

Lange's account does much of the work philosophers want. First, it clearly demarcates laws from mere universal generalizations. The latter are not sufficiently stable. Second, stability explains the (non-Humean) intuition that laws have a kind of necessity. Stability among counterfactuals allows us to determine those truths that are "naturally necessary," which in turn point to those generalizations that are laws (Lange 2009, chap. 2). Third, Lange argues that his account can explain a variety of related ideas: the immutability of laws, the nature of metalaws (e.g., conservation laws that govern other laws), and the relation of law to chance (Lange 2009, chap. 3).

While these are significant, there is one overriding problem with taking relations among possible worlds as the truth-makers for law-statements. It is not counterfactual stability that lets us make inferences about the laws. It is our knowledge of the laws that grounds predictions about counterfactual stability. How do I know that wearing a different shirt to class would not affect the charge of protons? Because we know the relevant laws. Our counterfactual judgments are parasitic in what we take the laws to be.[8] This, I believe, is why few have rallied to Lange's innovative approach. The metaphysical priority seems to be exactly the opposite of what it should be.

This third view takes the structure of possible worlds to be more fundamental than either laws or causal powers. Its implications for divine action are less clear. Several metaphysical and theological questions would have to be answered first. For example, what is the ontological status of possible worlds? Does God passively know counterfactual truths, or does God instead determine their content? If God knows each of the possible worlds but does not have a hand in shaping them, the laws of nature are not within God's control. While God will still choose which of the worlds to make actual, the relations between the worlds themselves simply are what they are. And it is these relations that are supposed to ground the laws.

One might say that since God does not ordain the laws in this view, there would be no conflict within God's will if he were to intervene in nature. On the other hand, since God chooses which possible world will be actual, God is determining the events in this world, and so any intervention would be contrary to what God had determined. Which is the more natural position for a nonviolationist is not clear to me.

In short, any account of divine action that takes laws to be grounded in possible worlds will first have to resolve several difficult metaphysical questions along the way, which is perhaps why no philosopher of religion has taken this approach, so far as I know.

I have argued that (i) Humean laws are too metaphysically lean to be laws of nature, (ii) causal powers are vague and do not comport well with the history of science, and (iii) counterfactual truths are dependent on more fundamental nomic relations. Nonetheless, each of these are live options that continue to be defended by theists and naturalists alike.

Let's now move on to the last family of views.

5.4 Nomological realism

According to *nomological realism*, laws have their own metaphysical standing. They cannot be reduced to law-statements. They do not supervene on events or causal powers. Laws are fundamental. This, I believe, is what most people have in mind when they begin to think about the issues raised in this chapter.

5.4.1 Universals and necessitation

The best-known type of nomological realism is associated with philosophers David Armstrong, Fred Dretske, and Michael Tooley. They take laws to be grounded in necessary relations between universals.[9] Consider the law-statement "all metals conduct electricity."[10] What is its truth-maker? In this view, the terms "metal" and "electric conductor" refer to universals – properties that cannot be reduced to something more basic. If this law-statement is true, those universals will be related in such a way that the former necessitates the latter.[11] For any true law-statement "all Fs are Gs," the universals F-ness and G-ness are related by way of necessitation. It is this relation that ultimately is a law of nature for Armstrong *et al.*

This answers several questions that Humean laws are unable to adequately address: First, what distinguishes a true law-statement from an accidental generalization – "all electrons have negative charge" versus "all my students are seated?" Only in the former case do the predicates refer to universals properly related. "My students" refers to a set, not a universal, and there is no necessitation between them and being seated. Any group of objects counts as a set, and as such it has little metaphysical significance. True law-statements, on the other hand, are tracking actual relations between universals. Second, this type of nomological realism supports the uniformity of nature and therefore the trustworthiness of induction. There is no chance, for example, that electrons will stop having negative charge given the relation between the relevant universals. The future will continue to look like the past *vis-à-vis* the laws of nature.

It is hard to say which of the alternatives that Humeans despise most, but this one is surely a candidate. In this case, I have some sympathy. We can detect metals, electrons, and charge, they say, but where are these universals to be found? If one already has reason to believe in universals, this is a good place to make use of them. If not, they seem like a metaphysical construct invented to solve a problem. Moreover, Armstrong leaves the necessitation relation as primitive and unanalyzable. But as Bas van Fraassen complains, "necessitation" seems like a name for something that is wholly mysterious (1989, 104–7). There is no explanation for how necessitation comes to influence *this* particular *a* that is *F* and this *b* that is *G*. If one is going to take something as important as necessitation as basic, why not play that card sooner? This, it seems, is what philosopher of science Tim Maudlin had in mind when positing the laws as foundational without any further need of analysis. We will take up that proposal in the next section.

Before moving on, there is an important presupposition about universals here that should be discussed. Armstrong *et al.* expect there to be relatively few properties that count as universals in physical laws. These are thought to correspond to common terms like "mass" and "charge" that appear in fundamental equations. A closer look at actual physics, however, reveals that *dynamical* properties are often the most important. Many of these are functions of position and momentum and have no handy description in either English or mathematics. Moreover, the language used to describe such properties varies between Newtonian, Lagrangian, and Hamiltonian formulations, none of which have a clear claim to being more fundamental (Wilson 2006, 260). The upshot is that if there are universals in Armstrong's sense, they do not correspond to a list of attributes that has been read off from some set of fundamental law-statements, as its proponents seem to expect.

5.4.2 Laws as primitive

Given the undeniable importance of laws in science, Maudlin takes laws of nature as primitive. After all, every ontology has some bits that are basic and unanalyzed. Mauldin thinks law and the governance-relation are as good a starting place as any other:

> My analysis of laws is no analysis at all. Rather I suggest we accept laws as fundamental entities in our ontology. Or, speaking at the conceptual level, the notion of a law cannot be reduced to other more primitive notions. The only hope of justifying this approach is to show that having accepted laws as building blocks we can explain how our beliefs about laws determine our beliefs in other domains.
>
> (2007, 18)

In other words, taking laws as foundational leads to an analysis of both dispositions and counterfactuals that is far more complete and natural than trying to analyze laws from some other standpoint. It is this explanatory power that justifies taking the laws as basic. We should believe in laws because of the explanatory work that they do.

This is a bold speculative move on Maudlin's part, but he is no doubt right about the role of laws in the history of science. As the long-term success of a scientific theory tends to support its truth, perhaps the same can be said for nomological realism. The concept of laws has proven itself, even if our knowledge about those laws changes as science has progressed.

5.4.3 Early modern laws

At this point it should be clear that the early moderns discussed in Chapter 4 were nomological realists. Descartes, Boyle, Newton and their contemporaries rejected Aristotelian causal powers in favor of law. What would they make of either Armstrong's universals or Maudlin's primitivism?

Surprisingly, they would reject both. As we've seen, there were several reasons why seventeenth-century philosophers moved away from Aristotelianism, including the obscurity of some of its main ideas. One important argument was that substantial forms were useless intermediaries between God and creation. An omnipotent being would not need such entities or powers to get nature to behave in the right way. Boyle in particular argued that they would make the creative activity of God less apparent (1744, 4:361). Instead, God, directly and without mediation, governs his creation. Laws are nothing more than patterns within God's will for how nature must behave. They were not thought of as autonomous agents that God created in order to govern nature.[12] If that were God's choice, substantial forms would be ideal. The early moderns did not exchange one set of governing entities for another; they rejected the middleman in favor of God's direct rule, which they referred to as laws.[13]

This is decidedly not how the laws of nature are understood today. It is often taken for granted that if we can explain some phenomenon by appeal to law, there is no longer any need for God. God and law are put forward as rival explanations, as if it were mutually exclusive that either God or laws govern the universe. Such a dichotomy would have been virtually unheard of prior to the nineteenth century.[14]

This, then, is why I think that the early moderns would have rejected the types of nomological realism presented thus far. Armstrong and Maudlin take laws to be responsible for ensuring nomic regularities. Despite their differences, they agree that laws have a kind of metaphysical autonomy over and responsibility for why the universe runs the way it does. I believe the early moderns would see these as every bit the intermediaries that they were trying to get rid of with their rejection of Aristotelian essences. In their view, the laws had no independent standing or power to bring about anything. The laws are no more than God's choices for how physical events shall proceed.

Alvin Plantinga has recently named this third type of nomological realism *decretalism* (2016, 135). This is where Newton, Boyle, Clarke, *et al.* belong on the overall map of options for the laws of nature. Let's consider it a bit further.

5.5 Decretalism

While decretalism is clearly a minority position today, there are several points to note. First, it is a form of nomological realism, which I have already argued is preferable to rival interpretations of law. Second, decretalism is a conservative position for theists. No additional ontology is needed to ground the laws of nature: no substantial forms, no universals, no dispositions. Third, it has much in common with one of the main views in the philosophical landscape today, namely, Maudlin's primitivism. Decretalism is therefore in good company. But while Maudlin leaves the governance relation unanalyzed, decretalism has an explanation. The laws are not abstract powers that must somehow be connected to actual events. God is directly responsible for the observed regularities in nature.[15]

One might question whether decretalism is really a type of nomological realism at all (Larmer 2017, 444n19). If there are no laws "out there" governing events, in what sense is this realism about the laws of nature? My only answer is that it fits better here than in any of the other camps. Decretalist laws transcend events themselves, and so the Humean will want nothing to do with them. Nor are they dispositions or capacities of natural entities. One could imagine a decretal dispositionalist who says that God created all causal powers by fiat and then embedded them in the corresponding entities,[16] but such a view would inherit all the problems discussed in section 5.2.1. Finally, all nomological realists agree that it makes sense to talk about laws even in a sparse or an empty universe. It would still be a law, for example, that like charges would repel even if God annihilated all charged particles. What this claim means precisely will differ for Armstrong, Maudlin, and Plantinga, but they each will be able to affirm it given the primacy of laws. If this isn't enough to justify including decretalism as a type of nomological realism, the only alternative is to see it as *sui generis*, without a home among the current list of options.

The Humean will no doubt be harrumphing at this point, complaining that we don't have any more epistemic access to God than to Aristotelian substantial forms. Perhaps, but this is just one more place where the intuitions of Humeans and non-Humeans clash. Staunch empiricists must make do with a small ontology. Their critics argue that inference to the best explanation and the need for truth-makers demand more from metaphysics. So no, the Humean does not like theistic explanations, but there's a lot the Humean does not like. I can only say that while it would be nice to have a concrete empirical basis for every claim one believes, that is an ideal that will never be realized. Physics itself cannot get by without unobservable entities or modality.

A related complaint is about obscurity: What exactly is the relation between God's decrees and events? What does governance look like at the point of contact? That's a perfectly good question, and there are two ways to approach it. One is to say that all how-questions eventually must come to an end. Take fundamental physics. Can anyone explain how the Higg's field bestows mass on elementary particles? What precisely does the causal joint look like? Can anyone say how an exchange of particles binds electrons to a nucleus? Everyone has a set of brute facts that belie further analysis, even the Humean. That there is always another how-question someone might ask does not constitute a defeater.

The other approach is to note that "point-of-contact" language is based on an intuition that something is needed to explain change. There must be an active causal agent – personal or impersonal – to move a system from one state to the next. The question that all sides are trying to answer in this chapter is, What ultimately accounts for changes of state within a system that occur according to fixed regularities? Non-Humeans have historically favored one of two replies. The first was that entities have been endowed with causal powers that enable them to do such and such. Causal powers/ capacities account for regular change. If that approach is rejected, there is a tendency to go looking for something else that does roughly the same work, and laws seem to fit. *They* are what ensure that a system will progress from one state to the next in a predicable fashion. Both responses share a common intuition: "There must be something that moves systems from one state to the next in regular ways, if not causal powers then laws." It is as if efficient causation were an office and the argument were merely whether laws or causal powers best fit that role.

Perhaps that's right, but there is an alternative approach for the work that laws do, one inspired by Murray Gell-Mann's so-called *totalitarian principle* in particle physics: Any process not forbidden will occur (1956, 859). What if the laws of nature do not compel change but rather forbid particular kinds of change? We are used to thinking of conservation laws working in this way, which is what Gell-Mann had in mind. Let's try to push that idea a bit further.

5.5.1 *Laws and constraints*

Some qualifications are in order. There are two ideas in this subsection that I do not, strictly speaking, accept but will use for ease of exposition. The first is that nature runs along levels. We saw this in Chapter 2 in the context of (strong/ontological) emergence and downward causation. In this picture, there is a level of mental states and causes that depends in part on the deeper level of neurophysiological states and causes, which in turn depends on an electrochemical level, and so on all the way down to fundamental physics. Sometimes causes at a higher level are said to influence events at a lower one, mental states typically being the prime example. While seemingly innocuous, this reified view of levels is what leaves emergentists open to the charge of causal redundancy discussed in section 2.5. To avoid this, all "levels-talk" here should be understood heuristically.

The second idea is a corollary. If, strictly speaking, there are no levels in nature, there will be no most *fundamental* level. The term itself, what philosopher Alan Love calls "the f-word," is a common bit of rhetoric to signal the importance of one's work ("I'm working on fundamental questions in _____"). Physics to date certainly has not discovered a fundamental level, although particles in the standard model, strings, and other contenders continue to be proffered. There may instead be an infinite hierarchy of theories, each of which works well in its own domain of applicability (Sklar 2002, 132–4). So once again, the imagery of levels here should be understood as a placeholder for an alternative, albeit messier, view of emergence (Bishop 2012), (Koperski 2015, sec. 6.6).

Nomological realists sometimes think of laws as being akin to Newtonian forces. Freshman physics is replete with blocks sliding on inclined planes where forces are decomposed and the power of vector mechanics is revealed. The lesson is clear: Forces make things go. At a slightly more advanced level of physics, we see that the Newtonian picture is nearly impossible to apply in many contexts. Consider a bead threaded onto a rotating wire (Figure 5.1). The bead is going to slide, but the changing forces that (i) hold the bead on the wire and (ii) make it move are mathematically intractable. Historically, classical mechanics moved from a Newtonian framework of

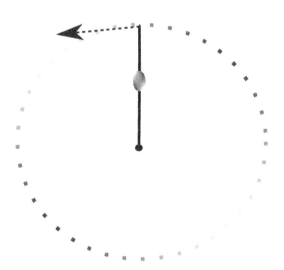

Figure 5.1 Sliding bead on wire.

impressed forces to the Lagrangian approach based on energy and constants of motion. The latter starts with a state space of possibilities. Each point in the space represents one overall state of the system. The goal is to find how the system evolves from one state to the next. Doing so depends on finding constants of motion in the relevant equations: variables that do not change over time. Each constant identified simplifies the mathematics. If a sufficient number can be found, there will be only one way the system can evolve from any given set of initial conditions. While that might not sound like a revolutionary advance, much of the power of classical mechanics – and to a lesser extent quantum mechanics – is due to this discovery. It is often far more useful to lay down constraints on the space of possibilities than to infer behavior from component forces. Keep that in mind.

The notion of constraints also comes up when one entity is incorporated into a larger system, as philosopher Robert Bishop details (2006, 49). Free-floating neutrons are not stable, having a half-life of eleven minutes. Contained in the nucleus of an atom and subject to an additional set of laws, however, neutrons are mostly stable, with a half-life in the millions of years. That individual atom alone in space obeys the laws of quantum mechanics and gravity. If this atom undergoes molecular bonding, further constraints will be imposed. The atom is no longer free to behave in ways that it might have previously. The range of possible states is narrowed still more if this molecule is incorporated into a strand of DNA. The move from the subatomic level to the atomic, molecular, genetic, and so forth imposes a series of restrictions on the neutron that we started with. The range of possibilities open to it is narrowed at each successive step.

A similar story can be told about most entities that are incorporated into systems of increasing levels of complexity (Bishop 2012, 68). Each level contains a new set of structures, relations, and laws. Those entities are most "free" in isolation, apart from whatever new restrictions are entailed by their inclusion into a larger system. Chemical and biological laws do not violate those at lower levels, but they do constrain the range of possibilities open to their constituent parts.

Bishop argues that this is the primary way of understanding laws as they emerge at different scales – as constraints on the less-restricted state space of free entities. The further up the ladder from fundamental physics one goes, the more constraints there are in terms of law.

Instead of thinking of laws merely as constraints emerging in higher-order systems, I suggest that we apply that idea all the way down. Laws *never* make things happen. That way of thinking, again, is rooted in a causal powers intuition. What, then, does account for change? There is no reason to turn to metaphysics for an answer. Forces and energy are responsible for moving systems from state to state, including forces that come into play at higher levels. Physics has solved the question of why particles, fields, and the systems composed of them are active. There is no need for causal powers, Aristotelian natures, or laws to answer that question.

So what, then, do laws do? Consider again the question that is at the center of this chapter: What ultimately accounts for changes of state within systems that occur according to fixed regularities? Laws are not needed to account for the change part of the question. They are needed to account for the fixed regularities. Why isn't the observable world a blooming, buzzing confusion? How is induction possible? These are the questions that laws are needed to answer. Nature is active.[17] Any process not forbidden might in fact occur. Laws constrain nature to act in regular, sometimes predictable ways. That is true in the emergent structures mentioned earlier, and it is true at the most fundamental level of reality (if there is one).

This, then, is what decretalism amounts to. It is not that by decreeing the laws of nature that God thereby *endows* forces/fields/particles/strings/energy – whatever precisely is most fundamental – with some sort of metaphysical *oomph* that makes things happen. That is not what laws do. At every level, laws impose constraints. When God decrees a law of nature, a range of possibilities is being fixed. Consider the four fundamental forces. It is as if there were a vast parameter space for how those forces would behave: strength, range, ways of coupling with matter, etc. The laws/decrees constrain that space to the point that we have the forces as they exist in reality.[18] On my proposal, all laws at the level of fundamental physics function this way.

While laws-as-constraints is a departure from the early modern view that I favor, it will be helpful in fending off the objection that decretalism is merely occasionalism, the doctrine that God ultimately causes all physical events (section 8.4).[19]

5.5.2 Decretalism and divine action

Turning back to the question of divine action, consider again the idea of "breaking the laws of nature." As we have already noted, the phrase is most naturally understood as an implication that there is some sort of entity or power that could possibly be broken. But the decretalist denies that when God ordains a law, something new comes into being. There is no structure or capacity that *is* a law that God might possibly disrupt. When nonviolationists talk about God's "breaking" or "violating" the laws of nature, they seem to have in mind some other type of nomological realism.

On the other hand, there is a sense of "breaking a law" that does not require the reification of laws themselves. There *is* something objectively wrong, say, about moving a chess pawn three spaces: It breaks the rules. "Breaking" here is a metaphor. It does not entail that rules exist as something other than social constructions. Likewise, God could break a law insofar as some new act temporarily contradicts a previously ordained regularity, even if laws do not have any sort of independent existence. Some nonviolationists see this as the main problem with intervention, not the metaphysics, as Robert Russell argues:

> [Since] God's intervention breaks the very processes of nature which God created and constantly maintains, it pits God's special acts against God's regular action, which underlies and ultimately causes nature's regularities.
>
> (2008, 584)

Whatever the precise metaphysics, the worry is that laws ultimately trace back to divine choices that interventions would contravene. Intervention therefore entails a conflict of the divine will, many nonviolationists argue, which is something that any model of divine action must avoid.

This means that decretalism does not by itself satisfy the objections of the nonviolationist, and so there is still a problem to be solved. As we saw in Chapter 2, however, it is not likely to be solved by an appeal to quantum mechanics or chaos theory. And if Everett's many-worlds interpretation continues its rise, the scientific consensus at the end of this century may be that nature is fully deterministic. Most nonviolationists believe that would signal the death of their program. Without ontological gaps in which God can act, the only remaining options are deism or naïve violationism. Nonetheless, I will argue in Chapter 7 that a third way is possible: a decretalist, nonviolationist model of divine action that does not depend on prior gaps in the natural order. Before that, there is one last, often unanalyzed concept in this literature to be discussed.

Notes

1 One reviewer asks whether the equation *is* the law, and that is the right question to ask. The answer depends on which view of laws discussed in this chapter that one holds. For most Humeans, the answer is "yes."

2 This point was repeatedly emphasized by an anonymous referee for *Philosophia Christi* in a previous version of this chapter, (Koperski 2017).

3 For the Humean, it makes no sense to say that God could have a created a universe just like this one, but with different laws – something that most theists wish to claim.

4 Those terms will be used interchangeably here.

5 Some dispositionalists allow for causal powers in configurations of matter, not just of material beings (Dorato and Esfeld 2016). Even so, they still have difficulty with quantum mechanical properties, especially nonlocality.

6 Free-fall experiments seemed to favor Leibniz. Inelastic collisions confirmed Newton's position.

7 See (Göcke 2015) and (Adams 2016) for models of SDA based on the priority of dispositions.

8 More precisely, the claim here is not that we always know the relevant laws in every case or even care. The ancients were making counterfactual judgments well before the notion of laws for nature was widely accepted. The point is one of

metaphysical priority: Counterfactual truths depend on law; laws do not depend on counterfactuals.

 9 See (Carroll 2016, sec. 3) for an introduction.

10 As we will see in Chapter 7, and as Robert Bishop notes (private correspondence), this is actually a poor candidate for a law-statement. The word "law" is often applied to models and families of differential equations that are not strictly speaking laws or law-statements.

11 At least in this possible world. For Armstrong, there are possible worlds in which these universals are not so related.

12 For better or worse, theists soon came to accept intermediaries once again, whether in the form of laws as independent powers, vital forces, or something else (Brooke 1992).

13 This is not to suggest that all natural philosophers at this time had a single well-articulated view of laws. As I argued in Chapter 4, the view presented here is most clearly represented by Boyle and Clarke.

14 As historian Matthew Stanley documents, Thomas Huxley intentionally and strategically set out to co-opt the uniformity of natural law from theism and recast it in terms of naturalism (2016).

15 Even critics of nomological realism argue that it is best understood – perhaps *only* understood – in light of theism (Cartwright 1993, 299; Ott 2009, 249).

16 This is close to Peter van Inwagen's view (1988). Yong and Smith (section 2.4) are also decretalists of some type, perhaps this one.

17 Instead of God first creating physical entities that then need to be constrained by laws, God's decrees could be made anytime before the Big Bang. The material universe would then evolve within the boundaries set by those laws, which in time leads to transparent space, the elements of the periodic table, and all the rest. The picture here is decidedly not Plato's cosmology, where a Demiurge imposes order on a preexisting chaos.

18 If the theoretical unification of forces is correct, this story will apply to one force but include the conditions for symmetry breaking.

19 While the arguments for decretalism are matters of philosophy of science and philosophy of religion, there is some biblical support for such a view, as theologian Daniel Treier has pointed out (private correspondence). In several places, the Old Testament describes God's creation act in terms of decrees and boundaries. For example,

> Job 38:4–11 (NRSV): Where were you when I laid the foundation of the earth? . . . Or who shut in the sea with doors when it burst out from the womb? – when I made the clouds its garment, and thick darkness its swaddling band, and prescribed bounds for it, and set bars and doors, and said, "Thus far shall you come, and no farther, and here shall your proud waves be stopped"?
>
> Proverbs 8:24–30 (NSRV): When there were no depths I [Wisdom] was brought forth, when there were no springs abounding with water. . . . When he established the heavens, I was there, when he drew a circle on the face of the deep, when he made firm the skies above, when he established the fountains of the deep, when he assigned to the sea its limit, so that the waters might not transgress his command, when he marked out the foundations of the earth, then I was beside him, like a master worker; and I was daily his delight, rejoicing before him always.

Works cited

Adams, Dani. 2016. "God and Dispositional Essentialism: An Account of the Laws of Nature: God and Dispositional Essentialism." *Pacific Philosophical Quarterly*. https://doi.org/10.1111/papq.12162.

Beebee, Helen. 2004. "The Non-Governing Conception of Laws of Nature." In *Readings on Laws of Nature*, edited by John W. Carroll, 250–76. Pittsburgh: University of Pittsburgh Press.

Bishop, Robert C. 2006. "The Hidden Premiss in the Causal Argument for Physicalism." *Analysis* 66 (1): 44–52. https://doi.org/10.1093/analys/66.1.44.

———. 2012. "Excluding the Causal Exclusion Argument Against Non-Redirective Physicalism." *Journal of Consciousness Studies* 19 (5–6): 57–74.

Boyle, Robert. 1744. *The Works of the Honourable Robert Boyle.* Vol. 4., 5 Vols. London: A. Millar.

Brooke, John Hedley. 1992. "Natural Law in the Natural Sciences: The Origins of Modern Atheism?" *Science & Christian Belief* 4 (2): 83–103.

Carroll, John W. 2016. "Laws of Nature." In *Stanford Encyclopedia of Philosophy*, edited by Edward N. Zalta. http://plato.stanford.edu/archives/spr2016/entries/laws-of-nature/.

Cartwright, Nancy. 1989. *Nature's Capacities and Their Measurement.* Oxford: Clarendon Press.

———. 1993. "Is Natural Science 'Natural' Enough? A Reply to Phillip Allport." *Synthese* 94: 291–301.

Dorato, Mauro, and Michael Esfeld. 2016. "The Metaphysics of Laws: Dispositionalism vs. Primitivism." In *Metaphysics in Contemporary Physics*, edited by Tomasz Bigaj and Christian Wüthrich, 403–24. Poznań Studies in the Philosophy of the Sciences and the Humanities 104. Boston, MA: Brill.

Dretske, Fred I. 1977. "Laws of Nature." *Philosophy of Science* 44 (2): 248–68.

Fodor, Jerry A., and Massimo Piattelli-Palmarini. 2010. *What Darwin Got Wrong.* New York: Farrar, Straus and Giroux.

Gell-Mann, Murray. 1956. "The Interpretation of the New Particles as Displaced Charge Multiplets." *Il Nuovo Cimento* 4 (S2): 848–66. https://doi.org/10.1007/BF02748000.

Göcke, Benedikt Paul. 2015. "Did God Do It? Metaphysical Models and Theological Hermeneutics." *International Journal for Philosophy of Religion* 78 (2): 215–31. https://doi.org/10.1007/s11153-014-9489-7.

Inwagen, Peter van. 1988. "The Place of Chance in a World Sustained by God." In *God, Knowledge, and Mystery*, edited by Thomas V. Morris, 42–65. Ithaca, NY: Cornell University Press.

Koperski, Jeffrey. 2015. *The Physics of Theism: God, Physics, and the Philosophy of Science.* Chichester, UK: Wiley-Blackwell.

———. 2017. "Breaking Laws of Nature." *Philosophia Christi* 19 (1): 83–101.

Lange, Marc. 2009. *Laws and Lawmakers: Science, Metaphysics, and the Laws of Nature.* New York: Oxford University Press.

Larmer, Robert. 2017. "Decretalism and the Laws of Nature: A Response to Jeffrey Koperski." *Philosophia Christi* 19 (2): 439–47.

Lewis, David K. 1973a. "Causation." *Journal of Philosophy* 70: 556–67.

———. 1973b. *Counterfactuals.* Cambridge, MA: Harvard University Press.

Maudlin, Tim. 2007. *The Metaphysics within Physics.* New York: Oxford University Press.

Mumford, Stephen. 2004. *Laws in Nature.* Routledge Studies in Twentieth Century Philosophy 18. New York: Routledge.

Ott, Walter R. 2009. *Causation and Laws of Nature in Early Modern Philosophy.* New York: Oxford University Press.

Plantinga, Alvin. 2016. "Law, Cause, and Occasionalism." In *Reason and Faith: Themes from Swinburne*, edited by Michael Bergmann and Jeffrey E. Brower, 126–44. New York: Oxford University Press.

Ratzsch, Del. 1987. "Nomo(Theo)Logical Necessity." *Faith and Philosophy* 4 (4): 383–402.

Russell, Robert J. 2008. "Quantum Physics and the Theology of Non-Interventionist Objective Divine Action." In *The Oxford Handbook of Religion and Science*, edited by Philip Clayton, 579–95. New York: Oxford University Press.

Sklar, Lawrence. 2002. *Theory and Truth: Philosophical Critique within Foundational Science*. Oxford: Oxford University Press.

Smith, Sheldon R. 2002. "Violated Laws, *Ceteris Paribus* Clauses, and Capacities." *Synthese* 130 (2): 235–64.

Stanley, Matthew. 2016. *Huxley's Church and Maxwell's Demon: From Theistic Science to Naturalistic Science*. Paperback ed. Chicago: University of Chicago Press.

Van Fraassen, Bas C. 1989. *Laws and Symmetry*. Oxford: Clarendon Press.

Wilson, Mark. 2006. *Wandering Significance: An Essay on Conceptual Behaviour*. Oxford: Oxford University Press.

6 Determinisms

Philosophy 101 didn't hold a lot of interest for me as a college freshman. Many of the ideas seemed obviously wrong, and I was more than ready to end the course once we got to Camus. One exception was the section on determinism and free will. While everyone's intuitions fall on the freedom side of this debate, there are arguments to the contrary in virtually every area of philosophy.

Let's say that the majority view is correct and our robust sense of freedom is an illusion. Why is determinism so bad? One reason is that it conflicts with ethical responsibility. A phrase that goes back to Immanuel Kant is "ought implies can." If we tell students that they ought to do their own work and they ought not plagiarize, we will imply that it is within their power to do so. The claim will make sense only if plagiarizing or not is within their range of options. We would never tell them that they ought to levitate and ought not have veins, since those matters are beyond their control. But if determinism is true and students plagiarize their papers, it will not be in their power to do otherwise. Ethical commands make no sense in a deterministic world since no one actually has a range of options from which to choose. The future, instead, has one fixed path. Theologically, the same goes for God's commands. It would make no sense for God to be angered by Israel's failure to, say, repent in response to the prophet Amos's warnings if they were literally not able to do so.

Examples like these explain why most philosophers take determinism as a problem to overcome. Physicists have a different attitude. For them, breakdowns in determinism are to be avoided. Indeterminism in physics typically signals that something has gone wrong in a theory or a model. Explaining this discrepancy is one of the goals of this chapter. To understand it, we must first see how the conventional wisdom about physical determinism goes awry. In the end, I will argue that insofar as physics is deterministic, it presents no obstacle to nonviolationist divine action. If there is a problem, it will lie elsewhere.

Let's start with a few varieties of determinism to see which type is of interest here.[1]

6.1 Types of determinism

"Determinism" is usually shorthand for causal determinism: Every event has a sufficient cause. More precisely, given conditions $\{x_1, x_2, x_3, \ldots, x_i\}$ and event C, effect E must occur. Every event in a deterministic system is covered by such a conditional. Given the antecedent conditions and cause C, there is one unique E possible. Nothing is left to chance and nothing escapes the network of causes and effects, including our "free" choices. This sort of determinism is now typically recast in terms of the laws of nature, as we will see.

God's omniscience leads to a second type of determinism, at least when it is taken *prima facie*. Omniscience traditionally includes knowledge of all future events. Let's say, then, that God now knows that you will have pizza for dinner next Friday. Do you have the freedom not to have pizza for dinner on Friday? If you did and freely chose to have chicken instead, God would have had a false belief, which would not be compatible with omniscience. God's beliefs about the future must come to pass. Hence, it seems that you do not have the ability to change the trajectory of the future and so do not have free will. While many solutions have been proposed to determinism grounded in God's knowledge of contingent events (Zagzebski 2017), the problem seems clear enough.

A third type of determinism comes from the philosophy of time, although fewer philosophers think this one poses a challenge to free will. In the *B-series*, *eternalist*, or *block universe* view of time, the future and the past exist as fully as the present does. There is no moment that distinguishes past from future. The entire timeline simply exists, and what we perceive as the flow of time is an illusion. The temporal slice of my drinking my coffee and writing this paragraph feels as if it's in the present, but so do each of my other temporal slices spread out over space-time. One upshot of the block universe is that what we think of as the future is fixed. There is a fact-of-the-matter regarding the exact number of copies this book will sell, the names of my great-grandchildren, and the other events I think of as being in the future, all of which are as unchangeable as those I think of as being in the past. It is in this fixedness that some find determinism:

> [The] worry regarding this doctrine is that if the future participates in the same degree of existence as the past (and present), then how can the future be non-fixed and open? Or, more concretely, if the event of the Third World War exists eternally, then in what sense is that event – prior to its occurrence – *not* inexorable?
>
> (Diekemper 2007, 429)

In other words, if there is an unchanging fact-of-the-matter regarding all events that I consider to be in my future, the outcome of which I have no ability to alter, it will be difficult to see in what sense I presently have free will.[2]

Of the three, causal determinism is the most relevant to special divine action. Nonviolationists typically believe that there is no room for God to act in a deterministic universe:[3]

> This determinism of physical causes involves the claim that the physical state of the world at a given time determines the physical state of the world for all future times. It is thus a *modal* notion. It denies that it is even physically *possible* that the present state of the world should give rise to more than one future state of affairs.
>
> Physical determinism is fundamentally a claim about causality – the claim, namely, that all that happens is a necessary effect of antecedent efficient causes. At the same time, it claims that all physical occurrences are lawful. The universe is such that a given set of physical events can give rise to only one successor set.
>
> (Clayton 2008, 187)

This explains in part why quantum mechanics is so important to nonviolationists. If its standard interpretation is correct, fundamental physics will not be deterministic, thus allowing the possibility of divine action.

Given the worries about determinism mentioned so far, philosophers and theologians are sometimes puzzled by the different attitude found in physics. Instead of avoiding determinism, physicists try to preserve it. Breakdowns in determinism are the problem. Why? Well, if one wants useful predictions, one will need the (nonprobabilistic) laws of nature to provide uniform results. Usually, when determinism fails, physicists think they have something wrong: either the theory is incomplete or a calculation is in error.[4] Singularities – places where the laws break down – are occasionally accepted, but only when no other option presents itself. This explains in part the early rejection of the Big Bang and ongoing proposals for eliminating it.[5]

How can we account for these differing attitudes between physicists on one hand and philosophers and theologians on the other? The answer is that they are no longer talking about the same thing. The latter do not fully appreciate how "[over] the centuries, the doctrine of determinism has been understood, and its truth or falsity assessed, in different ways" (Butterfield 2005). I will argue in the next two sections that the determinism of early modern philosophy is no longer the determinism of physics.

6.2 Causal determinism: the standard view

There were two main senses of determinism in play around the time of the scientific revolution: (i) as a law of universal causation and (ii) as the precise predictability of the future (Butterfield 2005). The first can be traced to Spinoza and Leibniz, the second to Laplace.[6]

Spinoza's view can be summed up in two quotes: "In nature there is nothing contingent, but all things have been determined from the necessity of the divine nature to exist and produce an effect in a certain way" (*Ethics*, Ip29); and "Nothing happens in nature that does not follow from her laws" (*Theologico-Political Treatise*, 6/19). Putting the two together, we find that everything that happens is necessary. Nothing is contingent. God has ordained the laws of nature, and all events follow necessarily from those laws. Since miracles would disrupt the fixed course of nature, there aren't any. Spinoza thought that belief in miracles was due to our lack of knowledge. If we understood all the causes involved, there would be no need to appeal to divine intervention.[7]

For Leibniz, the core idea was not nomological necessity but rather the Principle of Sufficient Reason, which says that, for everything that happens, there must be a reason that determines why it is thus and not otherwise. Physicists soon turned this into a doctrine about causation: Each thing that exists has a cause, and the state of every system is caused by the immediate prior state (van Strien 2014a, sec. 5). The Law of Continuity, a less well-known Leibnizian principle, said that nature makes no leaps.[8] More precisely, change from one state to another must go through all the intermediate stages. Hence, a ball rolling from point A to point B must continuously travel through all points in between. (This latter principle played a key role in the development of differential equations.) The Principle of Sufficient Reason and the Law of Continuity together imply causal determinism: All events form a continuous chain, no event "just happens," and each event is determined by some prior reason or cause.

Laplace, in contrast, famously tied determinism to prediction. If an intelligence knew all the forces involved and the state of every particle at a given instant in time, it would in principle be able to predict the exact state of the universe arbitrarily far into the future:

> We ought then to regard the present state of the universe as the effect of its anterior state and the cause of the one which is to follow. Given for one instant an intelligence which could comprehend all the forces by which nature is animated and the respective situation of the beings who compose it – an intelligence sufficiently vast to submit this data to analysis – it would embrace in the same formula the movements of the greatest bodies of the universe and those of the lightest atom; for it, nothing would be uncertain and the future, as the past, would be present in its eyes.
>
> ([1814] 1902, 4)

This vast intelligence has come to be called a "Laplacian demon." Such a being is an idealization, and not even modern supercomputers come close. Nonetheless, such predictions would be possible in a Newtonian world because its evolution is governed by deterministic laws. Or at least, that is the conventional wisdom on the matter.

Now consider two statements from theologians regarding determinism and divine action. The first is from Philip Clayton:

> The prior [i.e., more fundamental] question . . . is whether science even leaves a place for divine action. If Laplace were right, for example, and a strict determinism would allow us to predict all future states and retrodict all past ones, then there would truly be no place for divine action.
>
> (1997, 206)

The second is from Nicholas Saunders:

> [In] a totally deterministic world . . . the causal nexus of science is drawn so tight that there is no real freedom for either God or human beings. In such a world Laplace's famous demon reigns supreme. God cannot act in any creative way through the causality of science and still remain true to the deterministic rules put in place at creation.
>
> (2000, 254)

Notice how much they share with Laplace and Spinoza. Clayton appeals to Laplacian prediction; Saunders, to prediction plus universal causation. Neither of them believes that we live in a physically deterministic world, but they take it that determinism would be fatal for any robust model of divine action. They also take it that classical mechanics describes just such a world. If classical mechanics were true, there would be no room for God's ongoing causal influence within nature.

The conclusions presented in this subsection seldom meet with controversy. In light of how physicists now understand determinism, however, they are also mostly false. Seventeenth-century views on the matter have not held up well over time.

6.3 Determinism and physics

To make that case, let's revisit the Laplacian demon. The definition of determinism in terms of mechanics and unbounded prediction has been refuted by chaos theory. If chaotic systems, which are perfectly Newtonian and classical, are added to the mix of nature, the demon will require an infinite amount of information about the state of the system – precision to the level of real numbers. An infinitesimal error in the initial conditions guarantees that predictions made for a chaotic system will fail. Yet such errors are inevitable since no instrument is infinitely precise.[9]

Let's say there were some way to overcome this imprecision. Chaos would still thwart successful predictions because of limited computational capacity. Computers have finite memory. The Laplacian demon is in the same boat. Laplace described it as a vast intelligence, not an omniscient one. It does not have infinite computational capacity and would be as susceptible to round-off errors as any computer. Hence, its predictions about the future state of a chaotic system would fail. I believe that if Laplace had been aware of chaos, he would never have used this as an illustration of determinism. In what follows, we will ignore what any finite intelligence might be able to predict *vis-à-vis* determinism.

In modern physics, a theory is considered deterministic when, for any two systems S_1 and S_2 within the scope of that theory, if S_1 and S_2 have the same state at one particular time, they will evolve in precisely the same way for all future times.[10] So take two systems: two identical clocks, two billiard ball tables, or two solar systems with the same configuration of planets. Determinism requires that, for any of those pairs of systems, if they have the same state at one point in time, they will evolve in lockstep for all future times. Once synchronized, the two will remain isomorphic unless something interferes or one of the systems degrades.

Many of the clearest examples of deterministic physics come from classical mechanics. If we think of classical mechanics as point-particle physics – which we shouldn't, but let's ignore that for now – the laws of physics will be expressed as ordinary differential equations. The question of determinism can then be answered mathematically in terms of the existence and the uniqueness of solutions. For a set of equations and initial conditions, does a solution exist, and is that solution the only one? If the solution both exists and is unique, the model will be deterministic. A system correctly described by this model will always evolve in the same way from a given set of initial conditions. In terms of the system's phase space (section 3.2.1), this means that state trajectories never cross. Each point in the phase space (i.e., each possible state of the system) will be mapped to a unique trajectory into the future.[11] For first-order ordinary differential equations expressing functions that are suitably smooth, existence and uniqueness are guaranteed.

This, then, is the modern justification for saying that classical mechanics is deterministic. Classical mechanics is governed by differential equations, and the equations in textbook physics have unique solutions. In this light, determinism becomes a kind of metatheorem derived over the entirety of classical mechanics – something learned from or entailed by the physics itself. This metatheorem supports the idea that quantum mechanics was needed to introduce some measure of indeterminism.

One of the better-kept secrets in the philosophy of physics is that the conventional wisdom is wrong – or at least oversimplified. Determinism has a far more complex relationship to classical mechanics.

But wait. Do we really need to discuss this further? We know that classical mechanics is only an approximation in the actual world. Who cares about the details?

The answer is that insofar as classical mechanics is taken to be a clear example of determinism, one that motivates the need for quantum mechanics in the minds of many theologians and philosophers, it is important to see what is wrong with this characterization. Both the ways in which determinism fails in classical mechanics and the strategies used to restore it are important for understanding its place in modern physics.

Consider the qualifications already mentioned, which guarantee unique solutions to differential equations. Why should classical mechanics be limited to "suitably smooth" functions? Say that a point particle is situated at the top of a dome, with gravity but without friction. This seems like a perfectly acceptable classical system, one that might be discussed in freshman physics. Given well-behaved force functions, the particle will stay at the top of the dome forever unless perturbed. If not-so-well-behaved functions are permitted, specifically those that are not Lipschitz-continuous, the solutions to the equations will allow for the possibility that the particle moves off the dome at some arbitrary time without being perturbed (Norton 2008).[12] The easy solution is the one in which the particle remains in place forever. But there is a perfectly acceptable alternative in which it moves at some arbitrary time, thus violating the uniqueness of solutions to a simple initial value problem, which is a violation of determinism. Note that the motion "just happens" – no nudging, no new forces. The particle moves more or less of its own accord.[13] This is not the run-of-the-mill instability one finds in a pencil balancing on its tip. In a so-called "Norton's dome," the singularity at the top of the structure ensures that the particle will move at some time or another unless an infinite downward force is applied to keep it there (Malament 2008, 800). While this is not intuitive, there is no controversy over whether such solutions to the equations exist. Norton's dome is just not something that one is likely to bump into at the undergraduate level. If you still think this scenario is impossible and that the unperturbed particle must remain at rest, the question will become, Why is this impossible? Whatever the intuition, it must be based on something *other* than the laws of physics, which in this case are expressed by differential equations.[14]

What other solutions are not "suitably smooth" enough to guarantee uniqueness? Collisions, for one. A point-particle system is deterministic only if the particles do not collide, but we obviously do not live in that sort of world. In order to deal with collisions, physicists must replace point particles in their models with rigid bodies. The math for such systems is more complicated but not intractable. So maybe determinism can be preserved. That is, unless elasticity becomes important. If so, then rigid bodies will be replaced by the deformable ones found in continuum mechanics. But that takes us from the realm of *ordinary* differential equations to that of *partial* differential equations, which can be far more complex. The existence and the uniqueness of solutions for those equations are not so easily guaranteed.[15] This means that, in a world of fluids and deformable bodies, determinism can only be guaranteed for a handful of special cases. If one allows for fractures – which of course happen in the real world – there is nowhere, mathematically, to turn to preserve uniqueness, and all bets are off regarding determinism.[16]

This all leads up to something that is well-documented in the philosophy of physics: The pristine simplicity of classical mechanics is a myth.[17] It is simple and deterministic at the level of freshman physics, but only because of the restrictions and idealizations used to keep it that way.

Perhaps this is overstated. Perhaps some *parts* of freshman physics have it right. How about a world of point particles with mass and gravity, but where collisions are forbidden? Surely that is a deterministic system! It's nothing but Newton's laws of motion and universal gravitation.

Some readers will recall that the two Voyager satellites were slingshotted around the sun to increase their velocities – a maneuver used in the first *Star Trek* series. Using a similar mechanism, mathematician Zhihong Xia proved that, in a system of five bodies, a particle could be flung to spatial infinity in finite time (1992). Philosopher John Earman points out that if this is an acceptable Newtonian system, running the same solutions backward in time will be as well. This produces his "space invader" example, with particles appearing *from* infinity in finite time (1986, 34). Such a possibility thwarts determinism insofar as the system prior to the invasion must now adapt to the presence of something new.[18] The moral to the story is that in a "Newtonian space-time. . . [the universe] is not automatically 'closed' in the operative sense to outside influences" (Earman 1986, 34).

Finally, it is difficult to claim that classical mechanics entails determinism when determinism and indeterminism are to some degree mathematically interchangeable (Atmanspacher and Rotter 2008), (Werndl 2011). As Jeremy Butterfield notes, "there are many examples of a set of differential equations which can be interpreted as a deterministic theory, or as an indeterministic theory, depending on the notion of state used to interpret the equations" (2005). A system described using equations with unique solutions can be mapped to an indeterministic state space and vice versa. The choice of which to use is a matter of mathematical convenience. This means that "determinism is not a formal feature of a set of equations" (Butterfield 2005). In other words, not even the existence and the uniqueness of solutions are a guarantor of determinism.

The bottom line is that classical mechanics is not the realm of absolute determinism that so many suppose. Some of the breakdowns mentioned in classical mechanics are cleaned up by special relativity, but then general relativity adds new challenges. (Space-times that are not "well-behaved" [that is, globally hyperbolic] wreak havoc on initial value problems.) How is a physicist expected to make predictions under conditions such as these?

6.4 Rescuing determinism

Whether the subject is classical mechanics, special relativity, general relativity, or quantum mechanics, there are ways of preserving determinism in the face of counterexamples. If particles appearing from infinitely far away is a problem, one will impose new boundary conditions at spatial infinity that keep all our particles in-house and bar the door to space invaders. Xia's proof could also be negated by eliminating idealized point particles and infinite potential wells, even though neither of these is impossible in terms of classical mechanics alone (Earman 2007, 1386). That works, says Earman, but "smacks of making determinism true by making it a postulate of wishful thinking" (2004, 26). In other words, sure, it fixes the problem. But what is the physical basis for saying this cannot happen in a classical world?

A closely related approach would be to simply ignore these counterexamples. One might declare them physically impossible, even though they are perfectly coherent from a mathematical point of view. Physicists in the nineteenth century did just that in order to preserve determinism (van Strien 2014b, 180–82). In fact, the only way to ensure that determinism holds across the whole of classical mechanics is to *assume* it as an axiom, as V. I. Arnold does (1988, 2). And remember, there is a reason for this. Physicists and engineers need to solve equations, run simulations, and make predictions. Indeterminism gets in the way.

This, however, is a problematic response. The claim that classical mechanics is deterministic is never interpreted as "physicists have imposed determinism on mechanics for pragmatic reasons." Most believe that this sort of determinism is something that physics has taught us. Determinism is supposed to be entailed by classical mechanics – a state of affairs that would be true if not for quantum effects. Instead, determinism is invoked as a reason to ignore the counterexamples. The need to impose new constraints proves the point that *determinism cannot be derived from classical mechanics* (or from any area of physics, for that matter). Of course, if one assumes absolute determinism in the form of an axiom, the results will be deterministic. If *P* is a premise in an argument – even a hidden premise – one will certainly be able to derive *P* in the conclusion. But let's not pretend that we have learned anything from the exercise.[19]

In short, the role of determinism in physics is far more nuanced than it is commonly assumed to be. Laplace himself knew that there were breakdowns like the ones already discussed and that there was no way to prove the uniqueness of solutions across all of mechanics. In other words, the predictions of the Laplacian demon were not possible given what was known at the time about the laws of physics. So why did Laplace believe that the world was deterministic? In his famous paper, metaphysics, not physics, was the basis for determinism. In particular, he explicitly appealed to Leibniz's Principle of Sufficient Reason, which Laplace states as follows: "Current events are connected with preceding ones by a tie based upon the evident principle that a thing cannot come to existence without a cause which produces it" ([1814] 1902, 3).[20] So while it is widely assumed that Laplace was merely applying Newtonian mechanics to the whole of nature, he knew the mathematics could not guarantee determinism. But that was all right, he thought, since philosophy has already shown it to be true!

To introduce some jargon, Laplace was making use of a *metatheoretic shaping principle* (Koperski 2015, 25–29). Shaping principles are philosophical beliefs about the fundamental nature of reality and how best to understand it. Science depends on such principles to distinguish good theories, explanations, and methods from bad ones. Metaphysical shaping principles include concepts like the uniformity of nature, ideas about causation, and the view that reality is to some degree mind-independent and law-governed. In Laplace's day, one would have included Leibniz's Law of Continuity on this list, as well as others that we no longer hold. For Laplace and other physicists of his era, good physics was deterministic physics. Insofar as a theory failed to be deterministic, it was flawed. According to the shaping principles of the time, one should strive to isolate and remove any discontinuities from the description of God's mechanistic creation.

Maxwell also understood determinism as a shaping principle:

> If, therefore, those cultivators of physical science . . . whose style is recognised as marking with a scientific stamp the doctrines they promulgate, are led in pursuit of the arcana of science to the study of the singularities and instabilities, rather than the continuities and stabilities of things, *the promotion of natural knowledge may tend to remove that prejudice in favour of determinism* which seems to arise from assuming that the physical science of the future is a mere magnified image of that of the past [italics added].
>
> (1873, 823)

Maxwell takes determinism to be a "prejudice" brought to the table by his contemporaries, one that should be resisted in some cases. To see that determinism is not entailed by physics, however, one must get beyond the standard examples and into "the arcana of science."

Max Planck was more optimistic, but he concurred that

> the law of causality is neither right nor wrong; it is rather a heuristic principle, a guidepost, and in my opinion the most valuable guidepost we possess, to navigate the colorful confusion of events and to indicate the direction in which scientific research must proceed in order to achieve fruitful results.
>
> (1932, 26)

While "law of causality" is not strictly synonymous with "determinism," there is significant overlap between the two. Planck's justification for using it as a shaping principle was that it had shown its worth over time.

Like all shaping principles, this one can get push-back from new discoveries, which inevitably leads to controversy. The Bohr-Einstein debate is one famous case. Einstein's view of good science was rooted in the same basic intuitions as those of Planck. He believed that insofar as quantum mechanics implied indeterminism, nonlocal causes, and indeterminate values of state, it must be wrong. Bohr instead argued that the new physics required a change of shaping principles. In his view, good science would henceforth look different, at least at the level of fundamental physics. Bohr won, although the victory was less than absolute. Einstein still has his counterinsurgent supporters, along the lines of David Bohm (section 3.7.1).

Let's sum up the discussion thus far. For close to a century now, scientists have told us that there are important differences between the realm of quantum mechanical and that of observable objects. The quantum world is a menagerie of unintuitive goings-on, including irreducibly random events. In contrast, the realm of our experience is typically classical and deterministic. (This is why engineers are seldom taught much about quantum mechanics. It is irrelevant to almost all their concerns.)

But *why* do we believe that it took the discovery of quantum mechanics to break the grip of determinism? Two reasons. First, because Newton, Laplace, Euler, Boscovich, and the other heroes of classical mechanics said that the physical world is deterministic. As we have seen, however, they believed in physical determinism because of prior metaphysical commitments that few scientists now share, like the Principle of Sufficient Reason. Instead of inferring determinism as a consequence of scientific discoveries, they brought it with them as a presupposition.

Second, taking the breakdowns in determinism realistically would complicate our understanding of the classical realm. It is much easier to simply declare them "nonphysical events." After all, no one literally believes in classical mechanics anymore, so getting the details right is not all that important when teaching undergraduates. At the end of the day, physicists use determinism for the same reason engineers use linear models for processes that they know are nonlinear: It is what they need to do to get solutions to the equations. But these sorts of considerations are merely pragmatic, and pragmatism is a rather flimsy foundation on which to base belief in the unbroken determinism of the classical realm. In any case, philosophers and theologians ought not interpret these pragmatic uses of determinism as foundational truths entailed by the science itself. Butterfield sums up the current situation:

> [Formulations] of determinism in terms of causation or predictability are unsatisfactory. And once we use a correct formulation, it turns out that much of classical physics, even much Newtonian physics, is indeterministic; and that parts of relativity theory are indeterministic (owing to singularities). Furthermore, the alleged indeterminism of quantum theory is very controversial – for it enters only, if at all, in quantum theory's account of measurement processes, an account which remains the most controversial part of the theory.
>
> (2005, sec. 2)

In the end, determinism is like most ideas along the border of philosophy and science. It seems simple enough at first, but becomes increasingly complex once the details are considered, even within classical mechanics.

Determinism has played an important role in the literature on divine action since both noninterventionists and nonviolationists see it as an obstacle. But their worries are misplaced. If determinism is what Leibniz and Spinoza thought, yes, it will be a problem. God could not act within such a world without breaking the laws of nature. But if determinism is what modern physics takes it to be – a shaping principle supported by the existence and uniqueness of solutions to the governing equations – it will not be a bar to divine action. If some aspect of physics prevents divine action, determinism will not be it.

Another idea – one that is often conflated with determinism – might fit the bill. Let's consider whether *causal closure* can bear the weight that determinism cannot.

6.5 Causal closure

The idea shows up in two different contexts. The *causal closure of the physical* (CCoP) in the mind-body debate entails that causation at the level of physics is closed and complete in a way that biology is not.

> At first pass the causal closure of physics says that every physical effect has a sufficient physical cause. If this thesis is true, it distinguishes physics from all other subject domains. The biological realm, for example, is not causally closed in this sense, since biological effects often have non-biological causes, as when the impact of a meteorite precipitated the extinction of the dinosaurs.
>
> (Papineau 2009, 53–54)

CCoP says that if a physical effect has a cause, that cause will be physical. (The conditional allows for uncaused events and even nonphysical causes as long as they do not influence the physical.) Physicalists invoke closure as a way to fend off arguments from mind-body dualists and emergentists (see section 2.5). If CCoP is true, mental causes or causes above the level of physics will not have any effect on lower-level physical objects and events. The simplest physicalist position is to say that nonphysical causes will one day be reduced to physical ones.[21]

Theists typically reject CCoP insofar as they reject physicalism and ontological reductionism. Some also believe in downward causation, whereby causes at higher levels produce effects at lower ones, including the physical level. This would also constitute a violation of CCoP.

In the context of divine action, closure is a doctrine that applies to the whole of nature, not merely to the level of physics. The issue here is the causal closure of *nature* (CCoN), the completeness of the entire natural realm. According to CCoN, natural effects have only natural causes, but these might include causes that act across levels. It is this variety of closure that distinguishes noninterventionism from nonviolationism. The former accepts CCoN: Special divine action is not possible (in part), *because* nature is a closed network of causes. For the latter, CCoN is an obstacle to be overcome. If it were exceptionless, nonviolationism would collapse into noninterventionism. Finding ways to avoid or overcome causal closure was the underlying motivation behind each of the models of divine action discussed in Chapter 2. It is surprising, therefore, that it gets so little scrutiny. There is little in the way of "defense" anywhere to be found. CCoN is simply assumed to be part of the worldview handed down by science, or at least it was prior to the discovery of quantum mechanics. "As we know, in classical physics, nature is a closed causal system described by deterministic equations" (Russell 2008, 157).

The same lack of defense could describe CCoP thirty years ago, as Papineau discovered (2002, 45). Given its importance, he believed that closure could not be left as a bit of reductionist lore, and he has become its foremost defender. Since many of his arguments are also applicable to CCoN, we will consider the most important ones and draw out their implications for CCoN where appropriate.[22]

6.5.1 *Evidence 1: physiology*

Papineau's main argument in favor of CCoP is that all the empirical evidence is consistent with known physical forces. Physiology is a mature science, which after decades of successful research shows that there is no need to posit any sort of force or causation beyond the physical (2002, 255–56). Scientists who study the brain and the body have found no sign of minds or irreducible mental properties.

Papineau concludes that the case for CCoP is simply a matter of evidence, but this is misleading. It is instead an appeal to parsimony. Physiology has failed to find evidence of any nonphysical causes. If there were any, he says, there would at least be anomalies that could not be explained in terms of physical causes alone. Ockham's razor dictates that nonphysical causes be rejected or, at the very least, that they be recognized as inert *vis-à-vis* physical processes.

Noninterventionists like this argument and believe that it holds across the sciences, thus extending CCoP to CCoN. Nonviolationists do not. They believe in special divine action but typically in a way that remains hidden from scientific discovery. Hence, an absence of scientific evidence ought not be interpreted as evidence of the absence of divine action.

Here, I think, nonviolationism has it right. When it comes to CCoP, the truth is that dualism and all the other nonphysicalist programs were never refuted as much as they were ignored (Bishop 2010, 209). The physiological research that Papineau touts is all about the nonmental, either uncovering detailed mechanisms or understanding how one subsystem is integrated into a whole. Any question about the mind is carefully bracketed to the side, virtually guaranteeing that mental causes will not be detected (Lowe 2010, 74–75). That's fine in terms of scientific methodology, but let's not pretend that exhaustive knowledge of the interplay of nerves, muscles, and joints will ever be able to explain why my arm is moving. That event involves the mental: I *want* my coffee and *intend* to grasp the mug. Perhaps medical research should remain methodologically agnostic about the mental. But if scientists have tacitly agreed to not investigate that question, no amount of scientific progress would count as evidence against an irreducible mental realm. To claim that the matter has been resolved by the evidence begs the question.

What of Ockham's razor? Let's grant that physicalism has the leaner ontology. And let's agree that whether in science or philosophy, parsimony is a virtue. As the non-Humeans in Chapter 5 would be quick to point out, however, it is not the only one. Explanatory power and scope typically pull in the opposite direction from simplicity. Reductionist physicalism is parsimonious. Does it have the resources to explain what is currently known in science, let alone the mental? "Unlikely" is the charitable answer. ("No" is the correct one.) In any case, the argument has now turned to matters of metaphysics and explanatory virtues and away from the promise that the issue had been resolved by the evidence alone.

Is CCoN in any better shape? Again, it seems to beg all the interesting questions. Where is the evidence for CCoN? When has it ever been investigated? Under methodological naturalism,[23] researchers can probe every detail of nature, but they cannot consider the supernatural when forming scientific explanations. But if the question of divine action were disallowed from the start, the whole of science, no matter how advanced, would not constitute evidence against it.

6.5.2 *Evidence 2: conservation laws*

Papineau's second appeal to evidence in favor of CCoP points to conservation laws, especially our understanding of force since the nineteenth century (2002, 245). Unlike Newton's mechanics, which was compatible with all kinds of forces, including possibly mental ones, conservative forces have special properties. The events produced by conservative forces must allow key physical quantities to remain constant over time. The most familiar of these are total energy and momentum, which the four fundamental forces preserve.[24] Dissipative forces, like friction, are generally taken to be reducible to these four nondissipative ones. Papineau argues that conservation laws prevent nonphysical causes from having an effect on the physical unless those causes are able to store and release energy in a deterministic way (2009, 56–57). The qualifier could be met in principle but seems unlikely. After all, what sort of energy storage mechanism could a nonphysical force have?

Still, Papineau grants that nothing within physics guarantees that all forces will be conservative. The claim that there are no real nonconservative forces is based on the idea that any putative example can be reduced (2002, 249–50). This allows dissipation to be used heuristically by engineers and applied scientists without granting that it, strictly speaking, exists. In the end, this is an expression of faith in the reduction of nonfundamental forces, one often shared by those working in particle physics but doubted by specialists in condensed matter. There is a similar division among philosophers of science. Reductionists happily write promissory notes to cover unfulfilled reductions ("science will figure it all out in time"). Emergentists doubt this will ever be the case. Insofar as this matter involves difficult questions about metaphysics and reductionism, it is hard to see how the argument is merely a matter of the evidence, as Papineau claims that it is. In short, CCoP is not a truth that science has discovered.[25]

Even so, except for the reductionist language, this argument for CCoP does provide support for CCoN. Both noninterventionists and nonviolationists reject models of special divine action that require the breaking of a law. They would take seriously any argument based on conservation of energy and/or momentum that supports causal closure.

If the appeal to conservation is the best argument in favor of CCoP and, by extension, CCoN, as I believe it is, it will have an odd circularity. Nonviolationists say that special divine action will be rejected if it entails the breaking of the laws of nature. They then point to classical mechanics, which many believe entails determinism and causal closure. In a classical world, CCoN would pose a huge constraint on divine action. So far, so good. When pressed for arguments in support of CCoN, however, we find the best have to do with conservation laws. The argument started with the laws of nature, took a detour into closure, and ended up back in law. As far as I can tell, we could simply drop CCoN from the conversation. Any constraint on nonviolationism boils down to the relevant laws of nature. Talk of closure is an unnecessary complication.

Having sorted through the problems presented by determinism and causal closure, we have finally tracked down the real culprits, namely, conservative forces and conservation laws. If science presents an obstacle to nonviolationist divine action, this will be it. Conservation, however, is a big topic, one that my own model of divine action will have to address. A full treatment will be put off until the next chapter.

6.5.3 *Classical mechanics one more time*

Could one at least say that CCoN would have been a problem had classical mechanics continued to reign? It is still correct to say that current physics allows for divine action where previous science did not, right?

No. It should be clear from looking back over the counterexamples to classical determinism that closure runs into all the same problems. Classical mechanics does not entail CCoN, as Earman's space invader example shows. Classical space-times allow particles to appear from and exit to spatial infinity in finite time. As Earman concludes, once again, "[In a] Newtonian space-time. . . [the universe] is not automatically 'closed' in the operative sense to outside influences" (1986, 34). As we saw earlier, one can fix the problem by stipulating boundary conditions that forbid such influences. But if one needs to gerrymander the boundary conditions to ensure closure, the theory alone will not entail it.

This contradicts the familiar story that the discovery of quantum mechanics was needed to free us from CCoN and determinism. In my view, there is a kind of mythology that appears in the divine action literature. Determinism and closure will be seen as ancient foes to be overcome if we believe in theism instead of mere deism. But good fortune! We have discovered the new magics of top-down causation, quantum mechanics, and chaos, which can slay the beast and open the gate a bit so that God might act in the world.

But what if the pressing need for a hero in this story is misplaced? As we have seen, physics was never the abode of the type of determinism or closure that early modern philosophers had in mind. Polkinghorne gets it exactly right:

> It is clear that physical closure of the causal nexus of the world has not been established, so that claims that science has disproved the possibility of providential agency can be seen to be false. Belief in divine action is no more necessarily negated by an honest science than is belief in free human agency.
>
> (Polkinghorne 2006, 67; quoted in Göcke 2015, n. 5)

With those constraints now thrown off, we can turn our attention to a model of divine action that does not depend on exotic physics, that would have been viable in a fully classical world, and that will be viable if deterministic interpretations of quantum mechanics replace collapse-interpretations.

Notes

1 A third option that will not be discussed is *compatibilism*, which is usually advertised as a middle ground between (libertarian) freedom and determinism (Kane 2011, sec. IV). Libertarians prefer to call it "soft determinism," as it purports to establish a type of freedom but ultimately cedes all the important questions to the determinist.

2 One reply is that those future events depend in part on my decisions at the time (Kevin Timpe, private conversation). Say that the Templeton Foundation decides to support a third book of mine in 2025, which would be a wise and noble investment on their part. Even if that event is now ontologically fixed, it only comes about (in part) *because* of my decisions and actions leading up to it. Some argue that eternalism is therefore not in conflict with libertarian freedom.

3 As I mentioned in section 1.3, the exceptions to this rule tend to be philosophers such as Alston, Plantinga, and Larmer.

4 One famous example is the so-called "hole argument," which seemed to indicate that general relativity was not deterministic. Most physicists now believe that this apparent violation of determinism was due to a naïve understanding of gauge invariance, although the "history of physics shows that the primary reason for seeing gauge freedom at work is to maintain determinism" (Earman 2007, 1378).
5 The Steinhardt/Turok ekpyrotic cyclic model (http://wwwphy.princeton. edu/~steinh/npr/) posits another universe that collides with our own every trillion years or so. The energy released from the most recent collision is what we call the Big Bang, but such events would have happened repeatedly in the past according to this proposal. Penrose's conformal cyclic cosmology (2006) also posits many Big Bangs in the past and the future. The difficulty for Penrose is explaining the extreme low-entropy of the past. He does so by treating black holes as entropy eaters. It is widely believed that black holes have a fixed lifespan. Once they evaporate – a long, slow process – they take entropy with them, essentially recharging the battery of the universe. Neither has generated much support, but the search continues for ways to incorporate the Big Bang into a more holistic model in which it no longer appears as a singularity.
6 Although there are many examples of early modern philosophers arguing for one or the other. See (van Strien 2014a).
7 Elsewhere, Spinoza says,

> If a stone has fallen from a room onto someone's head and killed him, they will show, in the following way, that the stone fell in order to kill the man. For if it did not fall to that end, God willing it, how could so many circumstances have concurred by chance (for often many circumstances do concur at once)? Perhaps you will answer that it happened because the wind was blowing hard and the man was walking that way. But they will persist: why was the wind blowing hard at that time? why was the man walking that way at that time? If you answer again that the wind arose then because on the preceding day, while the weather was still calm, the sea began to toss, and that the man had been invited by a friend, they will press on – for there is no end to the questions which can be asked: but why was the sea tossing? why was the man invited at just that time? And so they will not stop asking for the causes of causes until you take refuge in the will of God, i.e., the sanctuary of ignorance.
>
> (*Ethics*, I, Appendix)

8 The Law of Continuity is arguably derived from the Principle of Sufficient Reason, although Leibniz himself never explicitly made that connection (van Strien 2014a, 29).
9 Both Pierre Duhem ([1906] 1954, 139) and Max Born (1969, 78–82) recognized this well before the term "chaos theory" was coined.
10 Cf. (Butterfield 2005). This definition can be amended in cases where gauge freedom complicates the notion of state (Müller and Placek 2018).
11 In dissipative systems, multiple states might all end on the same attractor and so are unique only up until then. Once on the attractor, the state trajectories will coincide.
12 See (Svozil 2018, sec. 17.4) for more examples of classical indeterminism once Lipschitz continuity has been relaxed.
13 Not everyone agrees with this characterization. A less provocative description is that, since the surface is infinitely slippery, the particle must move unless it is subject to an infinite gravitational force. But when it will move and in which

direction are not determined by the equations of motion. Hence uniqueness fails (and determinism along with it).

14 Robin Collins has objected (private correspondence) that this is an overly lean view of classical mechanical laws and that other principles must be brought into play to bridge the gap from mere mathematics to physics. Here, I adopt John Earman's position that "the field equations or laws of motion of the most fundamental theories of current physics represent science's best guesses as to the form of the basic laws of nature" (2004, 21). And while we might agree that still more "physical principles" are needed to get from the equations to mechanics, it is precisely the status and the justification of such principles that is in question in this chapter.

15 The Clay Mathematics Institute offers a $1 million prize for proving the existence of solutions to the Navier-Stokes equations in three dimensions (Earman 2007, 1384). These are the equations governing classical fluid flow.

16 The idea that determinism might break down in this manner is not new. The nineteenth-century French physicist Joseph Boussinesq suggested that mechanical systems involving singular solutions to differential equations might be the physical basis for free will (van Strien 2014b, 175–76). James Clerk Maxwell made similar explorations in this area (1879, 757).

17 For more ways that determinism can fail within classical physics, as well as the constraints added to preserve it, see (Earman 2007, sec. 3).

18 Parabolic partial differential equations in a Newtonian world, like the Fourier heat equation, present similar problems (Earman 1986, 42). There are also worlds with progressively smaller particles in something like a Newton's pendulum toy, with smaller and smaller bodies, where the last particle in the limit does not move at all (2004, 22–23). Like the space invader example, the equations are time-reversal invariant (i.e., they apply just as well if the whole process went in the opposite direction). Hence, if this is physically possible in a Newtonian system, so too is a string of particles at rest spontaneously beginning to collide.

19 There is a parallel set of issues in the philosophy of science literature on the use of causality in physics (Smith 2013). While some believe the idea that causes precede their effects is loosely based on an inductive generalization, others take it to be a constraint on good science.

20 For more discussion see (van Strien 2014a, 26–27).

21 "The biological, meteorological, and mental causes won't be eclipsed by the physical causes, simply because they will be one and the same as the physical causes – they will be 'non-physical' only in the sense that they are normally referred to using specialist (biological, meteorological, mental) terminology, and not because they are ontologically different" (Papineau 2009, 55).

22 See (Lim 2015) for a complete exposition and analysis of how these arguments in philosophy of mind mirror those in philosophy of religion.

23 The standard distinction to be made here is between ontological and methodological naturalism. The former is a metaphysical doctrine: All that exists is natural stuff; there is nothing supernatural. The latter says that although ontological naturalism might be false, scientific explanations must be restricted to natural events and entities. For arguments for and against methodological naturalism, see (Koperski 2015, chap. 5).

24 Two of the four are well-known: gravity and electromagnetism. The remaining two, the strong and the weak nuclear forces, are important for subatomic physics.

25 Papineau-critic E. J. Lowe argues that reductive physicalists no longer appeal to conservation, since it so clearly cannot close the argument the way they want (2010, 61).

Works cited

Arnold, Vladimir I. 1988. *Dynamical Systems III*. Berlin: Springer.

Atmanspacher, Harald, and Stefan Rotter. 2008. "Interpreting Neurodynamics: Concepts and Facts." *Cognitive Neurodynamics* 2 (4): 297–318. https://doi.org/10.1007/s11571-008-9067-8.

Bishop, Robert C. 2010. "The Via Negativa: Not the Way to Physicalism." *Mind and Matter* 8 (2): 203–14.

Born, Max. 1969. *Physics in My Generation*. 2nd ed. Heidelberg Science Library. New York: Springer.

Butterfield, Jeremy. 2005. "Determinism and Indeterminism." In *Routledge Encyclopedia of Philosophy*, edited by Edward Craig. London: Routledge.

Clayton, Philip. 1997. *God and Contemporary Science*. Edinburgh: Edinburgh University Press.

———. 2008. *Adventures in the Spirit: God, World, Divine Action*. Edited by Zachary R. Simpson. Minneapolis: Fortress Press.

Diekemper, Joseph. 2007. "B-Theory, Fixity, and Fatalism." *Noûs* 41 (3): 429–52.

Duhem, Pierre. (1906) 1954. *The Aim and Structure of Physical Theory*. Translated by Philip P. Wiener. Princeton, NJ: Princeton University Press.

Earman, John. 1986. *A Primer on Determinism*. Dordrecht: D. Reidel Pub. Co.

———. 2004. "Determinism: What We Have Learned and What We Still Don't Know." In *Freedom and Determinism*, 21–46. Cambridge, MA: MIT Press.

———. 2007. "Aspects of Determinism in Modern Physics." In *Philosophy of Physics*, edited by John Earman and Jeremy Butterfield, 2:1369–434. Handbook of the Philosophy of Science. Amsterdam: Elsevier.

Göcke, Benedikt Paul. 2015. "Did God Do It? Metaphysical Models and Theological Hermeneutics." *International Journal for Philosophy of Religion* 78 (2): 215–31. https://doi.org/10.1007/s11153-014-9489-7.

Kane, Robert, ed. 2011. *The Oxford Handbook of Free Will*. 2nd ed. Oxford Handbooks. Oxford: Oxford University Press.

Koperski, Jeffrey. 2015. *The Physics of Theism: God, Physics, and the Philosophy of Science*. Chichester, UK: Wiley-Blackwell.

Laplace, Pierre Simon. (1814) 1902. *A Philosophical Essay on Probabilities*. Translated by F. W. Truscott and F. L. Emory. New York: Wiley.

Lim, Daniel. 2015. *God and Mental Causation*. Springer Briefs in Philosophy. New York: Springer.

Lowe, E. J. 2010. *Personal Agency: The Metaphysics of Mind and Action*. Oxford: Oxford University Press.

Malament, David. 2008. "Norton's Slippery Slope." *Philosophy of Science* 75 (5): 799–816.

Maxwell, James Clerk. 1873. "Does the Progress of Physical Science Tend to Give Any Advantage to the Opinion of Necessity (or Determinism) Over That of the Contingency of Events and the Freedom of the Will?" In *The Scientific Letters and Papers of James Clerk Maxwell*, edited by P. M. Harman, 2:814–23. Cambridge: Cambridge University Press.

———. 1879. "Letter to Francis Galton, February 26, 1879." In *The Scientific Letters and Papers of James Clerk Maxwell*, edited by P. M. Harman, 3:756–58. Cambridge: Cambridge University Press.

Müller, Thomas, and Tomasz Placek. 2018. "Defining Determinism." *The British Journal for the Philosophy of Science*, 215–52.

Norton, John. 2008. "The Dome: An Unexpectedly Simple Failure of Determinism." *Philosophy of Science* 75 (5): 786–98.

Papineau, David. 2002. *Thinking About Consciousness*. Oxford: Clarendon Press.

———. 2009. "The Causal Closure of the Physical and Naturalism." In *The Oxford Handbook of Philosophy of Mind*, edited by B. McLaughlin, A. Beckermann, and S. Walter, 53–65. New York: Oxford University Press.

Penrose, Roger. 2006. "Before the Big Bang: An Outrageous New Perspective and Its Implications for Particle Physics." *Proceedings of EPAC*, 2759–67.

Planck, Max. 1932. *Der Kausalbegriff in Der Physik*. Leipzig: Barth.

Polkinghorne, John. 2006. "Christianity and Science." In *The Oxford Handbook of Religion and Science*, edited by Philip Clayton and Zachary R. Simpson, 57–70. Oxford: Oxford University Press.

Russell, Robert J. 2008. *Cosmology: From Alpha to Omega*. Minneapolis: Fortress Press.

Saunders, Nicholas. 2000. "Does God Cheat at Dice? Divine Action and Quantum Possibilities." *Zygon* 35 (3): 517–44.

Smith, Sheldon R. 2013. "Causation in Classical Mechanics." In *The Oxford Handbook of Philosophy of Physics*, edited by Robert Batterman, 107–40. Oxford: Oxford University Press.

Strien, Marij van. 2014a. "On the Origins and Foundations of Laplacian Determinism." *Studies in History and Philosophy of Science Part A* 45: 24–31.

———. 2014b. "The Norton Dome and the Nineteenth Century Foundations of Determinism." *Journal for General Philosophy of Science* 45 (1): 167–85. https://doi.org/10.1007/s10838-014-9241-0.

Svozil, Karl. 2018. *Physical (A)Causality*. Fundamental Theories of Physics. Cham: Springer International Publishing. https://doi.org/10.1007/978-3-319-70815-7.

Werndl, Charlotte. 2011. "On the Observational Equivalence of Continuous-Time Deterministic and Indeterministic Descriptions." *European Journal for Philosophy of Science* 1 (2): 193–225. https://doi.org/10.1007/s13194-010-0011-5.

Xia, Zhihong. 1992. "The Existence of Noncollision Singularities in Newtonian Systems." *The Annals of Mathematics* 135 (3): 411. https://doi.org/10.2307/2946572.

Zagzebski, Linda. 2017. "Foreknowledge and Free Will." In *Stanford Encyclopedia of Philosophy*, edited by Edward N. Zalta. https://plato.stanford.edu/archives/sum2017/entries/free-will-foreknowledge/.

7 Neoclassical special divine action

One danger of tying any philosophical program too closely to science is that science changes. Fundamental physics has stagnated in this generation. Resolving that stagnation might require theories not yet imagined. The model of special divine action presented in this chapter is less vulnerable to such changes. It does not depend on quantum mechanics or relativity and would be just as viable if classical physics were true, hence "neoclassical."

There is, however, one more controversy regarding the laws of nature that must be discussed. The issue is somewhat orthogonal to the issues discussed in Chapter 5. There, the question had to do with the metaphysics and the origin of the laws. Here, the goal is to demarcate laws in physics from a cloud of related ideas that are often called laws. What we will find is that the word "law" gets tossed around too freely. Although this imprecision is not normally a problem, if we are concerned about what constitutes the breaking of a law of nature, more care will be required.

The next section might seem like a detour, but distinctions made here allow the neoclassical model to be presented in a straightforward manner. The chapter concludes with an important objection based on conservation laws.

7.1 *Ceteris paribus* laws?

Let's begin with the difference between laws and law-statements. Newton's law of universal gravitation is often written $F = G\dfrac{m_1 m_2}{r^2}$.[1] But since it can be written down, that equation must technically be a law-statement. From the nomological realist's perspective, if a law-statement is (approximately) true, the law of nature that it describes – a part of the metaphysical landscape – makes it true. Law-statements are the best models we have for understanding the laws. The distinctions to be made in this section come from a close examination of how law-statements work in physics. That said, it is cumbersome to keep referring to law-statements instead of simply Boyle's law or Ohm's law. In this section, then, I will ignore the law/law-statement distinction for ease of exposition. The reader should remember, however, that any law that can be written down is actually a law-statement.

On to the controversy, in which philosopher Nancy Cartwright is a key voice. Her argument is based on the claim that the laws do not work as advertised. Consider universal gravitation. Is it true? Not of any charged bodies, she argues, since they are also subject to Coulomb's law. Given this additional influence, no charged body ever acts precisely as described by universal gravitation. In fact, no particle has ever acted in accordance with Newton's law of gravity, which considers only the force on two masses. Since gravity has an unlimited range, every object in the universe is attracted by every other particle that has mass.[2]

Cartwright's diagnosis is that universal gravitation, like all laws, contains an implicit *ceteris paribus* condition (tr: "other things being equal"). Colloquially, this clause means that laws hold only as long as nothing unusual happens. One can expect a tennis ball, when it is released, to fall toward the floor, unless my golden retriever is nearby. In that case, all bets are off. This, then, is what universal gravitation says:

> *If* there are no forces other than gravitational forces at work, *then* two bodies exert a force between each other which varies inversely as the square of the distance between them, and varies directly as the product of their masses.
>
> (Cartwright 1983, 58)

Except in a theoretical universe in which there are only two particles, the antecedent is never met, what Peter Lipton calls the "problem of instantiation" (1999, 157). An analogous situation holds for Kepler's laws of planetary orbits. No planet obeys Kepler's laws, which do not account for the perturbations of other planets in the solar system. The lesson some infer is that laws, strictly speaking, apply only to idealizations, including that of being a perfectly isolated system (Hüttemann 1998, 129; Lipton 1999, 155). "[There] are no exceptionless quantitative laws in physics. . . . [The] fundamental laws of physics do not represent the facts" (Cartwright 1983, 46, 58).

In Cartwright's view, this significantly weakens the case for nomological realism. Laws do not work the way we assume. Her alternative is to reject laws in favor of capacities:

> [The] logic that uses what happens in ideal circumstances to explain what happens in real ones is the logic of tendencies or capacities. What *is* an ideal situation for studying a particular factor? It is a situation in which all other 'disturbing' factors are missing. And what is special about that? *When all other disturbances are absent, the factor manifests its power explicitly in its behaviour.* When nothing else is going on, you can see what tendencies a factor has by looking at what it does. This tells you something about what will happen in very different, mixed circumstances – but only if you assume that the factor has a fixed capacity that it carries with it from situation to situation.
>
> (1989, 190–91)

So *ceteris paribus*, opposite charges attract, says Cartwright, but not because it is a law. Regularities in nature are due to capacities that can be made perspicuous in isolated circumstances, like lab experiments. The more common situation is for different capacities to be in play at once, producing the often complex behaviors we observe in the real world.

The claim that laws contain implicit *ceteris paribus* (CP) exceptions is now common. Among philosophers of science, it is also quite controversial. Cartwright *et al.* rightly note that there is some sort of contingency associated with the laws of nature. The question is whether this contingency is best understood as CP conditions built into the laws themselves. It is not.

Let's start once again with the idea that the most reliable law-statements in physics are the best models we have for the laws. Now recall the super-intelligence known as a Laplacian demon (section 6.2). One might think that a being with absolute knowledge of the laws of nature in a closed deterministic universe should be able to accurately predict the future. But that leaves out a crucial piece of information. For such a prediction to be possible, even in principle, the intelligence would need to know the absolute state of the universe at a point in time. In terms of the differential equations that the Laplacian demon would be solving, this information constitutes the initial and boundary conditions of the system. The first thing to note, then, is that these are not part of the laws. Even in a classical world, the laws of nature do not in themselves determine events. The future state of a system depends on contingent, nonlawlike information. That much is familiar.

As philosopher Sheldon Smith argues, this not an adequate place to stop. The distinction between laws, initial conditions, and boundary conditions is correct, but

> this taxonomy misses many features of modeling which are vital to the understanding of the role laws play in constructing concrete descriptions of motion. What is generally missed is the distinction between a differential equation, the solution of which describes the concrete temporal behavior of a system, and the laws (e.g. Newton's second law or Universal Gravitation) used to derive the differential equation.
>
> (2002, 243)

Let's unpack this. How do we get from laws to a model of some concrete, physical arrangement, from, say, universal gravitation to a textbook exercise about planetary motion?

The steps were codified by Leonhard Euler in the eighteenth century (Wilson 2016, Section 2).

A) Determine what sort of system one is trying to model: particles, rigid bodies, elastic bodies, etc.

Point particles are (typically) the easiest to model in terms of the mathematics. I limit the remaining steps to particle-based systems, although they have been extended to others.

B) Determine the relevant forces acting on these bodies: gravitational attraction, electrical repulsion/attraction, etc.
C) For each particle, determine how each force acts on that particle along some set of Cartesian coordinates.

This is the decomposition of forces one learns in freshman physics. Determine the degree to which gravity pulls on particle α along the x-axis, y-axis, and z-axis. Do the same for particle β, and so on down the line. Repeat this for each particle and every other force acting on the system, if there are any. The choice of axes is arbitrary, so at least one will be chosen to make the decomposition easiest (e.g., let the force of gravity act directly along the y-axis).

D) For each particle, sum up the forces along each axis: $\Sigma F_{\alpha x}$, $\Sigma F_{\alpha y}$, $\Sigma F_{\alpha z}$, $\Sigma F_{\beta x}$, $\Sigma F_{\beta y}$, $\ldots$
E) For each particle, set the sum of forces along the x-axis equal to its mass times the acceleration in the x direction. Do the same for each axis and repeat for each particle.

More precisely, set the force along the x-axis on particle α to $F_{\alpha x} = m_{\alpha} \dfrac{d^2 x}{dt^2}$, since acceleration is the second derivative of position. There will be three force equations for each particle, one for each axis, providing a set of differential equations to solve.

So, then, what is the law of universal gravitation, and what role does it play? Is it what Cartwright claims?

> *If* there are no forces other than gravitational forces at work, *then* two bodies exert a force between each other which varies inversely as the square of the distance between them, and varies directly as the product of their masses.
>
> (1983, 58)

No! The point of summing the forces along each axis is to allow for the possibility that *more* than one force is at work. In classical mechanics, there could in principle be many *types* of forces in play on the particles over and above gravity and electromagnetism, each one subject to the Euler procedure. Vector decomposition is designed to account for any number of forces on each particle. *There is no implicit* ceteris paribus *condition about the absence of forces other than gravity.* Universal gravitation provides one force vector for each particle in step (B). Other forces are incorporated in precisely the same way. There is nothing wrong, false, or CP-provisional about the force laws in (B).

The only place where something remotely like a *ceteris paribus* condition is involved is the choice of idealizations. That is, one must decide which forces are insignificant and what sort of system is to be modeled. Idealizations in step (A) might include taking a block to be a rigid body. Those in step (B) might include allowing that block to move on a frictionless plane. We may also choose to ignore the force contributions of all masses except Earth in a case where all other forces are negligible. Even in that case, universal gravitation is still not treated as false. The law is instead used to decide when the influence of other bodies can be safely ignored (Earman, Roberts, and Smith 2002, 285). In other words, we believe the law is correct. The only decision to be made is which bodies will contribute a measurable influence. One could always consider the gravitational pull of the moon, adding it to the decomposition of forces. Doing so will, however, (i) greatly complicate the mathematics and (ii) not register within the number of decimal places likely to be calculated. In any case, this pragmatic choice has nothing to do with whether the law of gravity is true.

Where are the laws in the Euler recipe? Two places. First, there are the force laws: universal gravitation, Coulomb's law, etc. If we move beyond point particles, friction and contact forces will be added to the list. Second, there are the laws of motion, here Newton's second law. What are *not* laws are the differential equations produced at the end of the procedure, which will be integrated for a solution. These equations cannot be generated without laws, but they are not themselves laws. Nor are the "nonnomic elements" needed to solve these equations: the initial conditions, boundary conditions, and idealizations (Smith 2002, 247).

Force laws, which get much of Cartwright's attention, are upstream in (B). To make a case for CP-laws, this is where the focus must be, not on the differential equations tracking the evolution of some individual system. Cartwright tries to show that universal gravitation is flawed given that no bodies behave in the way that the law dictates. The problem with this analysis is that universal gravitation by itself *says nothing about the behavior of bodies*. Universal gravitation is a force law. Force laws are essential in the Euler procedure, but it is the differential equation produced at the end that describes the behavior of a system. The force laws imply nothing about state changes over time. It is this conflation of laws with the differential equations that rely on them that leads to the misdiagnosis of CP-laws.

Let's draw some conclusions from this. First, not everything commonly called a law is one. (More precisely, some statements given the honorific "law" do not refer to a law of nature.) Consider Kepler's laws. Their corrected form can be derived by the Euler procedure from the equations for central-force motion. Kepler's laws are not laws, however. They depend on a set of conditions and idealizations. Given other initial conditions, the same

laws (central-force and Newton's second) will yield hyperbolic solutions –
e.g., some comets make a one-time pass around the sun, rather than an
ellipse, such as the planets do. If one is going to make a case for CP-laws, the
examples need to be legitimate law-statements, not merely generalizations
that are loosely called "laws."

Second, the Euler process requires both laws and nonnomic conditions
to derive differential equations. In addition there will be idealizations—
also non-nomic—regarding which particles to account for. A physicist or a
Laplacian demon armed with complete knowledge of the laws would not
be able to make any predictions, since the laws alone, again, entail nothing about the behavior of any concrete system. Predictions are based on
solutions to the differential equations produced at the end of the Euler procedure. For Kepler's laws and the other examples of supposed CP-laws in
physics, the examples are either mischaracterizations of what the law says,
like Cartwright's (this section, 127), or differential equations for some system or other, which are not laws.

Smith's conclusion is that if there are any CP-laws, they haven't yet been
discovered in physics (2002, 258). Moreover, any support that *ceteris paribus* language is thought to bestow upon capacities and causal powers is
likewise undermined.

The model of divine action we have been working toward might now
seem anticlimactic. So much ground has been cleared that the implications
may be obvious. In any case, there isn't much work left to be done.

7.2 The neoclassical model

The goal has been to find a model of nonviolationist special divine action
that allows for a significant degree of freedom on God's part but is not
dependent on the sometimes fickle interpretations of modern physics. Taking it from the top, then, it starts with decretalism, a type of nomological
realism. The regularities observed in nature are best explained by laws, but
those laws have no independent existence. They are not powers "out there"
in nature; rather, they are ultimately the decrees of God. Moreover, these
decrees are matters of constraint. The laws – not law-statements – of electromagnetism for particles and fields, for example, dictate that the relevant
forces apply only to specific types of entities with fixed degrees of strength,
range, etc. The laws don't "make things go," as it were. Electromagnetic
force does that, at least in this example. The law constrains the ways in
which this force behaves.

Of all the distinctions made thus far, the one between law and nonnomic
information is the most important *vis-à-vis* nonviolationism. Nothing in the
Euler procedure prevents the introduction of new influences on a system.
Consider two balls colliding on a pool table. If we assume a perfectly elastic
collision – an idealization – this will be a simple system to model. But what
if we tilt the table just prior to the collision? That will produce changes in

the decomposition of forces, the force of friction, and a couple of other factors, bringing about a new differential equation at the end. *But the laws will not change.* Universal gravitation remains what it is. The same for the laws of mechanics. (More precisely, the law-statements that appear in steps (B) and (E) are unchanged because the laws of nature to which they refer are unchanged.) All the nonnomic components in the Euler procedure are subject to change, but not the laws. We make such changes routinely, like the tilting of the table. If you want a slogan, it is this: The laws never break; they flow. The laws adapt to change. This was true when we thought that nature was Newtonian, and it remains true in the age of quantum mechanics and relativity.

In support of this last claim, consider two distinctively quantum phenomena: The first are vacuum fluctuations. Even in a universe devoid of matter, quantum fields would still exist and be subject to fluctuations that sometimes produce particles. This is related to the spontaneous emission of radiation: Particles appear in places where they had not previously been (Svozil 2018, sec. 14). Second, there is the phenomena of quantum tunneling. Consider an electron trapped in a negatively charged field. The electron cannot move if it is repulsed on all sides. Classically, this system would remain precisely as it is unless the field degrades. Given Schrödinger's equation, which takes the place of Newton's second law in the Euler procedure, there is a slight chance that the electron will "tunnel" through the barrier and appear elsewhere. In both examples, the appearance of particles from "nowhere" does not break any laws of nature. The gravitational and the electromagnetic fields adapt to these new particles, and they would do so even if much larger bodies were involved.

Changes to nonnomic conditions do not violate the laws of nature. Nature allows for change that the laws can seamlessly adapt to. We make such changes with every conscious act. If so, I see no reason based on physics to say that a divine person cannot likewise bring about change without breaking the laws – with one objection looming (section 7.3). Once the laws of nature are distinguished from behavior that is the *result* of those laws and nonnomic conditions, we find a vast space of contingency in which God can act. This is the neoclassical model of special divine action.

But how is it "neoclassical?" Isn't this contingency *somehow* dependent on the ontological openness introduced by quantum mechanics? If nature were classical and deterministic, surely any divine action would violate the laws.

The point of the previous chapter was that this intuition is based on a faulty understanding of determinism and causal closure. Deterministic systems are not the obstacle to divine action that they are often portrayed to be. The outdated view that I argued against, as Earman says, is

> contrary to the modern conception of determinism according to which laws allow for contingency in "initial conditions" and necessitate only

conditionals of the form "If the initial conditions are such-and-such, then the state at a later time will be so-and-so."

(2000, 9)

This "modern conception of determinism" fits into the same framework as that of the Euler procedure. The laws are needed to derive differential equations that model the behavior of particular systems. But those models are not themselves laws, nor are the nonnomic conditions Earman is referring to.

Having established that nonviolationist divine influence is possible even in a classical world, what does that influence look like? What does God *do*? The answer depends on matters of ontology. To say what influence God brings about depends on what exists to be influenced. Particles? That seems unlikely now that quantum fields have taken center stage in physics. Particle *physicists* take particles to be manifestations of excited fields. That view should survive whatever the outcome of research on string theory and its rivals. If fields lie at the foundation of all physical existence, divine action on this model will be directed at changing the states of those fields, which will then adapt to those changes as discussed. Note, however, that this answer approaches ontology from a reductionist point of view, as if the only "real" entities were whatever existed at the most fundamental level. Emergentists will complain – rightly, in my view – that what the other sciences study is as real as quantum fields. Not all phenomena can be reduced to fundamental physics, and our ontology should be expanded in order to accommodate this.

If the reductionist is correct, neoclassical divine action will be brought about when God influences the fields that underlie the rest of physical reality. If the emergentist is correct, God will also interact with higher-level phenomena in ways appropriate to them. For example, a relatively rigid macroscopic body could experience a contact force without touching another body. The range of divine influence depends on what exists and how emergent systems undergo change.

Noninterventionists will not be interested in this model, since it allows for divine action over and above God creating and sustaining of the universe. Fair enough. For my part, I think that while noninterventionism is not technically a type of deism, it is too near a neighbor to be of interest. Nonviolationists allow for a greater range of divine action as long as it does not break the laws of nature. That's fine, but worries about violations must be founded on what the laws of nature actually are, not on conventional wisdom. This is why so much of the work done here and in previous chapters involves the laws of nature. Airy generalizations about the laws invite pseudoproblems that dissolve under scrutiny.

But perhaps we have not yet considered all the relevant laws.

7.3 Objection: conservation laws

The account thus far has focused on force laws and laws of motion. There is an objection, typically aimed at interventionism, that seems to apply here as well. If God were to change any of these nonnomic conditions, that influence would thereby violate the conservation of energy and conservation of momentum:

> [The] laws of nature [do] not easily allow for divine intervention – at least not direct divine intervention – because that will involve an immaterial agent acting on or within a material context as a cause. . . . This is not possible; if it were, either energy and information would be added to a system spontaneously and mysteriously, contravening the conservation of energy . . . or God would somehow be acting deterministically within quantum indeterminacy.
>
> (Stoeger 1995, 244)

The literature on special divine action condemns violations of conservation laws as a fatal flaw given their status as "indispensable to science" (Kaufman 1968, 185n10).

> [Conservation of energy and momentum] are understood to hold without exception; they are not defeasible. . . . The notion that local energy and momentum are not conserved is a radical notion: there is no evidence for it in physical science, and massive evidence to the contrary.
>
> (Fales 2013, 299–300)

If the neoclassical model entails the violation of conservation laws, many will reject it out of hand.

There are three replies to this charge, which get stronger as we go.

7.3.1 Closed systems

As many have noted, conservation laws are not absolute. There are conditions under which they hold and others in which they do not. Any undergraduate text will point out that conservation of energy and momentum apply only to closed or isolated systems. If the system is influenced by outside forces or if particles enter or leave, conservation will fail.

As Plantinga argues, if God were to act on such a system, it would not *be* closed and so conservation would not apply (2011, 78).[3] Conservation laws are conditional. If God were to act on a system, the relevant conditions would fail to be met and so those laws would not apply.

While there is something right about this response to the conservation law objection, it is the weakest of the three. One reason is given by Hans Halvorson:

> [While] I agree with Plantinga's hedging of the Newtonian laws, I don't like the idea that these laws are hedged because the universe is an "open system" in the sense that local physical systems can be "open." Typically by "open system" we mean a subsystem of a larger *physical* system. But

since God is not physical, the universe is not a subsystem of some larger physical system.

(2013, 25)

The physicist's idea of an open system tacitly includes its placement within a larger physical system. This would not be the case for God's influence, and so there is something wrong with calling a system open when divine action is at work. Supernatural causes cannot change a closed system into an open one.

The second reason for preferring a different reply is that the closed/open distinction is not relevant in the more technical definitions of conservation. The closed system condition is used in undergraduate texts for pedagogical reasons, but specialists prefer the more rigorous approach discussed in section 7.3.3.

7.3.2 General relativity

The second reply will surprise many readers: Conservation of energy does not apply in general relativity with an expanding universe. There are several ways to approach this, but the simplest is that the total energy of the universe is continually increasing, and so it is not conserved (Misner, Thorne, and Wheeler 1973, 467; Wald 1984, 69–70; Jaffe and Taylor 2018, 414). Although there are ways of defining gravitational energy to mitigate the problem, most experts, like cosmologist Sean Carroll, think this is a fool's errand:

> It's clear that cosmologists have not done a very good job of spreading the word about something that's been well-understood since at least the 1920's: energy is not conserved in general relativity. . . . The point is pretty simple: back when you thought energy was conserved, there was a *reason* why you thought that, namely time-translation invariance. A fancy way of saying "the background on which particles and forces evolve, as well as the dynamical rules governing their motions, are fixed, not changing with time." But in general relativity that's simply no longer true. Einstein tells us that space and time are dynamical, and in particular that they can evolve with time. When the space through which particles move is changing, the total energy of those particles is not conserved.

(2010)

This is the majority view regarding conservation of energy in general relativity.[4] It agrees with the approach in the previous subsection in that conservation is not absolute. There are conditions for it to hold, and those conditions can fail. And when it fails, physics does not come crashing down.

If God is – putting it crudely – acting from outside the universe, the universe will constitute the system that God is influencing even if the effects are local. But that influence will not constitute a violation of conservation of energy, since conservation does not hold in our expanding universe.

While this reply is stronger than the one based on closed systems, there are some minority voices that raise concerns (Pitts forthcoming). It may be that general relativity offers still more technical reasons for being averse to divine action. Let's turn, then, to the best of the three responses to the conservation problem.

7.3.3 Noether's theorem

The three replies share the same basic logic: (i) Conservation is not a metaphysical given that all systems must adhere to, (ii) there are conditions for it to apply, and (iii) when those conditions are not met, conservation is no longer an issue. The roots of the third solution can be found in the second, but they can be put in a way that is independent of cosmology.

First, we need to consider some of the basics of *Lagrangian mechanics*. While the term might be unfamiliar, it is by no means exotic from a physicist's point of view. Lagrangian mechanics is largely equivalent to Newtonian mechanics, but it allows for solutions to equations that are otherwise intractable. One difference is that energy plays a central role. As Pitts argues (2019, sec. 2), if conservation of energy is going to hold, this will be the realm where it is evident. Moving to quantum mechanics will only raise new problems.

A Lagrangian L is a mathematical description of the energy of a system, both kinetic and potential. Take a simple example, such as a weight on the end of a spring moving back and forth along a surface (Marion and Thornton 1988, 193). Let's simplify further by stipulating that it is an ideal, frictionless spring oscillating in one dimension without gravity. The kinetic energy of the spring is the familiar $\frac{1}{2}mv^2$, where $v = \dot{x}$, the time derivative of position. The potential energy is $\frac{1}{2}kx^2$, where k is a constant that depends on the nature of the spring. The Lagrangian is the kinetic minus the potential energy, $L = \frac{1}{2}m\dot{x}^2 - \frac{1}{2}kx^2$. Instead of Newton's second law, Lagrangian mechanics uses the Euler-Lagrange equation. Having found L, one can plug it into the Euler-Lagrange equation in order to derive the model for a specific system, such as that of the moving spring. This is the Lagrangian analog to step (E) in the Euler procedure. Of course, it all gets far more complicated. The Lagrangians will become harder to find if we allow for motion in three dimensions, include gravity, have a system with many particles, or move to fields that are spread out over space. Moreover, getting from the Euler-Lagrange to the solutions of a given differential equation is difficult and sometimes impossible outside textbook examples. The best that physicists can often do is to simulate the behavior of the model on computers.

The relevance of all this to the question of conservation is due to a famous discovery known as Noether's (first) theorem. In 1915, Emmy Noether proved that conservation of various types could be inferred from mathematical symmetries. A symmetry or an invariance means that something remains the same while other things change. Look at a sphere that is all one color. If you move to the other side of the sphere or even peer at it from above, it looks the same. Not so for, say, a pyramid. The view from the side is different from the view from above. A sphere exhibits a type of spatial symmetry that a pyramid does not. How the sphere looks is invariant with respect to the angle at which you approach it.

Let's go back to the oscillating spring. Recall that $L = \frac{1}{2}m\dot{x}^2 - \frac{1}{2}kx^2$, the kinetic energy minus the potential energy stored in the spring. Notice that L depends only on the position x and velocity $\dot{x}$ of the spring. Although the state of the system is constantly changing, L remains the same. It is invariant with respect to time. Mathematically, if a function does not explicitly depend on time, when you take its derivative with respect to time, the result will be zero. In this case, $\frac{\partial L}{\partial t} = 0$.

According to Noether's theorem, we have just shown that conservation of energy applies to the ideal spring. The Lagrangian of this system is invariant with respect to time, a type of symmetry. Noether proved that if this symmetry pertains, conservation of energy will hold for that system.[5] (Another type of symmetry is related to conservation of momentum, but let's ignore that for now.) What is less well-known is that she also proved the converse albeit with a few more restrictions (José and Saletan 2006, 251): Roughly, if conservation holds, there will be symmetry. The conditional goes both ways. Taken together, Noether showed that if there is no time-translation invariance – if, in other words, that symmetry fails to pertain, then energy will not be conserved.

Back to the ideal spring. Let's now say that the mass is magnetic and we set the spring next to an electromagnet. Let the output of the electromagnet vary according to a simple sine wave, stronger and weaker over time. This means that L no longer applies. A new L^* will require another term representing the influence of the electromagnet and that influence is going to change over time. That new term will include sin t, which takes on different values at different *times*. Hence, L^* is not time-translation invariant, $\frac{\partial L^*}{\partial t} \neq 0$, and this is sufficient to show that, in this new system, conservation of energy fails. If there is no symmetry with respect to time, there will be no conservation of energy.

Once again, things will get more complicated in systems composed of many bodies or fields, but the basic relation between a Lagrangian time-translation invariance and conservation of energy is the same. If a Lagrangian explicitly involves time, the system's energy will change over time, translation symmetry will fail, and there will be no conservation of energy.

If a Lagrangian is independent of time, translation symmetry will hold, and the system will conserve energy.[6]

The bottom line is that it is not unusual in physics or engineering for energy not to be conserved. Conservation does not hold for mechanical systems with friction, aeronautical systems with drag, or any system subject to a time-varying influence. The most familiar parts of chaos theory pertain to nonconservative systems.[7] (Whether conservation can be restored in these examples is discussed in the following pages.) As Pitts points out (2019, 4.5), the physics of fields and continua employs mathematics (continuity equations) that quantify the *degree* to which conservation fails. It is not an all-or-nothing proposition, and the failure of conservation does not signal a catastrophe for physics.

The application of this to divine action is straightforward. Let's say that God primarily acts on fields – the "reductionist option" discussed in section 7.2. When God excites a local field, that system is being subjected to a time-varying influence. By Noether's theorem and its converse, the lack of time-invariance means that conservation of energy does not apply to that system during God's activity.[8] Conservation is not *violated*.

Although Noether's theorem was proved over a century ago, some will still be reticent to accept the arguments in this section. One reason is the belief that the examples can always in principle be changed so that conservation of energy is restored. In the case of the spring, one could rewrite the equations to include the electromagnet and the source of its electricity in one grand Lagrangian where time invariance would once again hold. In examples with friction or drag, the lost energy can be recaptured in the form of heat. Many believe that it is always possible to expand the system in question in such a way that conservation is restored. Fales makes this point:

> Take a gas in a closed, isolated container. The total energy and momentum of the gas molecules will remain unchanged over time. But if we heat the container over a flame, the energy content of the gas will increase; the system is no longer closed. However, we can restore the energy balance by extending the boundaries of our system to include the flame (the source of heat): the total energy for the gas plus the heat source will, once again, be conserved.
>
> (2013, 300)

This, then, presents a problem for divine action.

> Matters are different when God supplies energy (or momentum) to an otherwise closed physical system. If we now extend the "boundaries" of the system to include God, energy/momentum will *not* be conserved. For God has no mass/energy, and it makes no sense to speak of His having lost or gained energy in a transaction with nature. According to the theist, God creates energy *ex nihilo*.
>
> (Fales 2013, 300)

Hence, the appeal to Noether's theorem fails.

The question then becomes whether one can *always* redraw the boundaries of a system in this manner so as to restore conservation. Is that the case?

Not in cosmology, it is not. There is no way to redraw the boundaries so that the universe is part of some larger system.[9] If there were, the problem in section 7.3.2 would be solved. Nor would this idea restore conservation to the popular Ghirardi-Rimini-Weber (GRW) interpretation of quantum mechanics in which it fails (Gao 2017, 145). The belief that conservation can always be restored is reductionist. It assumes that measurable dissipative forces (like friction) can be completely reduced to conservative ones. Yet there is no theorem, theory, or observation that supports this. Although physicists are not always sensitive to philosophical distinctions, one popular textbook gets this exactly right:

> It must be reiterated that we have not proved the conservation laws of linear momentum, angular momentum, and energy. We have only derived various consequences of Newton's laws; that is, *if* these laws are valid in a certain situation, then momentum and energy will be conserved. But we have become so enamored with these conservation theorems that we have elevated them to the status of laws and we have come to *insist* that they be valid in any physical theory, even those that apply to situations in which Newtonian mechanics is not valid, as, for example, in the interaction of moving charges or in quantum-mechanical systems. We do not actually have conservation laws in such situations, but rather conservation *postulates* that we force on the theory.
>
> (Marion and Thornton 1988, 74, emphasis in original)

Note that last sentence again.

What Marion and Thornton describe here fits with an idea that we have dealt with before. Beliefs that are fruitfully imposed on scientific theorizing and practice are what I refer to as "metatheoretic shaping principles" (section 6.4). The uniformity of nature is one. The idea that effects never precede their causes is another. They are metaphysical theses that have proven their worth over time. The postulate that only conservative forces exist and that conservation of energy can always be restored in dissipative systems is another example. But like all such principles, this one is subject to challenges, suspensions, and changes (Koperski 2011, 34–39).[10] In the steady-state model of cosmology, Fred Hoyle, Hermann Bondi, and Thomas Gold explicitly rejected conservation of energy in order to avoid the Big Bang singularity and a finite age of the universe (Lowe 2010, 41). The idea that conservation is absolute gives it a status that it does not have in physics, as philosopher of physics Jeremy Butterfield sums up:

> [The] principle of the conservation of energy is not sacrosanct. The principle was formulated only in the mid-nineteenth century; and although

no violations have been established hitherto, it has been seriously questioned on several occasions. It was questioned twice at the inception of quantum theory (namely, the Bohr-Kramers-Slater theory, and the discovery of the neutrino). And, furthermore, it is not obeyed by a current relevant proposal . . . for solving quantum theory's measurement problem [i.e., GRW].

(1998, 146–47)

Even the best metatheoretic shaping principles can be traded off for other *desiderata*. The idea that conservation can always be preserved is no exception.

The neoclassical model allows for causal influences that are not time-invariant, but it is a misdiagnosis to say that conservation laws have thereby been violated. Noether's theorem sets conditions for conservation to apply. When these conditions fail to be met, there can be no violation of conservation laws.

7.4 Nearby views

I have at least three predecessors in the conceptual neighborhood: philosophers Alvin Plantinga, William Alston, and Robert Larmer.[11] The latter two point back still further to C. S. Lewis ([1947] 1978, 59).

Alston begins by making a now-familiar point. Determinism and causal closure are not metaphysical or scientific absolutes. Yes, scientists often assume them both, and this assumption has been fruitful. Nonetheless, "All our evidence is equally compatible with the idea that natural causal determination is sometimes, or always, only approximate" (1994, 48).

Alston treats determinism and closure as metatheoretic shaping principles – useful presuppositions in science, but not the sort of thing that one would expect to prove unconditionally or that stands irrefutable, come what may. His conclusion would have fit nicely into Chapter 6: "The upshot of all this is that, despite the enormous press given the thesis of determinism, I feel that it is not really a serious threat to the traditional way of thinking of God's actions in the world" (1994, 51). This traditional way of thinking about divine action, he says,

> does involve thinking of God as bringing things about other than they would have been had only natural factors been operative. But whether that implies a "violation" of natural laws depends on how we think of the latter. To suppose that it does is to presuppose that natural laws specify *unqualifiedly* sufficient conditions. . . . But we are never justified in accepting laws like this. The most we are ever justified in accepting is a law that specifies what will be the outcome of certain conditions *in the absence of any relevant factors other than those specified in the law.*
>
> (1994, 50)

While Alston does not explicitly mention *ceteris paribus* exceptions, that seems to be what he has in mind.[12] A law prescribes a given outcome unless something interferes. As I have argued (section 7.1), there is a better way to understand the contingency in nature that the laws allow, although that view had not yet been defended in print when Alston was writing. Under the Euler procedure, neither force laws nor the laws of motion themselves specify any outcome.

Plantinga likewise starts his analysis with determinism and causal closure:

> What we've seen so far is that classical science doesn't entail either determinism or that the universe is in fact causally closed. It is therefore entirely consistent with special divine action in the world, including miracles. Hands-off theologians [i.e., noninterventionists] can't properly point to science – not even to eighteenth- and nineteenth-century classical science – as a reason for their opposition to divine intervention. What actually guides their thought is not classical science as such, but classical science plus a gratuitous metaphysical or theological addition – one that has no scientific credentials and goes contrary to classical Christianity.
>
> (2011, 83–84)

The "gratuitous addition" is the imposition of the causal closure of nature as absolute. While the point is essentially correct, I reject the idea that determinism and closure are metaphysical/theological additions to science. All metatheoretic shaping principles lie in an overlapping conceptual space between theoretical science and philosophy. Science cannot do without such principles. While they can be misapplied or mistakenly thought to hold without exception, they are not gratuitous additions somehow foreign to science itself.

Plantinga goes on to take causal closure as a necessary condition for the laws to apply:

> Indeed, on this conception it isn't even possible that God break a law of nature. For to break a law, he would have to act specially in the world; yet any time at which he acted specially in the world would be a time at which the universe is not causally closed; hence no law applies to the circumstance in question and hence no law gets broken.
>
> (2011, 82–83)

The conditional nature of laws in view here works best for conservation laws. God's action negates closure, which in turn negates time-invariance, and so conservation of energy no longer applies. But this is not the way that force laws or the laws of motion work in the Euler procedure. Those laws always apply, but they adapt to changes made in nonnomic conditions. They do not depend on causal closure in the way that Plantinga has in mind here.

Robert Larmer's earliest work on divine action and the laws of nature predates that of Alston and Plantinga. He makes the clearest distinction of the three between laws and the contingent conditions upon which they depend:

> Scientific explanations must make reference not only to laws of nature but also to the material conditions to which the laws apply. . . . It is, for example, impossible to predict what will happen on a billiard table by making reference solely to Newton's laws of motion. One must also make reference to the number of balls on the table, their initial position, the condition of the felt, the angle the cue stick is held at, and so on. This means that, although we often speak as though the laws of nature explain the occurrence of an event, in and of themselves, this is not the case.
>
> (2014, 38–39)

Couching this in terms of explanation gives it an epistemological slant, but the idea that the laws are dependent on conditions that are not fixed in place is clear. Larmer then applies this to divine action:

> This basic distinction between the laws of nature and the stuff of nature suggests that miracles can occur without violating any laws of nature. If God creates or annihilates a unit of mass/energy, or simply causes some of these units to occupy a different position, then He changes the material conditions to which the laws of nature apply. He thereby produces an event that nature would not have produced on its own but breaks no laws of nature.
>
> (2014, 39)

In a field-based ontology, it would be better to talk in terms of excitation and dampening rather than creation/annihilation. Nonetheless, our two views can be harmonized except for Larmer's rejection of decretalism (2017).

While tensions remain between the accounts mentioned here and my own, there is a clear family resemblance. My contribution, if successful, will be to have placed these ideas on a somewhat more rigorous foundation, especially in the application of the Euler procedure and Noether's theorem. Still, the overall account contains a lot of moving parts, starting with decretalism and going down to the conservation of energy. I doubt that many will endorse the entire package. I do hope, however, that this model is able to move the needle a bit in the debate on special divine action.

Let's now turn to some objections not yet discussed.

Notes

1 Before a physicist has a chance to complain, this familiar version lacks the vector notation needed to form a differential equation.

2 That isn't quite right, given the restrictions on faster-than-light signals in special relativity, but the point still works for particles in the observable universe.

3 See also (Larmer 2014, chap. 2).

4 Philosopher Robin Collins and physicist Ulrich Mohrhoff explain this further in the context of conservation objections to mind-body dualism (Collins 2008, sec. IV; Mohrhoff 1997, sec. 3).

5 More precisely, time-translation invariance entails that *something* is conserved according to Noether's theorem, but it is not always energy (Smith 2008, 335).

6 A related set of conclusions applies to quantum mechanics, but the focus there will be on a Hamiltonian. If is time-dependent (i.e., lacks time invariance), conservation of energy fails (Jaffe and Taylor 2018, 405).

7 Any dynamical system with an attractor is dissipative (i.e., nonconservative), including strange attractors (section 3.2.1). As Ben Nasmith notes (private correspondence), the notion of a *conservative* force and *conservation* of energy are related, but they are by no means synonymous.

8 Some theologians will object that this sort of divine action is too "episodic" and that the notion of God acting "from outside" the universe fails to honor God's immanence. If so, one could change the account to say that all fields are continually subject to divine action, but only sometimes does this influence register as a measurable excitation.

9 Topologically disconnected universes within a multiverse, if there were one, would not be the sort of redrawing of boundaries in view here.

10 Consider another shaping principle: the uniformity of nature. This says that the laws of nature work the same everywhere in the universe, an undeniably useful bit of metaphysics presupposed by science. But there is no proof it is true without exception and will remain so. It is certainly not something that can be observed, nor does it follow from any scientific theory (hence the problem of induction). The more rigorously defined descendants of uniformity, the homogeneity and the isotropy of space, are common cosmological idealizations that are known to be false, strictly speaking.

11 Leigh Vicens has argued for a two-pronged approach to special divine action (2012, 334). The neoclassical view would fit within the second prong, as would Rope Kojonen's defense of Plantinga (2019).

12 See also (Alston 1999, 189–90).

Works cited

Alston, William P. 1994. "Divine Action: Shadow or Substance?" In *The God Who Acts: Philosophical and Theological Explorations*, edited by Thomas F. Tracy, 41–62. University Park: Pennsylvania State University Press.

———. 1999. "Divine Action, Human Freedom, and the Laws of Nature." In *Quantum Cosmology and the Laws of Nature: Scientific Perspectives on Divine Action*, edited by Robert Russell, Nancey Murphy, and C. J. Isham. 2nd ed., 185–206. Berkeley, CA: Center for Theology and the Natural Sciences.

Butterfield, Jeremy. 1998. "Quantum Curiosities of Psychophysics." In *Consciousness and Human Identity*, edited by John Cornwell, 122–59. New York: Oxford University Press.

Carroll, Sean. 2010. "Energy Is Not Conserved." *Preposterous Universe* (blog). February 22, 2010. www.preposterousuniverse.com/blog/2010/02/22/energy-is-not-conserved/.

Cartwright, Nancy. 1983. *How the Laws of Physics Lie*. Oxford: Clarendon Press.

Neoclassical special divine action 147

————. 1989. *Nature's Capacities and Their Measurement*. Oxford: Clarendon Press.

Collins, Robin. 2008. "Modern Physics and the Energy-Conservation Objection to Mind-Body Dualism." *American Philosophical Quarterly* 45 (1): 31–42.

Earman, John. 2000. *Hume's Abject Failure: The Argument Against Miracles*. New York: Oxford University Press.

Earman, John, John T. Roberts, and Sheldon Smith. 2002. "*Ceteris Paribus* Lost." *Erkenntnis* 57 (3): 281–301.

Fales, Evan. 2013. "It Is Not Reasonable to Believe in Miracles." In *Debating Christian Theism*, edited by J. P. Moreland, Chad Meister, and Khaldoun A. Sweis, 298–310. New York: Oxford University Press.

Gao, S. 2017. *The Meaning of the Wave Function: In Search of the Ontology of Quantum Mechanics*. Cambridge: Cambridge University Press.

Halvorson, Hans. 2013. "Plantinga on Providence and Physics." *European Journal for Philosophy of Religion* 5 (3): 19–30. https://doi.org/10.24204/ejpr.v5i3.216.

Hüttemann, Andreas. 1998. "Laws and Dispositions." *Philosophy of Science* 65 (1): 121–35. https://doi.org/10.1086/392629.

Jaffe, Robert L., and Washington Taylor. 2018. *The Physics of Energy*. Cambridge, UK; New York: Cambridge University Press.

José, Jorge Valenzuela, and Eugene Jerome Saletan. 2006. *Classical Dynamics: A Contemporary Approach*. Cambridge: Cambridge University Press.

Kaufman, Gordon D. 1968. "On the Meaning of 'Act of God'." *The Harvard Theological Review* 61 (2): 175–201.

Kojonen, Erkki Vesa Rope. 2019. "Is Classical Science in Conflict with Belief in Miracles? Some Bridge-Building Between Philosophical and Theological Positions." In *God's Providence and Randomness in Nature: Scientific and Theological Perspectives*, edited by Robert J. Russell and Joshua M. Moritz. West Conshohocken: Templeton Foundation Press.

Koperski, Jeffrey. 2011. "Metatheoretic Shaping Principles: Where Science Meets Theology." In *God in an Open Universe*, edited by William Hasker, Thomas J. Oord, and Dean Zimmerman. Eugene, OR: Pickwick Publications.

Larmer, Robert. 2014. *The Legitimacy of Miracle*. Lanham: Lexington Books.

————. 2017. "Decretalism and the Laws of Nature: A Response to Jeffrey Koperski." *Philosophia Christi* 19 (2): 439–47.

Lewis, C. S. (1947) 1978. *Miracles: A Preliminary Study*. Macmillan Paperbacks ed. New York: Macmillan.

Lipton, Peter. 1999. "All Else Being Equal." *Philosophy* 74: 155–68.

Lowe, E. J. 2010. *Personal Agency: The Metaphysics of Mind and Action*. Oxford: Oxford University Press.

Marion, Jerry B., and Stephen T. Thornton. 1988. *Classical Dynamics of Particles & Systems*. 3rd ed. San Diego: Harcourt Brace Jovanovich.

Misner, Charles W., Kip S. Thorne, and John Archibald Wheeler. 1973. *Gravitation*. San Francisco: W. H. Freeman.

Mohrhoff, Ulrich. 1997. "Interactionism, Energy Conservation, and the Violation of Physical Laws." *Physics Essays* 10 (4): 651–65.

Pitts, J. Brian. 2019. "Conservation Laws and the Philosophy of Mind: Opening the Black Box, Finding a Mirror." *Philosophia*. https://doi.org/10.1007/s11406-019-00102-7

———. Forthcoming. "General Relativity, Mental Causation, and Energy Conservation."

Plantinga, Alvin. 2011. *Where the Conflict Really Lies: Science, Religion, and Naturalism*. Oxford: Oxford University Press.

Smith, Sheldon R. 2002. "Violated Laws, *Ceteris Paribus* Clauses, and Capacities." *Synthese* 130 (2): 235–64.

———. 2008. "Symmetries and the Explanation of Conservation Laws in the Light of the Inverse Problem in Lagrangian Mechanics." *Studies in History and Philosophy of Science Part B: Studies in History and Philosophy of Modern Physics* 39 (2): 325–45. https://doi.org/10.1016/j.shpsb.2007.12.001.

Stoeger, William. 1995. "Describing God's Action in the World in Light of Scientific Knowledge of Reality." In *Chaos and Complexity: Scientific Perspectives on Divine Action*, edited by Robert J. Russell, Nancey Murphy, and Arthur R. Peacocke, 239–61. Berkeley, CA: Center for Theology and the Natural Sciences.

Svozil, Karl. 2018. *Physical (A)Causality*. Fundamental Theories of Physics. Cham: Springer International Publishing. https://doi.org/10.1007/978-3-319-70815-7.

Vicens, Leigh C. 2012. "On the Possibility of Special Divine Action in a Deterministic World." *Religious Studies* 48 (3): 315–36. https://doi.org/10.1017/S0034412511000266.

Wald, Robert M. 1984. *General Relativity*. Chicago: University of Chicago Press.

Wilson, Mark. 2016. "Mechanics, Classical." In *Routledge Encyclopedia of Philosophy*, 1st ed. London: Routledge. https://doi.org/10.4324/9780415249126-Q068-1.

8 Four objections

With any book-length project, there are bound to be many objections, and I do not pretend to address them all. Still, there are a few that I would like to discuss in this last chapter. The first is often aimed at nonviolationist models of divine action by noninterventionists. The worry is that any account in which God plays such a direct role improperly treats God as merely one more efficient cause among many. The second objection applies to the family of views of which mine is a part. Critics believe that such models allow for too much freedom on God's part. The third is a standard Humean criticism aimed at most theistic explanations. The final objection is an old problem for decretalist interpretations of the laws of nature: occasionalism.

8.1 God as efficient cause

In Chapter 7, I argued that both we and God have the ability to change nonnomic conditions in nature. In neither case are the laws of nature broken. The laws instead seamlessly adapt to such changes. Some will take this as one aspect of God and persons having libertarian freedom. Others will see it as problematic. The latter argue that when finite beings with free will make such changes, they are playing their ordained role within the created order. But to say that God acts likewise is to reduce God to one more efficient cause in competition with natural causes. Some claim that such a view is a type of idolatry: treating God as a mere creature (Burrell and Moulin 2008, 640–42). "The living God is not part of the causal nexus of the created world. Inserting divine action into indeterminate systems reduces holy Mystery who creates and sustains the whole world to a bit player" (Johnson 2015, 168).[1] This objection is most common among Thomist theologians, such as Ignacio Silva:[2]

> [It] is important to bear in mind that when someone objects that God is taken to act as a "cause-among-causes," the objector does not mean that God should not be taken to be a cause. Rather, what the objector means is that God does not act as a secondary cause among other

secondary causes. The objection thus wants to affirm the importance of God's transcendence; therefore it stresses the fact that when God causes, God always causes as a primary cause, and never as a secondary, created cause. In this sense, the main problem with seeing God as acting as a cause among causes . . . is that it limits God's transcendence, placing God's causality at the level of secondary created causes.

(2014, 13–14)

So while God causes events, "cause" is not a univocal concept that can be applied the same way to creatures as it can be to God (Silva 2014, 16). Failing to recognize the distinction reduces God to a secondary cause on par with other agents.

Of the four objections discussed in this chapter, I admit to having the least sympathy for this one. Perhaps it has greater force within an Aristotelian-Thomist metaphysic that I do not share. The critic allows for only two kinds of divine action. God caused all creatures to exist and continues to sustain that existence, including their causal powers (Silva 2014, 17). But that much is surely uncontroversial, apart from the appeal to Aristotelian causes. Virtually all theists – and many deists (Larmer 2017b) – agree that God created and sustains all beings other than himself. The only question is whether God is restricted to this sort of causation. William Alston's reply to this objection seems to me to be exactly right:

> These theologians seem to think that if God shares any activity, status, or category with creatures, that pulls Him down to their level. . . . But these scare tactics will not establish that position. In what respects does bringing about particular effects in the world reduce God to the level of creatures? It will certainly imply that both He and creatures are engaged in bringing about states of affairs; that is, they are both agents. But it is a mere rhetorical flourish to say that this puts Him on our level. Obviously there is a world of difference, all the difference there can be, between an infinite-source-of-all-being bringing about X, and you or me bringing about X. The fact that we are both engaged in *bringing about something* should not panic us into denying the differences between creator and creature that the Christian tradition has insisted on. In short, I see no merit whatsoever in these allegations.

(1994, 53–54)

In other words, what exactly is the problem here? If one is already committed both to the distinction between primary and secondary causation and to the idea that God directly acts only in the former, a number of nonviolationist models of divine action will be objectionable, including my own. Without that prior commitment, however, this sort of criticism loses its force. It is a problem only within a questionable metaphysical framework.

8.2 Anything goes

A second worry applies to any model that rejects the absolute causal closure of nature (section 6.5). Philosopher Kirk McDermid argues that doing so undermines the very notion of laws of nature. While taking aim at Robert Larmer, his objection applies equally to the family of views discussed in section 7.4:

> [Without] causal closure of the physical, it appears that almost anything goes! . . . [The] "open-systems" proponents' apparent motivation – to allow for the production of miracles, while minimizing interference with the lawful progression of physical events – seems laudable, but by denying CCP [i.e., causal closure] they have obviated *any* requirement for subtlety or discretion in divine intervention. Rejecting it wholesale makes natural laws metaphysically toothless – a result I am not sure they would be particularly happy with.
>
> (McDermid 2008b, 128)

This is the sort of argument more often used against violationism. The laws, McDermid believes, are greatly diminished if the universe is an open system. Moreover, the distinction between laws and contingent nonnomic conditions seems to entail that "the natural is never sufficient to determine the natural" (2008a, 161). We should instead be able to affirm the "determinative sufficiency of the natural in substantive respects" (162).

In response, I would first point out that the laws of nature remain unbroken and unchanged in the neoclassical model; hence, it is not "anything goes." Nonetheless, there is a certain aesthetic to the closed metaphysical determinism of Spinoza, in which the "determinative sufficiency" of nature is assured. Perhaps that is a bit further than McDermid would like to go, but on the spectrum of views between Spinoza's and that of naïve interventionism, his certainly seems to lean hard toward the former.

If one's intuitions are that God simply doesn't do all that much *vis-à-vis* creation other than sustain its existence, I do not have much to say. The one thing that I would insist on is that any criticism grounded in the laws of nature be based on physics and chemistry – those sciences where laws play a central role. We should be wary of either breezy generalizations or things that look suspiciously like metaphysical naturalism repackaged as SCIENCE.[3] I have argued that physics allows for far more contingency in nature than that which conventional wisdom dictates. That may both surprise and disappoint noninterventionists and some nonviolationists. Perhaps there are theological reasons for denying that God has so much freedom to act. If so, others are welcome to take up that debate. The issues addressed here are matters of physics and philosophy of science. If the arguments are sound, they will constitute a significant advance for the divine action literature.

8.3 Hume versus decretalism

The Humean has a standard complaint that was not addressed in Chapter 5. Decretalism explains the regularities in nature by appealing to God. But isn't that an inherently weak explanation given that one can use God to fix virtually any conceptual problem? Even a non-Humean might worry that such a move sounds like a God-of-the-gaps at the level of metaphysics.

Let's first note that, given the problems discussed in section 5.1, no one should take this objection as a reason to opt for a Humean interpretation of laws. If theistic metaphysicians and philosophers of religion reject decretalism, they will overwhelmingly favor dispositionalism or some other variety of nomological realism. No matter which is chosen, God will enter the picture at some point. Virtually all theists believe that God has ordained the laws of nature, regardless of whether one thinks the laws should be cashed out in terms of dispositions, relations between possible worlds, or nomological realism. The dispositionalist, for example, holds that God created the dispositions and causal powers and that events are influenced accordingly. The point is that every theistic view regarding laws will face the Humean criticism at whatever point God is involved. There is no unique problem here for decretalism.

Moreover, the objection implies that God has been brought into the question of laws in an *ad hoc* way to fix a conceptual problem that otherwise cannot be fixed. Is that true? It seems plausible from a contemporary point of view. That there are laws of nature is undeniable given a basic knowledge of science. Philosophers offer different ways to make sense of that idea, which we explored in Chapter 5. Given the need to account for the laws of nature, it might well seem as if the decretalist uses God to solve a prior conceptual problem.

That narrative, however, is wholly anachronistic. The idea that there are laws of nature arose in the seventeenth century from within a theistic framework (section 4.2). Natural philosophers were not invoking God to solve a standing problem of how to make sense of the laws of nature. They were bringing about a revolution in science and metaphysics by introducing the idea of laws and displacing the Aristotelian alternative. It is the Humean who needs to find inventive ways to underwrite the use of laws from a naturalistic point of view. As Nancy Cartwright observes, "I think in the concept of law there is a little too much of God. We try to finesse the issue . . . [but] in the end the concept of a law does not make sense without the supposition of a law-giver" (1993, 299). I would ask the naturalistic Humean why he needs make use of such a thoroughgoingly theistic idea – *laws* – in the first place.[4]

In the end, this objection is one more skirmish in the overall clash between naturalism and theism. If the latter is rationally justified, employing God to do metaphysical work should not be a problem. For the theist, it is unavoidable.

8.4 Occasionalism

As philosophy majors work their way through the history of philosophy sequence, they discover ideas that fall somewhere between implausible and laughable. One of these is occasionalism. Today, one might think of it as a type of antirealism about causation. This is due to the fact that occasionalists deny that there are any natural causes. They instead hold that the only being with the capacity to bring about change is God. If the laws are divine decrees and all events are subject to those laws, (it would seem) God will cause all physical events. As Nicolas Malebranche wrote, "there is only one true cause because there is only one true God; . . . the nature or power of each thing is nothing but the will of God; . . . [and] all natural causes are not *true* causes but only *occasional* causes" (*Oeuvres complètes de Malebranche* II, 312, translated in Lee 2016). Many early moderns held such a view.

Decretalism about the laws of nature is often thought to entail occasionalism.[5] Plantinga himself has embraced the label (2016), no doubt causing some consternation among his admirers. To many, occasionalism is, intellectually, a bridge too far.[6] If decretalism inevitably leads to occasionalism, the neoclassical model will have a problem.

This entailment makes sense from a historical perspective that recognized three options. The first is what Alfred Freddoso calls "mere conservationism":

> God contributes to the ordinary course of nature solely by creating and conserving natural substances along with their . . . causal powers or capacities . . . When [created] substances directly produce an effect. . ., they alone are the immediate causes of that effect, whereas God is merely an indirect or remote cause of the effect by virtue of His conserving action.
>
> (Freddoso 1994, 133)

This is the thinnest variety of theism, whereby God creates and sustains the universe but does nothing else. While it engendered a great deal of support in contemporary theology, "almost all the important figures in the history of philosophical theology have rejected it as philosophically deficient and theologically 'unsafe'" (Freddoso 1991, 555). The more popular position historically has been "concurrentism":

> [A] natural effect is produced immediately by *both* God *and* created substances. . . . [Secondary] agents make a genuine causal contribution to the effect. . . . [But] they do so only if God cooperates with them contemporaneously as an immediate cause. . . . which renders the resulting effect the immediate effect of both God and the secondary causes.
>
> (Freddoso 1994, 134)

This is the view of historical Thomism. Both concurrentism and mere conservation stand in opposition to occasionalism whereby "God alone brings about effects in nature; natural substances . . . make no genuine causal contribution at all to any such effect . . . God alone is a genuine efficient cause." (Freddoso 1994, 133–34).

Of these three, decretalism can only be a type of occasionalism. Mere conservation is what I have called "noninterventionism": There is no divine action other than creating and sustaining. Concurrentism is a variety of Thomism that was discussed in section 2.2. By process of elimination, only occasionalism remains. But I do not buy this entailment. Perhaps at one time this trilemma adequately captured the available options. Today, it is no longer sufficient.

Freddoso's occasionalist takes God to be continually intervening whenever there is causal work to be done in nature. A falling tree cannot snap a power line, says the occasionalist, because substances lack causal powers. Hence, God breaks the power line when the tree makes contact. A similar story holds for every instance of causation. But for the nomological realist, there is no need for such interventions. For most events described by physics, "cause" is just an imprecise way of describing how nature is evolving according to the laws, known or unknown. Moving from an explanatory framework where causes and causal powers take center stage to one where they have been replaced by laws solves the problem. There are no "missing causes" that God must make up for.

The critic has a ready response to this. The decretalist variety of nomological realism takes laws to just *be* matters of divine will. If that is so, Freddoso is correct. God is doing all the work, regardless of whether one calls it causation or something else.

But that doesn't capture the sort of decretalism in mind here. Nature behaves in regular ways, and that regularity is ultimately a matter of divine command. Does God therefore act within each sequence of events in order to sustain cause-and-effect relations? I don't see why. It is not the case that every time a force acts on a mass, God intervenes so that acceleration fits Newton's second law. Rather, God decreed once and for all that mass will accelerate in such and such a way under an impressed force. The relation between force, mass, and acceleration remains what it is henceforth. A law is a one-time decree that needs no further action on God's part. There is no special work regarding the laws for God to do apart from sustaining the universe in existence.

Larmer is not impressed by this response. He offers several criticisms of a paper that was the predecessor of Chapter 5 (Larmer 2017a). While I believe that his complaints can be rebutted without much difficulty, there is one exception. Let's start with an example. Consider two electromagnets attracting each other. Under the occasionalism of, say, a Malebranche, it is not the case that the generator causes the two magnets to attract each other – there is no such thing as natural causation. God instead causes the two to attract and move. In trying to avoid occasionalism, I deny that God steps in at this point. The decrees of God are issued once and for all, and nature acts accordingly. To emphasize my break with dispositionalism, I wrote that the magnets move by virtue of Maxwell's laws of electromagnetism. It is that last clause that Larmer focuses on:

> [It] is clear either these particles, bodies, and fields will have essential natures upon which the laws of nature supervene, or their actions will be caused by something external to them. If their action is caused by something external to them, then the cause will either be God directly or some intermediate created entity such as the laws of nature conceived in a nonoccasionalist way.
>
> (2017a, 446)

And so Larmer allows for three options: (i) dispositionalism and causal powers, (ii) some form of nomological realism other than decretalism whereby the laws have their own ontology, or (iii) God as the cause of all events in nature. Given the trilemma and my rejection of the first two options, Larmer argues that I am stuck with the third, which is occasionalism.

Perhaps, but label it what you will, the sort of decretalism explained here is not the causal anti-realism held by Malebranche and attacked by Freddoso. God does not step in at each point of contact to be the sole causal agent in nature. I see nothing incoherent about God's one-time-for-all decrees for what regularities nature will henceforth instantiate. A necessary condition is that God continues to sustain creation in existence, but that alone does not entail that God causes all events.

This does not deal with Larmer's central point, however. I did say with respect to the magnet example that electromagnetic laws are responsible for its motion. Yet in my view the laws are divine decrees. Hence, in some ultimate sense, God is the one making things go, as it were, which seems to be a type of occasionalism.

Clearly not all of the views expressed in that earlier paper are consistent with those of the model presented here. To say that the laws of nature are responsible for bringing about events wrongly gives in to the dispositionalist's intuition that something metaphysical must be responsible for change – if not causal powers, laws. And if the laws are divine decrees, God will be causally responsible. Many decretalists, including perhaps Plantinga, are fine with that, but there is a better approach.

In section 5.5.1, I argued that laws do not make events happen. Laws instead constrain the way that things go. For example, God has decreed that electrostatics will work *only* according to an inverse square relation. But the right answer to the magnet example is not that Maxwell's *laws* cause the magnets to move; rather, it is that electromagnetic *forces* do. Fields are real. From a reductionist perspective, quantum fields are the ground floor of physical reality. God's decrees regulate the behavior of those fields, but the decrees/laws do not bring about change. Laws are not efficient causes. Historian John Henry shows the proper approach for the decretalist to take:

> If God wishes to make a moving brick capable in its own right of break-ing a glass window, he can. God does not have to surreptitiously break the window for the brick, because he lacks the wherewithal to make the brick do it itself. For the [decretalist],[7] occasionalism is based on a pernicious absurdity (that God has to directly involve himself in absolutely everything that happens in the world, no matter how corrupt or degrading), deriving from an arrogant proscription of what God can and cannot do.
>
> (2009, 85–86)

Occasionalism, Henry rightly says, is an unnecessary type of hyperinterven-tion, one that decretalists need not accept.

Consider another example. Say that a conveyor belt lifts balls out of a bin one at a time and places them at the top of an inclined plane. The ball then rolls down the plane, but it is free to move left or right as the wind blows. Say then that I carve a channel straight down the plane so that the ball can-not move side to side. All the balls now roll in a uniform way. So why do the balls roll down the plane? Clearly, the answer is gravity. Why don't the balls move slightly to the side, as they had previously? Because the channel acts as a constraint on their motion. What we should not say is that I make the ball move. I made the channel but play no causal role in the process after that.

For the decretalist, laws are one-time decrees that act as constraints, in this case on the behavior of gravity. The gravitation constant must remain the pull of gravity must forever be proportional to the distance between masses, and so on. But it is gravity, not God, that pulls the ball down the plane. Physics is capable of describing change in terms of force and energy. There is no need for either causal powers or the metaphorical finger of God to continually move things along.

And so I hereby renew my denial: The version of decretalism presented here is not a kind of occasionalism. It is not the case that God is the efficient cause of every event.

8.5 Last words

Having reached the end of the story, do I believe that many readers will adopt the entire neo-classical model of divine action? Of course, they should, but sadly no. There are too many places where one might disagree. Perhaps it's the decretal view of laws. Perhaps it's the physics-based account of determinism. There are a lot of moving parts. But by laying out the enterprise from beginning to end, I hope to encourage others sympathetic to the Alston-Plantinga-Larmer approach. Take what you find useful and press on.

Notes

1 Elizabeth Johnson aims this criticism specifically at Russell's QM-NIODA, which I called divine quantum determination in section 3.1, but she makes it clear that the problem applies here as well (2015, 167).
2 Others include (Edwards 2010, 63) and (Dodds 2016,153). For a critique and more, see (Sollereder 2015).
3 This is one of Plantinga's (2011) main points. It has merit.
4 The concept of laws is the first on a long list of ideas in science with theistic roots. If the Humean naturalist wants to make use of them, he or she should give an account should be given in naturalistic terms. This challenge is laid out in (Koperski 2017).
5 Nancy Cartwright makes this charge explicit: "[Decretalism] is a kind of Occasionalism: the source of the necessity of the relations between force and mass and acceleration is that, whenever God sees a force acting on a mass, He ensures that the acceleration is what it's supposed to be. That would be the Occasionalist sense of calling the relationship between F, m and a 'necessary'" (2015, 119).
6 "Contemporary theologians, philosophers of religion and philosophers of science widely debate (and largely disagree) about what could be the best account of divine action. Nevertheless, they seem to have reached a consensus about what such an account should *not* be. The majority of the authors engaged in this debate refer to 'occasionalism' as the position that any satisfying account of divine action must avoid" (Sangiacomo 2015, 115).
7 Henry uses "voluntarist" here, which in context includes decretalism.

Works cited

Alston, William P. 1994. "Divine Action: Shadow or Substance?" In *The God Who Acts: Philosophical and Theological Explorations*, edited by Thomas F. Tracy, 41–62. University Park: Pennsylvania State University Press.

Burrell, David, and Isabelle Moulin. 2008. "Albert, Aquinas, and Dionysius." *Modern Theology* 24 (4): 633–49. https://doi.org/10.1111/j.1468-0025.2008.00490.x.

Cartwright, Nancy. 1993. "Is Natural Science 'Natural' Enough? A Reply to Phillip Allport." *Synthese* 94: 291–301.

———. 2015. "How Could Laws Make Things Happen?" In *Laws of Nature, Laws of God? Proceedings of the Science and Religion Forum Conference, 2014*, edited by Neil Spurway, 115–35. Newcastle upon Tyne: Cambridge Scholars Publishing.

Dodds, Michael J. 2016. *Unlocking Divine Action: Contemporary Science and Thomas Aquinas*. Washington, DC: Catholic University of America Press.

Edwards, Denis. 2010. *How God Acts: Creation, Redemption, and Special Divine Action*. Theology and the Sciences. Minneapolis, MN: Fortress Press.

Freddoso, Alfred J. 1991. "God's General Concurrence with Secondary Causes: Why Conservation Is Not Enough." *Philosophical Perspectives* 5: 553–85.

———. 1994. "God's General Concurrence with Secondary Causes: Pitfalls and Prospects." *American Catholic Philosophical Quarterly* 67 (2): 131–56.

Henry, John. 2009. "Voluntarist Theology at the Origins of Modern Science: A Response to Peter Harrison." *History of Science* 47 (1): 79–113.

Johnson, Elizabeth A. 2015. *Ask the Beasts: Darwin and the God of Love*. London: Bloomsbury.

Koperski, Jeffrey. 2017. "Theism, Naturalism, and Scientific Realism." *Epistemology & Philosophy of Science* 53 (3): 152–66. https://doi.org/10.5840/eps201753354.

Larmer, Robert. 2017a. "Decretalism and the Laws of Nature: A Response to Jeffrey Koperski." *Philosophia Christi* 19 (2): 439–47.

———. 2017b. "Doubting Thomists and Intelligent Design." *Sophia*. April. https://doi.org/10.1007/s11841-017-0593-x.

Lee, Sukjae. 2016. "Occasionalism." In *Stanford Encyclopedia of Philosophy*, edited by Edward N. Zalta. https://plato.stanford.edu/archives/win2016/entries/occasionalism/.

McDermid, Kirk. 2008a. "A Reply to Robert Larmer." *Religious Studies* 44 (2): 161–64. https://doi.org/10.1017/S0034412507009286.

———. 2008b. "Miracles: Metaphysics, Physics, and Physicalism." *Religious Studies* 44 (2): 125–47. https://doi.org/10.1017/S0034412507009262.

Plantinga, Alvin. 2011. *Where the Conflict Really Lies: Science, Religion, and Naturalism*. Oxford: Oxford University Press.

———. 2016. "Law, Cause, and Occasionalism." In *Reason and Faith: Themes from Swinburne*, edited by Michael Bergmann and Jeffrey E. Brower, 126–44. New York: Oxford University Press.

Sangiacomo, Andrea. 2015. "Divine Action and God's Immutability: A Historical Case Study on How to Resist Occasionalism." *European Journal for Philosophy of Religion* 7 (4): 115. https://doi.org/10.24204/ejpr.v7i4.90.

Silva, Ignacio. 2014. "Great Minds Think (Almost) Alike Thomas Aquinas and Alvin Plantinga on Divine Action in Nature." *Philosophia Reformata* 79 (1): 8–20. https://doi.org/10.1163/22116117-90000559.

Sollereder, Bethany. 2015. "A Modest Objection: Neo-Thomism and God as a Cause Among Causes." *Theology and Science* 13 (3): 345–53. https://doi.org/10.1080/14746700.2015.1053762.

Index